Intellectual, Humanist and Religious Commitment

Also available from Bloomsbury

Free Will and Epistemology, by Robert Lockie
Progressive Atheism, by J. L. Schellenberg
Skepticism: From Antiquity to the Present, edited by Diego Machuca
and Baron Reed
The Maturing of Monotheism, by Garth Hallett
Wittgenstein, Religion and Ethics, edited by Mikel Burley

Intellectual, Humanist and Religious Commitment

Acts of Assent

Peter Forrest

BLOOMSBURY ACADEMIC
LONDON • NEW YORK • OXFORD • NEW DELHI • SYDNEY

BLOOMSBURY ACADEMIC
Bloomsbury Publishing Plc
50 Bedford Square, London, WC1B 3DP, UK
1385 Broadway, New York, NY 10018, USA

BLOOMSBURY, BLOOMSBURY ACADEMIC and the Diana logo are trademarks
of Bloomsbury Publishing Plc

First published in Great Britain 2019

Cover design by Avni Patel
Cover image: Hope by George Watts © Ivy Close Images / Alamy Stock Photo

A catalogue record for this book is available from the British Library.

A catalog record for this book is available from the Library of Congress.

ISBN: HB: 978-1-3500-9771-1
ePDF: 978-1-3500-9772-8
eBook: 978-1-3500-9773-5

Typeset by Deanta Global Publishing Services, Chennai, India
Printed and bound in Great Britain

To find out more about our authors and books visit www.bloomsbury.com
and sign up for our newsletters.

For my grandchildren, Isabella and Theodore. May they find faith, hope and love.

Contents

Preface

If we are presented with good arguments both for and against some thesis, then for the most part we should suspend judgement. Sometimes, however, the topic is so important that we need to commit, making what William James famously called 'a passional choice'. In this book, I present a theory of when commitment is reasonable and apply it to three topics: reasoning, humanism and God.

Acknowledgements

I would like to acknowledge those who have influenced my work on this topic. For some reason Richard Swinburne's enormous influence is not reflected in the number of citations to his work. He is a splendid example of deep faith combined with intellectual integrity. Another who has been under-cited is John Bishop, who is the most prominent contemporary advocate of William James's passional choice, as well as a tireless critic of the omni-God conception. And I owe a great deal to John Schellenberg's work on belief. Less obvious influences, perhaps, are those unbelievers who find the very existence of reasonable believers surprising. I include among them my PhD supervisor, the late David Stove, and my beloved wife, Felicity.

Let me apologize in advance to any whose ideas I have borrowed without acknowledgement, either taken from articles I have forgotten I read, or, more excusably, from seminars and conference presentations.

Finally, I would like to thank the anonymous readers, Helen Saunders, Colleen Coalter and the rest of the editorial team for their assistance, and Joseph Gautham with his production team.

Introduction

The context: Loss of innocence

This book is a defence of commitment by those of us who have sceptical doubts, especially about religion, and who have lost their epistemic innocence as a result. My personal motivation is the loss of epistemic innocence among Roman Catholics, due to the manifest unholiness of the Church. That so many of its clergy were paedophiles is bad enough; that so many bishops sought to cover this up is a scandal egregious even for a scandal-prone organization. The Nicene Creed invites us to believe in the 'One, *Holy*, Apostolic and Universal Church'. How can we? We often describe this loss of epistemic innocence as loss of faith, but it is not so much loss of faith as loss of any purely passive, easy faith. So much for my motivation: my intended audience consists of all who, for whatever reason, have either lost or never had epistemic innocence on various disputed questions. I shall defend commitment and invite them to commit.

Roughly speaking, by a commitment I mean an act of assent. It is controversial to claim that we can ever freely choose to believe, but we can assent either publicly or privately, and these acts are as free as any others we perform. By epistemic innocence I mean the state of believing without critical reflection, that is, without seriously asking ourselves the question, 'But is it true?' One of the marks of epistemic innocence is to treat arguments against your belief not as genuine challenges but merely as problems to be solved or objections to be answered – the stuff of apologetics.

Lost innocence is nothing new. Among Greeks, Indians and, on moral and political matters, the Chinese, the response to lost innocence was speculation, and debate between resulting schools. We have grown weary of these debates, partly because of the contrast with the physical and biological sciences, which have, it would seem, progressed generation by generation, so we now know vastly more than we did a few hundred years ago. Many scientists insist this progress is the result of empiricism, basing our beliefs entirely on experience. But that just shows their own epistemic innocence. For those of us who lack this innocence, a commitment is required to the reasoning that underpins the sciences.

Our beliefs on many topics are epistemically innocent, but there is a Western philosophical tradition going back to Socrates that despises innocence. On the contrary, I hold that any belief is reasonable unless and until there is a known reason to doubt it, whereupon we should reflect upon it critically, bringing to bear other beliefs, many of which are themselves accepted uncritically (see Harman 1986). It does not matter much if readers think this standard is too lax, for my intended audience consists of those who have lost epistemic innocence, because they have taken seriously a reason to doubt.

My treatment of the topic is philosophical, which is appropriate because philosophy's history is a series of reactions to loss of conviction of one sort or another. That history is not, however, edifying and exhibits little of the sort of progress provided by the sciences. And you may hold – reasonably enough – that philosophers are obscure, out-of-touch pedants. This particular obscure, out-of-touch pedant is an old white guy to boot. I, therefore, need to justify my philosophizing about loss of innocence and subsequent commitment. To do so, I appeal to another tradition going back to Socrates: philosophy as intellectual midwifery. Explicitly, the social role performed by academic philosophers is not to be experts but to be guides to individuals in their own philosophizing. We are guides because we are heirs to a tradition that has already thought about most of the relevant issues (see Stove 1985). Nonetheless philosophy is primarily the individual's responsibility and a philosophical treatment of a topic is of value only if it guides individuals to make up their own minds.

Philosophy idealizes our situation by ignoring the murky subconscious forces that influence beliefs without regard to their truth. I take it for granted, then, that our philosophizing is to be guided by a respect for the truth or, more accurately, fear of falsehood.

Because philosophy in general, and commitment in particular, is the responsibility of the individual, not to be taken over by experts, the common view these days is that we should commit as it pleases us. Commitments are dangerous, however, often resulting in zealotry. Today we fear zealous Islamists. Yesterday it was zealous Marxists. So, we should remember William Butler Yeats: 'The best lack all conviction, while the worst / Are full of passionate intensity' ('The Second Coming'). Therefore, we should exercise due caution in making commitments, and that in turn requires fear of falsehood and hence attention to whether or not they are reasonable. (The circularity of a reasonable commitment to reason will be addressed in Chapter 3.)

Aims

In response to the loss of epistemic innocence I shall defend a threefold commitment: (1) to reason, by which I mean our ordinary human ways of seeking true beliefs; (2) to humanism and (3) to a God worthy of worship – in that order. I provide necessary conditions for a commitment to be reasonable and show that those three commitments meet the conditions. I then invite commitment. I do not, note, insist that it is unreasonable not to commit, nor am I able to show these necessary conditions are jointly sufficient. So, I am open to suggestions as to further conditions. Nor do I take these three to be the only reasonable commitments.

Here are simplified versions of rules governing reasonable commitment. They will be stated in more detail in Chapter 3.

1. The *Dilemma Condition*. The circumstances of a commitment should be an intellectual dilemma, with good arguments for and against the thesis to which commitment is made.
2. The *Pragmatic Condition*. We should only commit on matters that have good practical consequences.
3. The *Absolute Superiority Condition*. The content of the commitment should be better than rival commitments.

The scandal of epistemology

My personal motivation for this work is the epistemology of scandal, asking whether it is reasonable to continue belonging to the Roman Catholic Church, when you come to realize the hierarchy were more concerned for the church's good name than preventing abuse. But here is a warning about a different scandal, that of epistemology. It serves to assure readers that the author's arrogance is not of the Socratic kind mentioned earlier.

Most epistemology consists of general advice on how to discover the truth and properly applies in the context of answering questions for the first time. But it is too often misapplied to the context of judging a belief someone already has (see Harman 1986), for you may believe that by good luck you have achieved some goal ignoring the best advice, or you may have forgotten how you achieved it. In that case, it would be folly to say you should start again this time accepting the advice. It would be like counselling a happily married couple to get divorced because they married under parental pressure forty years ago as a result of pregnancy.

An example of scandalous epistemology would be the attempt to destroy an epistemically innocent faith by demanding reasons. I heard that a philosopher, whom I otherwise respect, asked a student why she believed in God. She replied that she had faith, to which his response was 'That's wanking!' For those with such innocent faith, the rather lax rules of Reformed Epistemology hold, I believe, and the only reasonable philosophical attack on innocent faith is by way of conclusive or almost conclusive objections. So, her innocent reply should have been, 'Why not?' For an example of a conclusive objection, showing just how hard they are to find, suppose a mathematically competent fundamentalist misunderstands 1 Kgs 7.3 to imply that $\pi = 3$. Then I am entitled to lay out the proof that $\pi \neq 3$. In any case, my intended audience is not the innocent. It consists of those for whom neither religion nor irreligion is epistemically innocent. In particular, I am speaking to those of us for whom the question of having faith, once answered in the affirmative, has become unanswered again.

Distinguishing the Universe from universes, Time from time, and God from god

A final introductory note: we can use upper case letters to specify a narrower sense, *sensu stricto* as the biologists say. I shall do so in three cases. First, by the 'Universe' I mean the sum of all physical things, by a 'universe' I mean one of the many universes that make up the Multiverse. To avoid confusion, it helps to think of each of these universes as a spatio-temporal system of four dimensions, ignoring the possibility of extra dimensions in which there is extent only on the exceeding small scale. If there is just one universe then the Universe is the universe. Otherwise the Universe is the Multiverse.

The second case is that of 'Time' and 'time'. By 'time' I mean the fourth dimension of space-time, as described by Minkowski or as in General Relativity. By 'Time' I mean genuine time, which is often called 'hypertime'. I shall speculate that there are many spatio-temporal universes each including what is thought of as the future, but that at later moments of Time there are fewer such universes than at earlier moments. So, we may think of these universes as enduring for different spans of Time. Details will be provided in Chapter 2.

Finally, by 'God' I mean a being worthy of worship, while 'god' is a being who is powerful and knowledgeable enough to be worthy of worship if good enough. Hence a creator is god but not obviously God. I stipulate that a theist is someone who believes there is a god, an atheist someone who denies there is a god and an agnostic someone who suspends judgement. This leaves scope for theists to deny that God exists.

Between Innocence and Commitment: Speculation and Experience

Both collectively, as attested by the history of philosophy, and individually we react to the loss of innocence on a topic with the Epistemological Turn, thinking about what is reasonable to believe. The obvious criticism of this reaction is that the Turn is from epistemic innocence to innocent epistemology. That is, the epistemology is no more secure than the topic in question, such as the trustworthy character of the church, which we lost innocence in. Historically, the epistemological debates of modernity have resulted in loss of innocence about epistemology, a loss which is the key to postmodernism – thank God we are post postmodernism! Because of this loss of innocence about epistemology I shall be urging *commitment* to reason, that is, to our ordinary human ways of reasoning even when they go beyond what is obvious.

There are, however, two reasons for exploring epistemically innocent epistemology. The first is that there is no *general* objection to innocence, for critical inquiry is both difficult and fallible. Moreover, it usually results in further dissension. Therefore, we should not demand it on every occasion. Hence, the case against an innocent attitude towards epistemology has to be made in some detail. This case is partly collective and historical and partly individual. At the collective level, philosophy in modernity was bedevilled by disputed attempts to state the epistemological principles intended to settle disputed questions. Likewise, at the individual level if we start thinking how we should investigate the disputed topics about which we have lost innocence, then all we can be sure of is a core of epistemology, which constrains but does not settle the disputes. This core consists of what is *evident*, that is obvious to us, rather than merely *intuitive*, that is, what we tend to believe but without complete conviction.

One disputed topic was the occurrence of knowledge that is *a priori* in the sense of either occurring without experience or, if occasioned by experience, not undermined by a subsequent discovery that the experience was illusory. An example is the claim that every change must have a cause. While we may have doubts about whether these *a priori* claims are genuine pieces of knowledge, they do count as intuitions.

Our inability to settle the question of the correct epistemology, apart from this core, might suggest a fallibilist approach in which, abandoning consensus, individuals, reflecting on the history of epistemology, nonetheless reach tentative conclusions about how we should reason on disputed topics. This is an explication of the rules implicit in our innocent epistemology once it has used itself to correct itself. Now, the history of philosophy in modernity exhibits a nice dialectic: in different ways, the rationalist reliance on the *a priori* and the empiricist reliance on experience are both antitheses to the scholastic thesis that placed great weight on tradition. These two antitheses were then synthesized by Kant. Without endorsing Kant's deflationary account of the a priori, I take this synthesis to be *reason*. Thus, the second justification for examining innocent epistemology is to make the case for the synthesis as reason, namely, the human way of reasoning.

The fallibilism of this sensible synthesis undermines, however, the innocence of epistemology. Consider Faith, a woman who has lost her innocent Christian fundamentalist belief in the literal truth of the Bible. If Faith relies on reason, she will not return to fundamentalism. Her fundamentalist friends point out to her, though, that she might instead reject reason, of which they have a rather poor opinion. Faith re-commits to fundamentalism and rejects the rules for reasoning as I describe them. She is sane, and so she accepts core epistemology, allowing for instance, that there are a few corruptions to the text, which explain any blatant inconsistencies. Recognizing the coherence of Faith's re-commitment, I – her would-be critic – cannot retain my innocence about the epistemology that judges her. To be sure, I can tell her she is unreasonable. But she can retort that my arrogance is taking me to Hell – Ouch! There is no neutral point to adjudicate from. She has committed to the Scriptures understood literally; I have committed to reason. This stand-off will be discussed after I present some rules for reasonable commitment.

Innocent reactions to loss of innocence: Speculation

A natural response to loss of innocence is to be a 'free thinker', daring to think for yourself. Unfortunately, as the history of Greek and Indian philosophy illustrates, this results in a profusion of incompatible theories, all advocated with conviction. Although arrogant this is of benefit, for it is reasonable to think of these theories as *speculative hypotheses*, hopefully providing a complete range between which we may choose. I shall use as an example the various hypotheses about the origin of the physical universe. At least among those who retain some innocence about epistemology there is an agreement that we should prefer theories that explain more with less. As the case of the origins of the universe shows, this results in limited progress, based on (1) compatibility with what we claim to know, namely, common sense and established science and (2) some, limited, agreement about what is intuitive or counter-intuitive.

A spirit who created

I start with the most familiar speculation about the origin of everything physical, one that I reject. Prior to advances in brain science it was sensible enough to suppose *Cartesian* or, as I prefer to call it, *radical* dualism, which was a gift for religion.[1] By radical dualism I mean the thesis that a human being has a non-physical part, which we might as well call a 'soul', and which can have complex thoughts and emotions without the body. On this thesis, the brain is a means of interacting with the physical world, and hence other souls. If we hold there are such things as souls then three speculations become tenable. The first is that we survive death disembodied. The second is that there are angels as traditionally conceived of. The third is that the physical universe was created by a soul that differs from ours only in its vastly greater power over the physical. I hasten to note that this is not how Thomists, and scholastics more generally, think of god. I also grant that if we accepted the tenability of radical dualism there would still be much work to do when arguing for the existence of a God who was not merely creator but worthy of worship.

My reason for rejecting radical dualism is the usual one. Brain structure explains the details of our mental lives including memory and thought. To be sure, animal, especially human, consciousness resists complete explanation in terms of neural structure or activity, as does our capacity to act rather than merely behave. But that is a general mystery, leaving no need for non-physical *details*. Thus, brain damage does not merely affect capacity to interact with others: it can alter a person's whole mental life. This alteration would be quite mysterious if radical dualism were correct.

If we reject radical dualism we may reasonably speculate that all complexity and structure derives from the complexity and structure of the physical. Hence, we should be attracted to the supervenience thesis that there are no possibilities that differ in non-physical respects without differing in physical respects. The best known argument against this supervenience thesis is the Conceivability Case, as advocated by David Chalmers (1996). The argument is that philosophers' *zombies* are conceivable, and that conceivability provides a case for possibility. These zombies are molecule for molecule replicas of ordinary human beings but lacking consciousness.[2] They would occur if the supposed psycho-physical laws were different. Their possibility would show supervenience to be incorrect but not imply radical dualism. To establish radical dualism, we need the conceivability of the opposite of philosopher's zombies, the supposition of an animal that is conscious although its brain does not have the requisite structure, or has complex conscious thoughts in spite of an unsuitable brain, say Don Marquis's Archy the cockroach, who uses a typewriter (Marquis 1950). Archy is conceivable only in the weak sense of being describable without contradiction, whereas the zombie is positively conceivable in that we can make sense of the supposed psycho-physical laws relating brain to mind states and fill in the details of how they might fail (see Chalmers and Jackson 2001). Moreover, we know what it is like to have been a zombie: it is to have a fugue episode. I judge therefore that we should reject radical dualism, treat the supervenience of the mental on the physical as a tenable speculation but, out of respect for Chalmers and his zombie friends, not take it to be established. [3]

There can be an *embodied* God, and hence theists have no need to rely upon radical dualism. This will be argued for in Chapter 7.[4] Meanwhile, here are some further, more acceptable, speculations.

Necessary laws

Naturalists understand the universe in terms of the laws of nature, which science seeks to discover. This is, I grant, a good way of understanding, for four reasons. First, the sciences have explained much, so it is reasonable to expect them to explain more. Second, the laws of nature are candidates for the sort of thing that can be posited without further explanation; for they are necessary in some sense, and if we require unexplained truths to be metaphysically necessary then there is no good objection other than theism to the thesis that the laws are metaphysically necessary (Swoyer 1982; Fales 1990; Shoemaker 1998). Third, we may reasonably hope for a unified systematic theory of the laws, the 'Theory of Everything'. Finally, we might hope that the total absence of anything is a situation incompatible with the laws (Tryon 1973). In that case the laws would explain not merely how the state of the universe follows from earlier states but why there is something rather than nothing.[5]

This hypothetical explanation in terms of the laws coheres with science, although it is based on some fairly optimistic predictions about the sort of theory of everything we might come to discover. And it is not contrary to common sense, provided it is clearly recognized that this is not a total way of understanding but one that takes the laws for granted without further explanation.

The Multiverse

I shall rely heavily on the speculation that there are many universes making up the one Multiverse. These are to be thought of as parallel universes in the sense that (1) some of them are nearby universes and (2) the spatio-temporal locations in nearby universes can be correlated, at least to a good approximation. The most straightforward way of achieving this is to think of the universes as occupying four-dimensional (hyper-)surfaces in a much higher dimensional Universe, 'the Hyperverse'. Think of the universes as (infinite) pages of an (infinite) book in which each page is similar to but not exactly the same as the next. In the analogy, each page is a complete story of all events in four-dimensional space-time.[6]

This speculation is a latter-day variant on the theme of plenitude, traced by Arthur Lovejoy (1936) back to Plato. It has been taken seriously as a way of understanding quantum theory, because of Everett's Relative State Interpretation (Everett 1957; De Witt and Seligman 1970; Deutsch 1998), and it has recently been discussed by analytic philosophers of religion (Kraay 2015; Harper 2016). I shall rely on this speculation when discussing agency and the afterlife. Here I merely want to defend it as a speculation. To that end, I first note the way it can be used to explain away quantum-theoretic indeterminacy, which is illustrated in the famous thought experiment of a single electron going indeterminately through two slits. On the Many Worlds Interpretation, it is said to go through one slit in some universes and the other in others. The indeterminacy results from the way we, the observers, are extended across many universes. Hence the phrase 'in our universe' ambiguously refers to the many universes in which the electron goes through the slit. If it is subsequently observed which slit the electron goes through, then, on the standard Many Worlds Interpretation we, observers, have undergone fission: in some universes, we have observed the electron going through the first slit; in others our counterparts made the other observation.

Next, although plenitude does not, to be sure, explain why there is a physical universe, it does explain why our universe is fine-tuned to have peculiar life-friendly features – we couldn't be in a life-hostile one. Moreover, if we took the basic laws of nature for granted as metaphysically necessary truths, Plenitude explains the derived laws as due to the way our universe subsequently developed, say by one rather than another symmetry-breaking.

To any who complain that the Multiverse is a luxuriant growth to be shaved off by Ockham's Razor, I concede that is a problem for a plenitude of all metaphysically possible universes, a problem that I shall address in Chapter 7, when I consider alien possibilities. But for much of the speculative use of the Multiverse, all that is required is the existence of many universes with the same fundamental laws of nature, which is a dapper ontology. Moreover, this is the same razor violation as required for the naturalist explanation of fine-tuning as due to there being a multiplicity of universes with the same underlying fundamental laws but varying 'constants'. To be sure, that naturalistic explanation does not require the parallel universes of the Many Worlds Interpretation of quantum theory, but (1) the extent of the violation of Ockham's Razor is much the same even if these universes are parts of the one four-dimensional Universe and (2) it would be strange to violate Ockham's Razor in this mild way without taking advantage of the Multiverse to explain quantum-theoretic indeterminacy.

The Multiverse has much to commend it, then. It is, however, usually coupled with the No Collapse Many Worlds Interpretation of quantum theory, which is contrary to common sense, for, according to it, each of us has many counterparts living in universes that differ from ours only in what is occurring far away. Even worse, there is repeated fission of each of us into many distinct future individuals, for this is a corollary of the way the puzzling Twin Slit experiment is explained. To reconcile the Multiverse with common sense I now present a variant.

Universe termination and the Delayed Collapse Interpretation

No Collapse has the consequence that experimenters (and the rest of us) split into very many actual counterparts who have made different observations. This is contrary to common sense. Instead, therefore, I propose a Delayed Collapse Interpretation based on *universe termination*. In the beginning, there was a multiverse that contained everything possible (on one variant everything compatible with the laws of nature and on another everything metaphysically possible including rival laws of nature). Initially, then, there is indeterminacy between all the universes. But there is a succession of *universe terminations*, so the resulting indeterminacy is only between those that survive. After the electron passes through the twin slits, a termination eliminates those universes in which it goes through one of the slits, leaving the other as the observed result.[7] This interpretation requires that we think of the many universes as four-dimensional with 'past', 'present' and 'future', much as Boethius thought of creation spread out before the eternal creator. Genuine Time is something different, namely, the succession of states in which fewer and fewer universes survive termination. The correlation between the 'temporal' aspects of the four-dimensional universes and genuine Time is that at a given moment of Time there is a region of macroscopic indeterminacy and another region in which there is almost complete macroscopic determinacy. That is, the many universes agree in the latter but disagree in the former about the macroscopic details. We call the former region the future and the latter the past, with the present a transitional region between the two. To use the book analogy, suppose we tear off pages in such a way that at genuine time T, the stories on the remaining pages agree, at least in all macroscopic details, about a large region of space-time, a 'block', and the later T is the larger the block. In this way, the block grows. On this theory, the fission implied by the standard Everett-inspired interpretation begins to occur but is frustrated by the termination of the universes that are inhabited by one of the products of fission.

One way of thinking about termination is to consider *time-dependent possibility*: the still-possible decreases with the passage of time, whereas the now-necessary increases. The now-necessary corresponds to the determinate past, and the still-possible to the indeterminate future. Combining this modal theory of Time with realism about possible universes results in the speculation of universe termination.[8] There is a variant, based on the possibility of philosophers' zombies. We may think of the universe termination as a process by which consciousness retreats from billions of universes. The zombification hypothesis respects common sense more than destruction, for, contrary to traditional theology, we tend to assume an ur-conservation law: stuff cannot just cease to exist. But either way of taming the Multiverse will do.

Axiarchism

By axiarchism I mean the Platonist principle that one, perhaps the only ultimate, way of understanding is to be aware of the good, including the beautiful. According to this axiarchist principle, theocentric understanding is not ultimate but penultimate, with god's existence being explained by the divine goodness and beauty.[9] On the other hand, scientific understanding would be ultimate if naturalism were correct and if science is based on the appreciation of the beauty of the natural order. Axiarchism may be conjoined with the rationalist principle that understanding is the guide to truth – either reliance on the Principle of Sufficient Reason or the rather weaker Inference to the Best Explanation – to imply that we should expect what is good and puzzle at deviations from goodness.

John Leslie's (1979) version of axiarchism states that things are as they are ethically required to be. This abandons common sense by supposing that being ethically required could operate without there being an agent aware of ethical obligations. By contrast, the speculation I consider, and what I mean by axiarchism, is that we directly understand something by being aware of its goodness, where goodness includes beauty and is not the same as being ethically required.[10]

In the next chapter, I require that we commit ourselves *as if* axiarchism is correct. This is a principle of cosmic optimism, if you like. I shall not in fact commit to axiarchism, but I defend it as a speculation. I start with a special case, aesthetic understanding (Forrest 1991). This special case is a thesis about theory choice, about which I now digress. Given two theories with the same observable consequences, how do we choose between them? Further observation might help, but let us suppose it is beyond our powers to discriminate in this way. The sceptical empiricist will refuse to select one theory as more likely to be true than the other, but reason – to which I shall commit – goes beyond this sceptical empiricism. The classic example is the comparison between Omphalism and Evolution as an explanation of the geological fossil record. Omphalism is Philip Gosse's (1857) hypothesis that God created the whole Universe a few thousand years ago as if it had had millions of years of history. The logical positivists used to solve the problem of choosing between empirically equivalent theories by identifying them. But Evolution and Omphalism are not, strictly speaking, empirically equivalent. For the first sentient animals, many millions of years ago, daily made observations inconsistent with the Universe's not existing. But we cannot *now* distinguish Omphalism from Evolution by observation. Nonetheless it is unreasonable not to reject Omphalism as far less probable than Evolution. Even worse than Omphalism is its secular variant, that the universe came into existence spontaneously a few thousand years ago with the fake evidence of the past in place. To reject silly theories such as Omphalism we rely upon Inference to the Best Explanation, or its technical explication in terms of probabilities, asserting that the theory that best explains is most likely to be true. That shifts the problem to that of deciding how we explain or, if that is more general, how we come to understand.

I know of three ways we might choose which theory helps us understand better: reliance on simplicity, coherence or aesthetics. The choice between these three ways of going beyond the empirical must, trivially, be a priori. But the *a priori* is not divorced from experience: very often what we find intuitive is occasioned by experience, even though the intuition survives the discovery that the experience is illusory. (Consider, for instance, learning geometry as a result of an interactive virtual reality geometry game.) Hence an examination of the actual practice of great scientists like Albert Einstein helps inform our *a priori* judgements. I submit that informed *a priori* judgement favours aesthetic understanding over simplicity or coherence. The case for aesthetic understanding is largely defensive; therefore, meeting the obvious objection that the capacity to make true comparisons of simplicity or of coherence is less mysterious than the supposed capacity to make true aesthetic judgements. My defence of aesthetic understanding is what John Mackie calls a 'companions in guilt' strategy: comparisons of simplicity and coherence are no less mysterious than aesthetic comparisons.

Consider simplicity. I grant that we reasonably rely on *a priori* appeals to simplicity as in various razor arguments (Forrest 2009a). This is compatible with aesthetic understanding because underlying simplicity is a requirement for elegance. To show that simplicity is a 'companion in guilt' with aesthetics, I note that simplicity is relative to a way of classifying or describing things. Hence, if simplicity is the guide to truth there must be objectively more and less natural predicates, those that 'carve Nature across the joints'. That undercuts the objection to aesthetic understanding, for both it and the appeal to simplicity require claims to objectivity, which I find intuitive but are widely questioned.

That simplicity is relative to a way of classifying things is shown by considering a simplified historical example, the superiority of Kepler's description of the orbits of planets as ellipses to the Copernican description using epicycles. This requires that we grant that ellipses are objectively natural shapes. A less accessible but even more striking example is General Relativity, which is an elegant theory provided we grant that differentiable manifolds are objectively natural,[11] for if we state General Relativity in terms of coordinates it is a mess.

The next question, then, is how we come to know of the objectively natural. We must as small children already have some 'innate ideas' – tendencies to describe and classify in one way rather than another. Experience then adjusts our innate tendencies reinforcing those classifications that result in accurate predictions, and weakening others. In this way colours and other 'secondary qualities' are judged not to provide as natural a classification as shapes. Our discovery of how things are to be classified and described is part of reason, that is, our ordinary way of reasoning, to which I shall urge commitment. It does not, however, explain how we come to know that ellipses and other elegant mathematical shapes are natural and definitely does not explain how we learn that differentiable manifolds are natural. What is required is a human capacity for *reflective judgement* as Kant calls it, and one that extends beyond childhood. This is a way of finding the universals to which particulars belong (see Ginsborg 2014: §1). Or to avoid appearing to presuppose realism about universals, we have this capacity to discover new natural classes, not just the capacity to describe the world using those that are innate. Kant's insight is that reflective judgement operates especially in judgements of the beautiful. This may be illustrated by my reaction to artists' 'breaking the rules'. Initially I judge them harshly as 'showing off', trying to be original. But in some cases, after a while it 'grows on me', and I acknowledge that the artist has discovered something objectively natural. An elementary example is an asymmetrical vase. Traditionally vases were symmetrical, often with circular symmetry, but some asymmetrical vases are remarkably elegant. We should judge their shapes natural *because* we judge them beautiful. Kepler, surely, was motivated by the beauty of ellipses.

The remaining alternative to aesthetic understanding is the appeal to coherence, that is, the way the different parts of a theory support each other. It has recently been proposed by Paul Draper as an alternative to simplicity, and he submits that although the criterion of simplicity supports theism, coherence supports naturalism (Draper 2016).

I have doubts as to whether coherence is enough to dismiss Omphalism, as all right-minded thinkers should, for Omphalism coheres with various other fundamentalist alternatives to genuine science, such as rapid geological change. A further criticism is that coherence is applicable only to scientific theories that have not been unified in a rigorous way. It seems strange to suggest that General Relativity is supported by the coherence of its rather few observable consequences, such as the gravitational red shift, gravity waves and the advance of the perihelion of Mercury. Instead, it is supported by its elegance together with its capacity to explain widely differing phenomena. By contrast, the criterion of coherence applies when the explanations are of similar phenomena.

Putting those criticisms to one side, I claim that coherence like simplicity presupposes that we know how to 'carve Nature across the joints'; that is, we can distinguish between more and less natural classifications.[12] Suppose, for instance, that we want to know how carnivorous plants 'solve the problem' of not eating all their pollinators. That a certain plausible strategy, say the spatial and temporal separation of flowers and traps, is an adaptation in one genus supports the hypothesis that this strategy has evolved for another and vice versa. This helps establish coherence only because we dismiss the sceptic who complains that the two genera have evolved on different continents, or at different times. Such dismissal illustrates our shared understanding of the relevant natural classification.

My case for aesthetic understanding is that it is *a priori* intuitive and not as mysterious as might have initially appeared. This case can be supported in two further ways. Not all mathematical theorems are equal, and a certain piece of mathematics is judged to be at best a useful lemma if it lacks elegance. This is an aesthetic judgement. Therefore, good mathematics is beautiful. But good mathematics also often finds application to physics. This, otherwise perplexing truth, can be explained provided the *a priori* judgements on which physics depends are themselves aesthetic. Because physics is beautiful in a rather abstract way it uses beautiful mathematics.

The other way of supporting aesthetic understanding comes with a warning: Achtung! Kant! It relies on the premise that the mark of an objective classification is the aesthetic joy we have in contemplating the *beautiful* in the partly stipulated sense of excellent specimens of natural kinds;[13] for in that case, judgements of simplicity and coherence depend on aesthetic judgements and the objection to aesthetic understanding is demolished. Because of the human tendency to get bored, this premise is especially clear when the kind is novel and we are introduced to the kind by an excellent specimen.

In support of the Kantian premise I note that, apart from philosophers, we do not think in terms of naturalness or 'carving Nature across the joints' when exercising reflective judgement, but we do use aesthetic vocabulary – 'elegance' is the mathematicians' term of choice.

Achtung! Mehr Kant! Further support for the Kantian premise may be obtained by considering Kant's *Third Critique*, although some readers might like to treat this as a digression to be skipped. The *Third Critique* concerns both aesthetics and teleology, which is a peculiar combination if we think of a thing's *telos* as what it was designed for, or maybe what it was as if designed for. But there is a different way of thinking of a thing's telos. It concerns what it is for the thing to be an excellent specimen of its objectively natural kind. This is what the postmodernists – may they rest in peace – call the *essence*, when they criticize essentialism, the thesis that various characteristics are required to be a good specimen of, say, a human being. To be sure, we may note the fallacy of *biologism*, trying to infer the 'essence' in this sense from what is required to be a good specimen of some broader class, such as a placental mammal. And we may also grant that some kinds, notably humanity, can have multiple essences: there is not just the one way of being excellent. But these concessions do not undermine the idea of a telos as a description of features that make something an excellent member of a given natural class. For example, the human telos requires that we be social animals not anchorites. The discovery of a telos can be aesthetic in two ways. First, there is the pleasure or joy of discovery of an objectively natural class, and second the pleasure or joy occasioned by observing an excellent specimen of the kind. We say that the features that bestow excellence are *fitting* for the kind.

Having travelled thus far with Kant, I should say something about the *sublime*, the aesthetic as transcendent, pointing to something beyond the ordinary human condition. The experience of the sublime prompts the judgement that we are in the presence of something more important than us, and just as, I say, science rests on aesthetic judgements, it also presents the cosmos as sublime. Many would say this is illusory. Many others would interpret it in religious terms. The puzzle is that although we contrast the sublime and the beautiful we also think of both as matters of aesthetics. My speculation is that to experience the sublime is to discover that in the objectively natural classification of things, we humans are of the same natural class as the transcendent: we are divine but not excellent specimens of the divine. I shall avoid relying heavily on this, because it is too conjectural, but it coheres with the *sensus divinitatis*, the human tendency to believe in something metaphorically beyond or above the ordinary, namely, excellent specimens of the natural class of the divine.

If we grant that we understand by discovering objective beauty, we might go further in either or both of the two ways. First, we might claim that understanding is itself an aesthetic experience. Second, and more relevant to this work, we might generalize to include the sense of something being *fitting* as a way of understanding. Such generalized axiarchism can be stated as saying that the only ultimate explanation for things is goodness, where goodness here includes the beautiful and the fitting, but is not taken as narrowly moral in the sense of concerning right action, or the even more narrowly ethical in the sense of concerning fairly precise rules for right action. To be sure the moral might be grounded in tele, but that grounding is not to be assumed when judging axiarchism.

To summarize this lengthy digression, the case for axiarchism, other than its direct intuitive appeal, is a generalization from the ways we ordinarily choose between theories that we cannot, at this time, distinguish empirically. Axiarchism is not, however, a complete way of understanding, for there are incommensurable values, that is, situations that are good but in different and incommensurable ways. For example, consider aesthetic values, the value of intellectual discovery and the value of a happy pleasurable life. Aesthetic understanding reconciles the first two of these, but the last is not commensurable to the first two. Thus, there could be identical twins one of whom lives a happy prosperous life and the other that of a poverty-stricken artist. Which is better? Neither, but nor are they of equal value.[14] It is plausible, then, that there is no best possible world, or universe, because some exhibit more of one value and others more of some incommensurable value. In Chapter 8, I shall provide a theodicy based on these incommensurable values. For instance, god must decide between (1) the aesthetic appeal of fairly simple laws of nature admitting no exceptions and (2) more complicated laws that result in less pain. If one is better than the other, then the choice is obvious, and in that case the creator is redundant, for if one is better than the other then we can give the axiarchist understanding of why the better occurs, that is, precisely because it is better. If they are incommensurable, then neither the theistic nor the axiarchist way of understanding is complete. I shall argue in Chapter 8 that the theistic lack of completion is, however, less serious than the axiarchist one.

The defensive role of speculation

I have expounded some speculations at length, partly because I shall need to refer to them later. But the obvious conclusion is that we are at a loss as to how to decide between them. This obvious conclusion needs qualifying: even if we cannot discover which is the best of a range of speculations, we still need to separate those that are tenable, that is about as good as any other, from those that are clearly inferior. (Thus, I rejected radical dualism as untenable.) For a tenable speculation is as a way of replying to an objection, a way that is better than a mere defence. Here I am using the defence/theodicy distinction introduced by Plantinga when considering the Argument from Evil (1965). A defence does not attempt to show that the thesis being attacked is probable, but merely that it is consistent with what we know. A theodicy attempts to give the correct explanation. I say a theodicy is speculative if it is being proposed as the best or equal best theodicy we can think of, and one that is good enough if there is no better. Generalizing from theodicy, the criterion for a speculation to be satisfactory is that it is good enough as a hypothesis, so that if it is better than rivals, we would propose it as the truth relying on an Inference to the Best Explanation, and not merely the best of a bad bunch.[15] If there are several explanations of which none are superior to the others, then the criterion is that in the absence of better ones they are good enough for us to believe that one of them is correct.[16] Because there may turn out to be other, rival, hypotheses, the speculation is not clearly the best (or a best) explanation, merely a hypothetical way of understanding. Usually, successful predictions are required for a hypothesis to achieve the status of the uniquely best explanation, and metaphysics is not good at prediction. Nonetheless a satisfactory speculation can provide a defence against an objection. Consider again speculations intended to explain why God's creation is so prone to evil. Suppose there are two or three satisfactory ones. Then we may grant that we do not know why God permits or causes evil, but unless there is a better explanation, one of the satisfactory speculations is the correct explanation of evil.

Innocent reactions to loss of innocence: Experience

Bacon's bell, evangelicals and confident empiricism

Francis Bacon's idea that careful experiment can resolve centuries of fruitless argument is of obvious appeal, and has been vindicated by scientific progress. This progress depends on the way rival scientists can perform the same experiment and agree on the results, even though they might disagree on the explanation. There is no strict analogue for religion, except when assessing meditation techniques. There are, however, religious movements that stress the role of experience. An important example is Evangelical Christianity with its emphasis on the 'born again' experience, a vivid sense of your own sinfulness followed by an equally vivid sense of having been forgiven by God as a result of the atoning work of Jesus Christ. It is not hard to understand why a born-again Christian might despise 'arid' philosophical and theological discussions of what seem minutiae.

The assessment of Baconian empiricism is likely to be influenced by our knowledge of David Hume's scepticism about induction, that is, extrapolation from the observed to similar unobserved cases (Hume 1975). But that is irrelevant because here I am discussing the epistemically innocent reaction to loss of innocence on certain specific topics, notably religion: our ordinary use of induction is not in question. Moreover, we may take Hume's sceptical solution to his sceptical doubts as itself a way of acknowledging that induction is an ineliminable part of reason in my sense.

The religious example illustrates the genuine problem with reliance upon experience, its theory-laden character. I know of no good argument against the plausible thesis that background beliefs influence experience itself. But even if that thesis is rejected, the background beliefs constrain our interpretation of the experience. Born-again Christians interpret their sense of guilt and relief at forgiveness in Protestant terms. Contrast a Catholic who confesses a specific case of sinning and is relieved by the assurance of divine forgiveness when absolved by a priest. Or, for an even greater contrast, compare someone who, influenced by the *Course in Miracles* (Schucman 2007), would interpret a similar experience as a matter of self-forgiveness and the realization of unity with the divine.

The experience of the divine is likewise theory-laden. Christian mystics tend to report an ecstatic union with God. Many Hindu mystics report a blissful state of identity with God. A Buddhist might offer an interpretation in terms of *sunyata* (emptiness but without the negative connotation). I conclude that innocent prior beliefs enable someone to rely upon experience, but if these background beliefs are themselves subject to critical examination, experience ceases to be decisive. This holds not just for the experience of individuals but for traditions based on the experience of those long dead, and the scriptures that record these experiences. These are influenced by the prior beliefs, both of those who had the experience and of those who recorded them. Something similar is true of science, although the point has been exaggerated by Kuhn (1962) and Feyerabend (2010). A good example is the interpretation of the red shift in distant galaxies as a Doppler shift, indicating their speed of recession. For galaxies to which we have assigned a velocity that is comparable to the speed of light the observation is theory-laden in two ways. First, as Harold Brown (1993) points out, we assume Special Relativity rather than Newtonian mechanics. This is not problematic because we have independent reasons for that preference. But second, we have to assume that other causes of the red shift are negligible. Instead the red shift might be due to the gravitational attraction of distant galaxies (López-Sandoval 2008). What this example shows is that either we should be sceptical about the widely accepted thesis of the recession of distant galaxies or we should rely heavily on the wisdom of scientists to compare speculations prior to experience.

An example in which scepticism is less plausible is provided by the recalcitrant geocentrist who argues that General Relativity permits a frame of reference in which the Earth is stationary and then insists that this frame is privileged as the only correct one. This is contrary to our use of parallax to measure the distance to nearby stars such as Alpha Centauri. The recalcitrant geocentrist will insist, however, that such measurements are theory-laden and based on the assumption that the 'fixed' stars do not undergo a yearly oscillation. Another example is provided by the dating of ancient rocks using radioactive decay. Potassium 40 is radioactive, with a half-life of over a billion years. About 10 per cent of it decays into the inert gas Argon 40, which is retained by solid rock but not when it is molten. Hence, we can use the ratio of Argon 40 to Potassium 40 in a rock to determine when it was last molten. This and other dating methods are based on the principle that the rate of radioactive decay is unchanging. How can we exclude the hypothesis that the rate of all radioactive decay is controlled, say, by *phantom energy*, a proposed candidate for dark energy whose density changes with time (Baum 2007)?

As if

I invite readers to conclude that reason relies heavily on the *a priori* dismissal of certain hypotheses as highly improbable. That undermines the Baconian reliance on experience to replace *a priori* speculation, showing the need to combine the two. The alternative is to retain the empiricist reliance on experience and rejection of speculation, conceding that this is, however, a sceptical position. This alternative is instrumentalist in the sense that we treat theories as ways of systematizing observations and making predictions without believing them true. It can be given a Kantian gloss by saying that we should be agnostic about things in themselves but rely on our best theories to predict experience. Bas van Fraassen (1980) has presented it in a different way, one which reconciles instrumentalism with common sense and which is in the spirit of Bacon. We do know about the familiar organisms and objects around us, he says, but our confidence in a scientific theory should decrease as we consider less directly observable entities. I call all versions of instrumentalism, *as-if* interpretations with acknowledgement to Hans Vaihinger (1924). They tell us that for all practical purposes it is as if 'well-confirmed' scientific theories are correct.

As-if theories exert an enormous attraction for religious sophisticates – a pox on sophistication! And these days there are many who think of religion as a metaphor. I shall consider as-if interpretations further in Chapter 5, where I discuss how the self-correcting nature of reason tends to generate them. Here, though, I note that they do not avoid the a priori, for they replace a choice between theories by a choice between their as-if variants.[17] Instrumentalists tell us to pick the best theory and give it the 'as if' gloss, but to choose between theories that cannot now be distinguished empirically is to speculate a priori. And if the theories themselves cannot be distinguished at this time nor can their 'as if' variants. I used an example in which the red shift of distant galaxies was not due to an expanding universe but to gravity. A variant theory might be that the gravitational red shift should be far greater than observed except that the gravitational red shift is being corrected for by a Doppler blue shift indicating a universe collapsing so rapidly that there will be a Final Crunch far sooner than we would otherwise expect. Lovers of apocalypse will tell us that the end of the world is nigh. But its being as if nigh has the same practical consequences as its really being nigh, which are quite different from those of the orthodox position. Hence a choice has to be made, and it is made in the same way as between the theories without the 'as if' qualifications.

Logical probabilities

The last, best chance of rescuing empiricism is to admit an *a priori* judgement, but to insist that this is the judgement of *a priori* ignorance not *a priori* knowledge. We may then use this judgement to generate 'logical' probabilities. This approach goes back to the Principle of Insufficient Reason implicit in the work of Jacob Bernouli and Pierre Simon Laplace. It assigns equal probabilities to rival hypotheses prior to any empirical information. Rudolph Carnap's attempt to provide a theory of logical probabilities based on the empiricist *a priori* ignorance that illustrates the problem with this. How do we choose the range of mutually exclusive jointly exhaustive hypotheses to which equal probabilities had to be assigned? (Carnap 1950). Treating distinct but indiscernible situations as different failed to justify ordinary inductive extrapolation, whereas reliance of Leibniz's highly speculative metaphysics of the Identity of Indiscernibles conformed much better with our intuitions.

A more promising version of the theory of logical probabilities has been provided by Edwin T. Jaynes, with his Maximum Entropy Principle (1982). The idea is that the probability distribution for various hypotheses relative to some empirical data is that which has the least information among all those compatible with the data. This is a convincing way of expressing *a priori* ignorance. Because information content is measured by negative entropy, Jaynes uses this to justify the assignment of entropy in statistical mechanics. If we apply Jaynes's theory more generally, then we may note that simpler hypotheses require less information to state than more complicated ones. Consequently, this provides an empiricist justification for preferring simpler theories. Hence empiricists should prefer the simplicity criteria over the aesthetic. Unfortunately for empiricists it does not remove the need for *a priori* judgement, for, as discussed above, our discovery of which classes are objectively natural is presupposed by our judgements of simplicity. Therefore, it is also required if we are to apply Jaynes's approach more generally than to the foundations of statistical mechanics. The very same intellectual capacity (Kant's reflective judgement) is required for discovering a class to be objectively natural as for making an objective judgement of beauty. Hence empiricism cannot fulfil its promise of banishing the a priori. The probabilities obtained using (tacit) priori knowledge of naturalness but constrained by what is reasonable, including core epistemology, will be referred to as probabilities, without qualification. If, in addition, we incorporate controversial judgements as to what leads to truth I call them 'epistemic probabilities'. Probabilities will play a minor role in this work, epistemic probabilities almost no role at all.

Innocent reactions to loss of innocence: Reformed Epistemology and Presuppositionalism

Innocent Reformed Epistemology

The Reformed Epistemology of Nicholas Wolterstorff (1976) and Alvin Plantinga (1983) began as a critique of Classical Epistemology, namely, the thesis that to be reasonable religious beliefs must be derived as conclusions of an argument from premises that are either evident to the senses or self-evident.

Plantinga (1993) has further developed Reformed Epistemology to argue that beliefs based on divine inspiration count as knowledge. I have no quarrel with either of these claims and shall return to Plantinga's further development in Chapter 4. In its original formulation, Reformed Epistemology may also be interpreted as a defence of epistemic innocence. Again, I have no quarrel, for I do not hold the cold shower school of education that scepticism is good for you, and that anyway it is such fun to corrupt the innocent. What educators should do, and what gives philosophy a place in the curriculum, is equip students to deal with any future loss of epistemic innocence, in the hope that the enlightened post-innocent stage will turn out to be an improvement on unenlightened innocence.

Reformed Epistemology and loss of innocence

Reformed Epistemology is an accurate description of a certain kind of epistemological innocence, but may it be taken as a reaction to loss of innocence? The Classical Epistemology that it rejects is a plausible enough account of what is beyond reasonable doubt or dispute, provided we grant as evident what is highly probable and not just what is certain. It is a mistake to assume, however, that we may reasonably believe only what is beyond reasonable doubt. As Plantinga gleefully points out, that thesis does not meet its own standards. I express this self-refutation by pointing out that it is not beyond reasonable doubt to suppose all reasonable beliefs are beyond reasonable doubt. Hence the critique of Classical Epistemology survives loss of innocence concerning religious or other (non-epistemological) beliefs.

The positive assertions of Reformed Epistemology cohere with the evangelical movement's emphasis on religious experience, asserting that the results of experience or inspiration can be reasonably held without further argument, provided rebuttals are countered. The problem with Reformed Epistemology is that, for those who have lost epistemic innocence in their religious beliefs, the rebuttals will include both the awareness of other religious faiths and a proper appreciation of a secular naturalist world view. And, as discussed above when considering Evangelical Christianity, experience alone is not enough to meet these objections. Some consideration is required of the background religious beliefs in terms of which the experience is interpreted. No doubt a reformed epistemologist could point out the impossibility of checking all background beliefs that inform experience. Quite so, and that is one reason for granting that Reformed Epistemology is an adequate account of innocent religious faith. But I am here considering the innocent reaction to loss of innocence.

Presuppositionalism

Presuppositionalism, as I understand it, is the thesis that the use of reason presupposes trust in divine providence.[18] Cornelius van Til (1967) proposed the implausible stronger thesis that reason presupposes Christianity – and a fundamentalist-inclined Protestantism at that. The basic idea of Presuppositionalism is that having lost the innocence even about epistemology there is no obstacle to committing to a providential God as the grounds for reliance on reason. This does not tell us the content of reason, but it would show that any use of reason (going beyond core epistemology) to argue against theism refutes itself. Now, the constraints provided by Reformed Epistemology are, it would seem, as severe as core epistemology can provide. Therefore, Presuppositionalism would justify Reformed Epistemology even for those who have lost innocence.

The providential justification for our reasoning reverses my order of commitment, which is to reason first and then to faith. First, I argue that the bounds to reason provided by Presuppositionalism serve to protect theism only from objections to theism not from objections to Presuppositionalism. Hence, without in any way objecting to theism, diminishing the providential role of god, or even rejecting conservative attitudes to scripture and to tradition, the case for Presuppositionalism may be undermined by providing an alternative providential hypothesis. This is that God does not so much simplify the universe so that even dummies like us can understand but rather grants us god-like minds so that, with time, effort and humility, we can understand without limits. This is just as plausible as Presuppositionalism, which requires not just a commitment to divine providence but also one to the limits of reason. Moreover, this alternative shows that we should not reason from our reasoning powers to Presuppositionalism. By contrast I propose a commitment to reason first, with further commitments within the bounds of reason. And I do so without prejudging the limits of reason. This is quite compatible with using an Inference to the Best Explanation from our reasoning powers to a god who wants us to understand. But that is quite different from the thesis I reject, namely, taking reason to be limited by its presupposition of providence. Therefore, the order of commitment is not reversed, and, disregarding euphony, I declare myself an anti-Presuppositionalist.

Innocent epistemology as synthesis

What I describe as innocent epistemology is much like W. V. O. Quine's program of *Epistemology Naturalized* (1969). This describes how human beings actually reason without considering how we *should* reason. Innocent epistemology is self-correcting in that we naturally, without explicit critical reflection, respond to inconsistencies, as for instance when we note the self-refuting character of Classical Epistemology, or the inconsistency between strict empiricism and our intuitive dismissal of silly but empirically adequate theories such as Omphalism. Hence the problems resulting from over-reliance on experience support the thesis that innocent epistemology is a synthesis of speculation with experience. We use experience where possible to favour one over another plausible speculation, but absent experience we have to rely on the a priori ranking of the speculations.

As part of this synthesis we should attach some, albeit fallible, authority to *common sense*. I take this to be what we collectively believe, itself based to some extent on experience and on *a priori* insight. Another authority endorsed by innocent epistemology is that of well-confirmed science, although it is not always clear just what is well confirmed and what is speculative. I have, for instance, no significant doubt about the use of radioactive decay to date rocks, but I do have doubts about using the red shift to infer the expansion of (our part of) the universe. The authority of common sense and of science should be sufficient to exclude those speculations that are not confirmed experientially but conflict with science or with common sense. It was for this reason that I rejected the standard No Collapse Many Worlds Interpretation of quantum theory in favour of Delayed Collapse.

Philosophy in Modernity was dominated by various attempts at critical reflection about epistemology, with rationalists proclaiming as knowledge the *a priori* intuitions we use to judge speculations, empiricists totally rejecting the role of the a priori, and Kant deflating the *a priori* to compromise with empiricism. Quine's reaction is to replace this dismal history with a descriptive account. But once we start thinking critically, once we lose our innocence, there is no going back. The synthesis may, however, be committed to, in which case it will not be innocent and it will be an account of how we *should* reason.

There should be consensus about the self-evident, namely, what is obvious once we think about it. This constitutes what I call 'core epistemology'. It includes the need that there be some synthesis, judging rival hypotheses both *a priori* and by their experiential consequences. So, there is no need to *commit* to there being a synthesis. Even so, there would be no consensus about the details of this synthesis, including which *a priori* judgements to make. For example, should we rely on the *sensus divinitatis* understood as the sense of something greater than us? Again, there is the problem of weighing up the empirical against the a priori. The dispute over the relative weights given to *a priori* and to empirical considerations is illustrated by the problem of anomalies: To what extent should we continue backing a theory that seems to be refuted by experience, because of its *a priori* support?[19] An interesting example is the Problem of Air, which Peter van Inwagen compares to the Problem of Evil (1991: 153). He imagines an Aristotelian arguing with a Greek atomist thus: 'Suppose air were made of tiny solid bodies as you say. Then air would behave like fine dust: it would eventually settle to the ground and become a mere dusty coating on the surface of the earth. But this is contrary to observation.' The atomists could have responded that it was a splendid theory, and they expected that eventually a solution would be found to this anomaly. Another example is provided by the Kant-Laplace theory of the origin of the solar system, which was rejected for a while but has evolved into the current Nebular theory. The chief anomaly was the slow rotation of the sun (less than once in three weeks) – not what was expected from a contracting spinning disk of gas and dust. How ready should we be to abandon theories that are *a priori* supported by their elegance? Should we say the Greek atomists, and Kant and Laplace were vindicated? Or is it just luck that similar theories are now accepted? It follows that even if it is core epistemology that there be a synthesis, the details of that synthesis require commitment.

Suspense of judgement, epistemological anarchy or commitment?

The previous sections show how, once we reflect upon the ways of arguing over the disputed issues about which we have lost innocence, we discover further disagreements and so lose innocence in epistemology itself, apart from a core. If as a consequence we suspend judgement about disputed questions in epistemology, then we should suspend judgement on the topics, notably those concerned with religion, in which we lost innocence in the first place. Or, suspending judgement on disputed epistemology, we could equally well adopt an 'anything goes' approach reminiscent of Paul Feyerabend (2010) or even New Age thought. Or, as I shall urge, we might commit in ways we judge to be reasonable. The chief core epistemological constraint on commitment that survives the disagreements over epistemology itself is that the criteria for commitment do not suffer self-refutation. That is, we must be entitled to commit to our criteria for commitment.

Reasonable Commitment

In this chapter I provide three conditions for commitment to be reasonable, or, as we say, within the bounds of reason, by which I mean the ordinary human ways of reasoning. I begin by explaining why commitment is sometimes reasonable. Then I justify the three conditions. After further clarification, I reply to some objections, notably the circularity of proposing rules for reasonable commitment that will then be used to commit to reason.

Is commitment ever reasonable?

The case against commitment

In the previous chapter I considered some epistemologically innocent reactions to loss of innocence in religion and other disputed topics. The unsatisfactory nature both of empiricism and of the *a priori* reliance on speculation leads to the synthesis that is reason. We should rely upon speculation to arrive at fairly plausible hypotheses, and then rely upon experience to confirm some hypothesis as such that no reasonable person would doubt it.

The method of speculation and experience underpins a large amount of science, namely, that which a cautious but not overly sceptical thinker will believe true. That gives science a certain authority, which our speculations should in its turn respect. Reason is somewhat messy in that it grants authority not just to science, but to common sense, on the grounds that it is our collective speculation and experience.

Because reason is self-correcting but not always the product of explicit self-criticism, it is hard to be precise as to what is within the bounds of reason in intellectual disputes, where there are arguments for and against a given thesis.

History embarrasses philosophy by showing these disputes can go on for millennia without much progress. Initially this suggests the following:

> *The Weighing Up Rule:* If a good case can be made for and against a thesis but neither outweighs the other then we should suspend judgement.

This rule is contrary to the idea of reasonable commitment that I am advocating, for one of the following must hold true:

(1) No good case can be made for either side of the dispute.
(2) A good case can be made for one side of a dispute but not the other.
(3) A good case can be made for one side of a dispute that outweighs the other. (So overall there is a fairly high probability, say over 75 per cent.)
(4) A good case can be made by both sides but neither outweighs the other.

It would be capricious to commit in case (1), where a 'leap of faith' would indeed be a 'jump in the dark'. Consider some extraterrestrials proclaiming with great earnestness that a black hole is moving at near the speed of light towards the solar system, which it will gobble up. The extraterrestrials refuse to reveal the evidence, and we find the predicted catastrophe rather implausible. There is a debate between those who are impressed by the extraterrestrials' intelligence, and so trust their prediction, and those who interpret their behaviour as showing they are having a joke at our expense. In this case neither side of the debate has a good argument. We should suspend judgement. There is no need for a commitment in cases (2) and (3) and the Weighing Up Rule excludes commitment for case (4). I argue against the Weighing Up Rule by dividing case (4) into (4a) and (4b), which will be clarified in the next section.

(4a) The cases for and against can be combined to make a good case for a judgement of probability around 50 per cent, say between 25 per cent and 75 per cent.
(4b) The cases for and against are *incommensurable*.

An example of (4a) occurs if one extraterrestrial wearily explains what the evidence is, clearly impatient that we are so slow to understand. But then another extraterrestrial disagrees, providing an equally convincing case that the black hole will pass right through the solar system doing no harm. We understand just enough to judge that both cases would, taken in isolation, be strong. But because the cases for and against are of the same kind they cancel each other out. The Weighing Up Rule holds for (4a) because respect for the truth should prevent commitment if we judge there is a roughly 50 per cent chance of truth. To be sure we might decide to act *as if* some claim is true, hitching a ride on the extraterrestrials' flying saucer, even though it is not probable, because of likely benefit if it turns out to be true. But to assert it as true because of the benefits disrespects the truth.

I conclude that if the Weighing Up Rule fails, it fails only in the case (4b). In that case talk of weighing up is misleading because it is a metaphor suggesting an objective procedure for discovering weights, not just the objectivity of the weights themselves. We think of the scales of justice or maybe lifting up an object in the right hand and another in the left to find which is heavier. But the weighing up of arguments or reasons is not always like that even if there is something objective to be discovered. If an intellectual argument cannot be resolved, the judgement as to which case is of greater weight is usually precisely what is being disputed. In such cases, I submit, reason fails to settle the dispute. Instead it sets up an *intellectual dilemma*, by which I mean an intellectual debate with two features. The first is that each side of the debate has a *pro tanto* convincing case, that is, an argument that would be convincing in the absence of counterargument. The second is that neither argument objectively defeats the other. Faced with an intellectual dilemma, the requirement to be reasonable fails to settle the issue and so the Weighing Up Rule is not well motivated. I draw the corollary, however, that in cases (1), (2), (3) and (4a) commitment is not reasonable. Hence the Dilemma Condition is a necessary condition for commitment. It is not sufficient, however, for there are other conditions including the pragmatic one, namely, that the commitment be useful.

Must commitment take effort?

Ordinarily, we think of commitment as hard. While I am not assuming this, I note that the circumstances of an intellectual dilemma will, for truth-respecters, be distressing and the commitment likely to be a matter of emotion and effort.

Intellectual dilemmas

Pro tanto arguments

The idea of an intellectual dilemma is of pro tanto arguments for each side of a debate neither of which defeats the other. Typically, neither case will, however, be conclusive. If both are, then we have a genuine antinomy, but these are rare. If you examine one of Kant's 'antinomies', for instance, neither case is conclusive, even if Kant took them both to be. But they might well be genuine dilemmas.

For a dilemma neither argument is objectively *defeated*. Now, John Pollock distinguishes two kinds of defeat. First, the argument may be *undercut* (Pollock 1986: 39). That is the argument is shown not to support the thesis even ignoring the opposing argument. In the previous chapter I considered the theory-laden character of observation, and these examples also illustrate undercutting. The argument from religious experience *without additional metaphysical premises* to the existence of God as traditionally conceived of (all-powerful, all-knowing and morally good) is undercut by the counterargument that reports of, memories of or even the experience itself is influenced by antecedent beliefs. The other way in which an argument is defeated is if it is *rebutted* (Pollock 1986: 40). That is, the only reasonable judgement is that the counterargument is more powerful, equally powerful or at least about as powerful. In the previous chapter I used an example of scientific orthodoxy, explaining the red shift of distant galaxies as due to the expansion of the Universe. The appeal to orthodoxy is rebutted, I say, by an alternative hypothesis, but readers might prefer their own examples. A dilemma is like mutual rebuttal except that the opposing arguments go past each other without interacting.

An example of a dilemma

Intellectual dilemmas provide the context for intellectual commitment, notably the commitment to reason. An example is provided by the Liar Paradox, based on the sentence 'This sentence is not true'. It is true if and only if it is not true. Hence, it is either both true and not true or neither true nor not true. Both alternatives are paradoxical. The intellectual dilemma is that on the one hand the logic used for deriving the paradox seems impeccable, but on the other hand the conclusion seems absurd: we have an *a priori* intuition that nothing can be both true and not true, and an equally firm one that nothing can be neither true nor not true. This illustrates the features of a dilemma. First, the two arguments would in isolation be considered conclusive, which is even stronger than my requirement of being beyond reasonable doubt. Second, they do not defeat each other. This mutual non-defeat is shown by the way the thinker tends to oscillate between thinking that there must be something wrong with the logic because the conclusion is absurd and thinking that the logic is impeccable, so the apparent absurdity must be accepted. In this case, however, there is no need for commitment, for the paradox has no important consequences, so we are entitled to suspend judgement. This example also illustrates the potential for a dilemma to set up a dialectic with the impeccable logic being the thesis and the absurdity of the conclusion being the antithesis. There should be a way out of here, a synthesis – or so we hope.[1] But the dilemmas that are the occasions for commitment are those that defy synthesis.

Intellectual and moral dilemmas

Intellectual dilemmas are comparable to moral ones, in which there is an undefeated pro tanto case for acting and also one for not acting. My example, the Hostage Dilemma, is a variant on Bernard Williams's (Smart and Williams 1973: 247). Ten hostages including a baby have been taken by someone brought up to treat murder lightly but never lie and never break a promise. The hostage-negotiator is given a choice, kill the baby and the other nine will be released; otherwise they will all be killed. No amount of thought will help the decision. As with other dilemmas it is natural to pray even if you do not do so regularly. This supports the sense that there is an intellectual impasse, an *aporia*, if you insist, for, typically, those who seldom pray, pray for guidance when all else fails.

The Hostage Dilemma illustrates a further feature of dilemmas. The weak-willed but virtuous person will do nothing. A strong-willed person will be more likely to kill the baby to save the other nine. It would be tendentious to describe the weak-willed as cowardly, for that would be to judge it right to kill the baby. There should be no shame in being weak-willed in the face of a moral dilemma nor any pride in being strong-willed.

Now consider an intellectual dilemma concerning, for instance, the existence of God. If we find that thesis distasteful, then we will not commit in the face of a dilemma. If we find it attractive, then the more weak-willed of us will more easily give in and so commit themselves, for the hard option is to resist our emotions and suspend judgement. As in the case of moral dilemmas we should neither be proud of strength nor ashamed of weakness. Sometimes to be weak is to exhibit proper humility while to be strong is to 'kick against the goads'.

The conditions for reasonable commitment

I propose three necessary conditions for reasonable commitment.

1. *The Dilemma Condition.*
   The circumstances of a commitment should be an intellectual dilemma, with undefeated pro tanto cases both for and against the thesis to which

commitment is made. Each case must be such as would be convincing beyond reasonable doubt if considered in isolation. The dilemma must be genuine in the sense that we have diligently examined both sides of the argument and that we have failed to find the desired synthesis.

2. *The Pragmatic Condition.*

   We should only commit on matters that have good practical consequences. Practical consequences include attitudes of love, hate or considered indifference.

3. *The Absolute Superiority Condition.*

   The content of the commitment should be absolutely better than rival commitments.

I hold that these conditions are individually necessary for it to be reasonable to commit to a given thesis. Tentatively, I propose them as jointly sufficient. Even if they are satisfied you might reasonably choose not to commit, although I commend prayer for inspiration to those who hesitate.[2] In Chapter 4, I make some comparisons, which will show that I am, however, requiring rather stricter conditions for commitment than most do.

These conditions owe much to, but will be contrasted with, William James's account of the passional choice in his 'Will to Believe' (1896) as well as recent discussion of intractable philosophical disagreement (see Feldman and Warfield 2010).

More on the Dilemma Condition

The first condition is that the circumstance of a commitment is an intellectual dilemma, with good pro tanto arguments both for and against the proposition that is the content of the commitment.[3] The case for this condition was made in the first section, in which commitment is otherwise criticized as unreasonable. The Dilemma Condition may also be treated as a response to William Clifford, to whom James was replying. Clifford famously sums up his paper 'Ethics of Belief' (1887) thus: 'It is wrong always, everywhere and for anyone to believe anything on insufficient evidence.' Intuitively he is correct, if we have insufficient reasons for belief and insufficient reasons against. Intellectual dilemmas result, however, not from too little evidence but from too much, for there is a pro tanto case for belief and one against.

The first condition is, then, that the cases for and against the thesis are the horns of a genuine intellectual dilemma. That is, either side would, but for the other side, be convincing. The requirement that the dilemma is genuine is obvious, for it would be silly to commit in the face of a dilemma if one of the cases involved would fail on feasible further examination, or if there is some synthesis that incorporates the best features of the cases for and against. The cases made on both sides of the dilemma are *incommensurable* in the sense that weighing up the reasons is itself a disputed judgement. Otherwise one side would defeat the other. This contrasts with the situation considered in Section One of no, or only very weak, arguments for either side, in which to commit would seem capricious. Another way of expressing the incommensurability is to say that in a genuine dilemma the sides not only disagree about what is true, but there is a further significant disagreement about which case is stronger– something that should not occur in cases of commensurable arguments for and against. The judgement is inevitably disputed because the only respect in which I hold that I am superior to dissenters is that I judge that I have made the correct decision *in this case*. And, likewise, those who disagree with me believe themselves superior only in that they judge that they have made the correct decision *in this case*. Let me repeat that disputed judgement is compatible with the content of what is judged being quite objective. Indeed, if the content is subjective (e.g. that hot spicy food is good) then there is no dispute.

On the Pragmatic Condition

The second condition, one that James would accept as part of his pragmatism, is that we should not commit on inconsequential matters, which we should treat as mere speculations. To be more explicit, there should be good practical consequences of the commitment. For instance, there are competing scientific theories about the origin of life on Earth. Such speculative research is worth funding, but it seems silly to commit, because there are no practical consequences. Among practical consequences I include our attitudes of love, hate or indifference towards things, including friends, neighbours, other living people, future generations, other animals, the environment and, for believers, God. When I say that these consequences should be good I mean what is good for us not what we desire.

The necessity of the pragmatic requirement is easily demonstrated: to commit is to disregard those who disagree and so would be arrogant if inconsequential, and worse if of bad consequence. Therefore, I take this second condition to be, in part, an ethical rule, expressing proper humility.[4] It is not purely ethical, though, because intellectual arrogance leads to false beliefs. Hence, I treat it as a requirement for being reasonable.

The third condition

The Absolute Superiority Condition is more controversial. It is that the thesis committed-to is absolutely better than rival theses, not just better for us. I understand goodness to be the most generic positive value of which moral goodness (righteousness) and beauty are species. It was discussed when considering axiarchism in the previous chapter. Absolute Superiority may then be defined thus: X is absolutely superior to Y only if it is objectively the case that X is better than Y, and only if it is not (just) better for me or better for us, but better without qualification.

The case for the third condition is in two parts. First, I show the need for *some* further condition. Then, less securely, a case is made for the detailed condition that I propose. Part of the case for requiring some further condition is that we should heed the generally accepted warning against wishful thinking. For instance, I believe in an afterlife. Is that just because death scares the whole Bristol Scale out of me? Such wishful thinking is unreasonable, but the Pragmatic Condition by itself permits it. More generally, if there is no extra condition, then, in a dilemma, the Pragmatic Condition would be sufficient for reasonable commitment. Hence, we could sometimes commit just because it is useful. That is loathsome. Because the Pragmatic Condition is necessary but not sufficient, we should instead say that we sometimes fail to commit because it is useless to do so.

Another reason for requiring some extra condition is that to accept ordinary human ways of reasoning is to grant that they tend to lead to the truth. Because of the self-correction of these ways of reasoning, we should make the proviso that where reasoning permits contrary conclusions a person should suspend judgement. Hence the conditions for commitment should not allow contrary conclusions. More explicitly, we should not both judge it reasonable to commit to X and judge it reasonable to commit to Y, where X and Y are believed incompatible. Consequently, commitment is only reasonable when it is a choice between committing and not committing. The Pragmatic Condition is not sufficient to exclude contrary commitments, and hence some third condition is required. Its insufficiency is illustrated by a commitment to a religion because it is the faith of our forebears. Imagine an island divided into two nations. They distrust each other but, after a war many years ago, live at peace. This peace depends on each nation's cohesion, which is in large measure due to religious unity – or so we are to suppose. They are well aware of the difference in their religions, and adolescents often query why their nation should have the true religion. They are urged to commit for the general good. That would satisfy the Pragmatic Condition, and we may fill in details to make the decision as to which religion to accept a genuine dilemma.[5]

Core Epistemology shows, then, the need for some third condition but not its content, which I arrive at by non-evident but intuitive reasoning, in this case the method of reflective equilibrium (Rawls 1971; Daniels 2013). That is, the Absolute Superiority Condition both has intuitive examples and is shown to be plausible by a combination of four arguments (see Chapter 5 for an intuitive non-religious example, that of human reasoning).

The weak axiarchism argument

The first argument for the Absolute Superiority Condition is that it is a way of weakening axiarchism that does justice to it, without commitment to it. This argument is further supported by the plausible thesis that scientific reasoning is itself a special case of axiarchism, namely, aesthetic understanding, discussed in the previous chapter. Understanding is, I suggest, both an aesthetic experience (Forrest 1991) and a guide to truth, as in inference to the best explanation (Harman 1986). If we were to commit to axiarchism, then everything I propose as an intellectual dilemma would be a disagreement about value. Moreover, there would be no genuine further commitments because we would have already decided to as-if commit whenever there would otherwise have been a dilemma. Instead I advocate a case-by-case decision to commit or not, for a general commitment to axiarchism fails to meet either the Dilemma or the Pragmatic Conditions. The Dilemma Condition fails because neither the case for it nor that against it would be totally convincing even without the opposing case. Hence, even if we do commit it would only be to the probability of axiarchism. As for the Pragmatic Condition, I can think of no consequences of axiarchism that do not already follow from individual commitments in accordance with the Absolute Superiority Condition. Instead of a commitment, then, I take the appeal to the plausibility of axiarchism as part of the case for the plausibility of the Absolute Superiority Condition.

The anti-pluralist argument

My anti-pluralist stand is central to my theory of commitment, and in the next chapter I criticize various accounts of commitment as pluralist. Here I rely on anti-pluralism to demonstrate the need for a third condition for reasonable commitment. First, then, core epistemology assures us that two contrary commitments cannot both be true.[6] Because reason is the guide to truth, it follows that reason has failed if contrary commitments made in similar circumstances are both reasonable. Consider, for instance, two rival dilemmas: atheism versus agnosticism and theism versus agnosticism, and suppose those deciding whether to commit are in similar circumstances. If both dilemmas met the conditions for reasonable commitment, then both theism and atheism would be reasonable. Because reason is a means to the end of arriving at truths, the commitment I shall be making to reason requires confidence that failures of reason are exceptional and occur only when the intuitive rules fail. In cases where we might as easily commit to a thesis as to its negation, there is no such failure – we should suspend judgement. If, however, there is a dilemma in which we might accept a thesis or else suspend judgement, we cannot suspend judgement as to whether or not to suspend judgement. I conclude that reason fails in such dilemmas, but only in such dilemmas. In the next chapter I return to the topic of pluralism, considering the suggestion that religious pluralism is an exception to my general condemnation.

To avoid pluralism the conditions for reasonable commitment must be stringent. This is why I require absolute superiority rather than absolute goodness. In addition, I throw out the challenge to provide a plausible alternative that is just as stringent. Please don't suggest an Absolute Inferiority Condition – that is not merely counter-intuitive but incompatible with the Pragmatic Condition.

The stubborn disagreement argument

The third argument for the Absolute Superiority Condition is that it locates stubborn disagreements among intellectual peers as ultimately due to different judgements of value. This is an area of disagreement where we all concede that judgements are disputed. With some relish, perhaps, we dismiss those who disagree as 'benighted' – they just don't get it.

The analogy with moral dilemmas

Finally, the Absolute Superiority Condition is supported by the analogy with moral dilemmas, such as the Hostage Dilemma mentioned above. In such cases there is an ethical rule and a pro tanto good reason for breaking the rule. All too often the rule is broken for pragmatic reasons, concerning say the good of a nation, but clearly it is wicked to break a rule deliberately for pragmatic reasons, saying the ends justify the means, unless you are completely satisfied that breaking the rule has better consequences than any other action you can perform. For instance, on a variant of the Hostage Dilemma the negotiator is given the choice to kill the baby or to commit suicide or watch all ten hostages die. In that case suicide is absolutely superior to infanticide, which would be wicked.

Committing to absolute values

In the special case in which the commitment is to a judgement of absolute value, the third condition is trivial. Suppose something is good, for instance, the understanding provided by science. Then is it better that it be good than that it be not good? For if it were not good there would be fewer good things, which is a less good situation. Moreover, this is as objective as the thesis that understanding is good. Nor is the value of there being more good things just a means to an end; it is intrinsically good. Therefore, the Absolute Superiority Condition is trivial when applied to absolute values.

The only objection I can think of is that iterated evaluations – it is good that it is good – are not so much trivial as meaningless. If so, then the Absolute Superiority Condition is a meaningless prohibition and so may be ignored. Hence the objection would be a pyrrhic victory, for a meaningless condition functions just like a trivial one.

No commitment to completion

There could be grounds for thinking you have a complete theory on some topic, one to which nothing could be added. The hoped-for Theory of Everything in physics might in the future provide an example. These grounds would include the sense that everything was understood. Absent such understanding it is not absolutely good that the theory you have is complete, in the sense that it cannot be improved, for it would be better if more could be added so that more was understood. Hence regardless of the practical benefits we should never commit to completion. This is quite compatible with holding that a religion is true, even that it is the 'one true religion' in the sense that the truths within any other *currently* existing religion are contained within it.[7]

The Absolute Superiority Condition for reasonable commitment is somewhat tentative, and I urge readers who reject it nonetheless to agree that we should not commit to completion. This reflects the judgement that commitments fail to count as knowledge because they are always somewhat tentative.

Divine guidance?

I do not propose any additional necessary conditions for commitment. One suggestion that comes to mind, though, is divine guidance. If that is merely a matter of praying for guidance then I say 'Amen', but that does not affect the intellectual discussion. But if the idea is that commitment is unreasonable unless there is a sense of divine guidance, then this is open to the obvious objection that the sense of guidance is only relevant if it is evidence of genuine guidance. The sense of divine guidance is shown to be unreliable, however, by the diverse, and often bizarre, claims accompanied by the sense of guidance. If nonetheless some case could be made for this sense-of-guidance condition then the case for and the case against would set up a further dilemma, but one in which the Pragmatic Condition is not satisfied, for there are practical benefits in commitments, such as those to humanism, that are made without this sense of divine guidance.

Replies to objections

Acknowledging rivals?

Suppose we replaced the Absolute Superiority Condition (3) by the variant (3*). The content of the commitment should be absolutely good.

That would be stronger in one respect, but weaker in another. That (3*) sometimes constrains more than (3) is illustrated by the situation of someone who judges none of the options to be good but commits to the least bad. That would satisfy (3) but not (3*). An example might be commitment to free will. You might judge having free will to be neither good nor bad because freely doing good is very good but freely doing bad is very bad. Nonetheless you might think the absence of freewill to be definitely bad. In such a situation, commitment seems just as reasonable as if you take freewill to be absolutely good. So, if we reject condition (3) it should not be in favour of (3*) but the disjunction, (3) or (3*).

The more serious objection to the Absolute Superiority Condition, (3), is that it is too strict. Does not tolerance require permitting situations in which several incompatible commitments are reasonable, say to various different religions? The case made for above for there being some third condition answers this objection, but it is worth expanding, for it seems intolerant and arrogant to grant that your judgement is disputed by those who are at least as able and as experienced as you are, and yet insist that your position is superior to rivals. Suppose you and I disagree. Then we might be able to do the philosophical thing, and either come to agree or uncover a deeper disagreement. But once the argle bargle is over we may well have an irreducibly disputed but reasonable disagreement. At this stage, there are no further intellectual reasons for intellectual peers to disagree. If I then commit to the disputed position, I do so because it attracts me not because I am arrogant and think I am superior. If my opponent does not commit even though the position is attractive our dispute is not intellectual, so the question of intellectual ability is irrelevant. If, however, more than one position is attractive then the choice between them is unreasonable because, by the rules governing reasonable commitment, the one position is as likely to be true as the other. This problem does not arise, however, if the choice is between commitment and suspense of judgement, for it makes no sense to say these two options are as likely. I conclude that we may avoid suspending judgement if it is a choice to commit or not to commit, but that there should be only one candidate for commitment. Hence, I prefer the condition (3) both to its variant (3*) and to their disjunction.

The objection from circularity

The objection is that the conditions for reasonable commitment themselves presuppose commitments:

1. The Absolute Superiority Condition presupposes the controversial thesis that some things are absolutely better than others, and
2. Reason, that is, ordinary human ways of reasoning, has been used when formulating the conditions for commitment.

The circularity is genuine in that someone who is sceptical about reasoning apart from core epistemology will find nothing in that core to support the conditions that I have stated. But it does not show that it is contrary to that core to accept the reasonable requirements for commitment, for if we initially suspend judgement about those requirements as general rules, we may then commit in ways that are in fact in accordance with them, including commitments to the general rules. Likewise, if we initially suspend judgement as to the objectivity of values we may commit to that objectivity. This coheres with the method of reflective equilibrium, in which the judgements of particular cases both support and are supported by the general rules, but there is no circularity in relying on particular judgements prior to the formulation of the general rules.

Core epistemology does provide some constraint, however, for it includes, I submit, an injunction against arbitrary or capricious commitment. Suppose I think it would be great if my granddaughter was a reincarnation of my grandmother and so, on a whim, decided to assert this. That would be an example of an arbitrary commitment. There are, however, different ways of ensuring that commitment not be arbitrary. One suggestion, my own, is to rely on the constraints of ordinary human reasoning, formalized in the conditions I propose. An alternative would be to abandon the Pragmatic Condition but keep Absolute Superiority. Other alternatives should, however, be definitely rejected, for instance, the strict, Cliffordian rule of always suspending judgement unless there is a convincing case for and none against, for, acknowledging Alvin Plantinga's influence, I gleefully point out that the Cliffordians are hoist by their own petards: there is no convincing case for the Cliffordian position except by standards, such as appeal to intuition, lax enough to allow a convincing case against.

The collapse objection

This is the objection that no reasonable commitment is ever made, because to be reasonable the Absolute Superiority Condition must be satisfied, but if it is, then the position 'committed to' is in fact objectively judged superior, relying on the axiarchist principle that the absolutely better is more probable than the less good.

This objection would, if cogent, remove all need for the pragmatic requirement and would result in a multiplication of scare-quotes, around 'dilemma' and 'commitment'. I reply in two ways. First, I note that judgements of absolute and hence objective value are themselves sometimes disputed in the sense that my only reason for believing myself superior to dissenters is that I claim that I have made the correct judgement (see Chapter 6). My second reply is that the collapse of the dilemma only occurs if and after we have committed to axiarchism, which I have not recommended.

The insincerity objection

A familiar objection is that we cannot commit because we cannot directly choose to believe. This is misguided because commitment is an act of assent, either public or internal. There is, however, a successor objection, namely, that assent that does not arise from prior belief is insincere. This objection has force only insofar as insincerity is a defect, and I grant that it is defective to assent to something inconsistent with what you already believe. But it is far from clear that there is any defect in assenting in the context of previously suspending judgement. It is mischievous, therefore, to call such assent insincere, because that invites condemnation. On the contrary, one of the states we call belief in a given proposition is the *habit* of assenting to that proposition. And clearly a habit of assenting is caused by repeated assent, not the other way around. I shall return to this in the final chapter, when considering the topic of faith, where the idea that faith is passive is a common mistake.

That the choice to assert can be sincere is further supported by the not too speculative thesis of parallel processing: the brain generates several scenarios, leading to several possible ways of behaving (cf. Dennett 1991). In that case a choice to act is a favouring of some over other scenarios, and a choice to assert is sincere if it is a decision to favour a scenario according to which what is asserted holds true. This will not express a prior belief when there are other scenarios in which it is false.

Not committing to angels

There is one further objection to the rules for commitment, namely, that the rules are too lax, and it is hard to find any commitment people actually make that does not meet these standards. On the contrary, the study of religions provides many examples of unreasonable commitments, but here I provide an illustrative example that I hope is not too controversial and is of independent interest.

The case for angels is widespread experience, which would be convincing but for the opposition of Ockham's Razor, since angels even if physical would not be organisms of familiar kinds (Phillip Pullman – 2008 – treats then as beings of light, which is insightful). For those of us who have not met angels, this sets up an intellectual dilemma where any reasonable judgement would have to be a commitment. I am not sure why Christians should care, but critically reflective participants of Yoruba religion might well identify the small 'g' gods, or Orisas, with the angels of the Abrahamic religions, even though in Santeria, the fusion of Yoruba religion with Catholicism, they are identified with saints (see Kerade 1994). For those Yoruba, then, who have not met angels but have lost their innocent religious beliefs, the role of angels, that is gods, in their practice presupposes commitment.

Commitment to angels fails, however, to satisfy the Pragmatic Condition. Not only is there the moral hazard of using the 'Satan made me do it' excuse, there is the diversion of effort from practical methods to seeking the intercession of angels or gods. To be sure this 'opiate of the people' criticism can be made of religion generally, but it does not succeed if petitions are made only to the worship-worthy being, for worship implies submission, and that is not compatible with the attempt to manipulate or persuade that is characteristic of petitions to lesser deities, angels and saints.

If we ignore the Pragmatic Condition there remains the question of whether it is absolutely good that there be angels. It is indeed absolutely good that there be many kinds of rational creatures and not just our own kind. Hence it is good that there be extraterrestrials. But angels have two characteristics that distinguish them from extraterrestrials. The first is that even if physical they are not, strictly speaking, material. The second is that they can interact with us by preternatural means. While I have no objection to speculations about angels, I fail to see why their existence, as opposed merely to extraterrestrials evolved on distant Earth-like planets, is good. My judgement here illustrates a rather general feature of commitments. Although I am judging absolute goodness, which is mind-independent, my judgement is itself subjective in the sense that others, such as adherents of Yoruba religion, might well disagree, and I have no reason for asserting superiority of judgement over them other than the fact that I judge myself right and them wrong.

Conclusion

The three proposed conditions for commitment to be reasonable are individually necessary and, tentatively, jointly sufficient. Even their necessity is in principle defeasible but I know of no defeater. I shall argue that commitment to reason and science, to positive humanism, and to the worship of God meet these conditions.

Some Comparisons

Comparisons with similar accounts of commitment justify having developed my own theory of reasonable commitment rather than, say, relying on William James's. The points of divergence also help to clarify my theory. Nonetheless readers may well decide to skip some of the many comparisons, for my criticisms are somewhat repetitive, being mostly based on the stand I take against pluralism.

Fideism

Clarification

The contrast between faith and reason is confused by the ambiguity between the following:

1. The contrast between the 'heart' and the 'head';
2. The contrast between testimony-based faith and reasoning abstracted away from testimony on religious matters; and
3. The contrast between faith that goes beyond reason, that is, ordinary human ways of reasoning, and those ways of reasoning.

I delay discussing the 'head'/'heart' contrast until I consider Pascal, below. The second contrast can be quickly dealt with: to ignore testimony is contrary to reason. It is the third contrast that I take to define fideism. An additional complication is that when asked to justify their religious beliefs many will say 'I have faith' partly as a way of stopping a conversation that embarrasses the epistemically innocent. Unfortunately, this conversation-stopper can prepare the way for the confusion of saying, 'I have lost my faith', referring to a loss of innocence.

I mean by fideism, then, the position of favouring faith over reason, that is, over our ordinary ways of reasoning when they go beyond *core epistemology*, namely, that which is evident, so we cannot help accept it. I distinguish moderate from extreme fideism, with moderate fideists denying that their beyond-reason faith contradicts reasoning. I take both Stephen Evans (1998) and John Bishop (2002, 2007) to be recent examples. My own position could be thought of as a moderate fideism that is not restricted to religion. The three proposed conditions for commitment show how ordinary human reasoning restricts the scope of fideism, especially the condition that commitment is only reasonable when we are faced with an intellectual dilemma.

As an example of extreme fideism, I consider the fundamentalist theologian Charles Ryrie. He does not reject reason but rather takes faith to be decisive when they clash. For instance, in answer to the objection that the children of Adam and Eve must have had incestuous sex to reproduce, he defends this incest because there would have been no harm in inbreeding (Ryrie 1999: 110). If I were a fundamentalist I would argue that in this situation these children were faced with a moral dilemma: incest was wrong but so, in the circumstances, would be abstinence. I would draw the conclusion that, had there been no Fall, God would have saved them from a moral dilemma, say by miraculously creating other human beings (from other ribs of Adam?). That Ryrie does not draw this conclusion shows that he is an extreme fideist trusting the Bible as a religiously complete teaching. But that he argues that incest was prohibited only because of the detrimental effects of inbreeding exhibits ordinary human reasoning about divine commands.

The rejection of extreme fideism can be argued for in two ways: either by considering the individual making the commitment or by considering disagreement with unbelievers. The first way is based on the multiplicity of fideisms to choose between. No doubt the epistemically innocent fideist is faced only with a choice of faith over unbelief, but anyone aware of the multiplicity of faiths realizes, however, that faith is not enough to choose between competing religious claims, such as Protestantism, Catholicism, Islam, Hinduism or even non-theistic religions such as Theravada Buddhism. For reasons that need not detain us, only conservative or literalist religious views tend to be held in an extreme fideist fashion. But the point remains that reason has to be invoked to decide between faiths. All that survives of fideism is the basic trust in something other than the purely human. But that residue of fideism is captured by the cosmic optimism implicit in the Absolute Superiority Condition. I conclude that extreme fideism has nothing to contribute.

Because commitment is an act, but belief is passive, I follow the Catholic tradition in taking faith to be an act of assent (Herbermann 1913).[1] But what if we took faith to be a combination of passive belief with an act of trust? That would affect the role of reason and protect extreme fideism from the criticism I have just made, for then the answer to 'Why do you believe in this rather than that religion?' would be 'I cannot help it, thank God'. Now there are many things we cannot help believing, including all that is *evident*. Hence, I have no quarrel with those who cannot help believing – or disbelieving. And that is precisely the situation of many who have an innocent religious belief. For those who have lost this innocence, an act of assent is, however, required. So, I reach the unsurprising conclusion that extreme fideism is for the epistemically innocent.

The second way of arguing against extreme fideism is based on respect for those unbelievers who are epistemic peers. They find fideists smug, but that is scarcely a reason for rejecting it. And, as I say, again and again, epistemic innocence is not my target, so insofar as the response 'I just have faith' is an innocent conversation-stopper I am only criticizing it as sloppy. The innocent should instead say, 'Why do you think faith requires justification?' But for those who have lost innocence there is the problem of respect. If others disagree with you, then you cannot coherently take your present commitment to be true by good luck. Instead you must assert your epistemic superiority over your peers. You might appeal to divine guidance, but even so you have to assert some superiority over other religious believers who likewise appeal to divine guidance and reach incompatible conclusions. Nor should you take yourself to be superior unless there is something you are judging better than your rivals. For instance, you might think your opponent is clever but rather silly, or has not studied enough relevant literature or has a narrower background experience having led a sheltered life. But none of these responses are fideistic. Those who believe in a providential God who inspires must be relying on some grounds, however intuitive or inarticulate. Otherwise, we may criticize their faith as blind. The Absolute Superiority Condition that I propose is a way of explicating the intuitive processes that prevent faith from being blind.

Wittgensteinian fideism

As I understand it, Wittgensteinian fideists dissolve the third of the contrasts between faith and reason by taking 'language games', and hence human reasoning, to vary from domain to domain, with religion providing just one domain among many.[2] If they are right, then my project of using uniform rules to govern all commitments is undercut. My response is that they use the wrong way to divide human communications into the domains. Some talk is primarily for socializing. Other talk is intended as edifying. Again, there are research programs. And we curse and swear. But in addition to all these, there is the domain of individual assent to that which is proclaimed as objectively factual. This *domain of facts* is centred on metaphysics and includes science understood realistically. It is because religion overlaps metaphysics that the same rules of commitment hold. And the ultimate reason for this is that it is contrary to core epistemology to worship if the domain of facts does not contain a worship-worthy being. Incense is no substitute for metaphysics.[3]

Wittgensteinian fideism does, however, exhibit a natural enough reaction to loss of innocence, that of deliberately pretending, make-believing or acting as if something is true that we would like to be true. An object of worship must, however, be literally worthy of worship if we are to avoid idolatry: neither as-if, nor metaphor, nor pretence of worth suffice.

Descartes

Descartes responded to his loss of epistemic innocence by proposing a thorough review of all his beliefs to decide what he genuinely knew. He also aimed to establish the growing corpus of knowledge (science) on firm foundations. He thought that a day's hard thought in a well-heated room would do the trick – nice work if you can get it, but you can't. Nonetheless he may be reconstructed as making a commitment to reasoning, aware that an evil demon could manipulate even what seems a valid deduction.

Or, closer to the text of *Meditations*, we could take Descartes to have faith in a God who will not allow us to be deceived, provided we purge reason of morally culpable defects. My objection to that thesis is that sometimes, by bad luck rather than by being overconfident, morally conscientious scientists do make mistakes. Examples are not easy to give, for we are tempted to say, in hindsight, that they were overconfident. An example might be the assertion that there were no chemical compounds of the 'inert' gases, such as xenon.

Pascal's Wager

Pascal's Wager concerns a situation in which a religious doctrine is of some positive probability, and there is an antecedent belief that commitment to the doctrine has an infinitely better outcome if it is true than if the alternative is true.

This would also apply to an intellectual dilemma, in which no definite probability can be assigned, provided it is definitely non-zero. And the circumstances of the Wager are such that the Pragmatic Condition is satisfied. The reason, then, why I reject Pascal's Wager is that, as usually formulated, it requires no further condition, such as Absolute Superiority.

I begin by distinguishing the Wager in a strict sense from the wider application of risk-taking to matters of faith. The Wager in the strict sense is relevant if an atheist or agnostic assigns some small positive probability to the thesis that there is a God with whom we can enter into loving relations in the afterlife. You might also suppose that (1) this would be the highest good for humans and (2) non-belief in this life is a serious obstacle to achieving that goal in the next life. In that case, you might well want to become a theist. And it would be priggish not to manipulate your own beliefs. In any case the Wager would also concern others, for you would want to educate your children in such a way that they are likely to be theists.

The Wager presupposes that deliberately rejecting faith for intellectual reasons prevents, or at least jeopardizes, salvation. But a worship-worthy God would not, I insist, require faith in that sense, even though I grant that the rejection of faith for other than intellectual reasons might well be a spiritual hazard. More specifically, I say that the situation of Pascal's Wager arises only from the wrong sort of anthropomorphism applied to a god or the gods, in which these beings are not worthy of worship or trust but nonetheless have some virtues – those of a warrior caste maybe. In that case, although given to anger and vengeance, the gods are true to their word. But, as has been widely pointed out, there are very many varieties of theism, with various combinations of virtues and vices with no guide to choosing between them. Such hypotheses, especially that of a god of malicious supreme power, are scary, but they have no practical consequences and are, moreover, highly improbable. They are best ignored. To any not persuaded of its improbability I recommend a commitment against supreme malice.

I have objected to Pascal's Wager, because of its relaxation of the third, condition, Absolute Superiority. I anticipate three replies. First, my dismissal of the idea that faith is required for salvation might seem arrogant to those who accept either the Lutheran and Reformed doctrine of *Sole Fida* or the Roman Catholic one of *Nulla Salus*. My rejoinder is that John Schellenberg (1993) has provided all the argument we require. He argues that God would want relations of mutual love with all humans and concludes that the occurrence of sincere and intellectually able atheists refutes the existence of God. There are two ways of undermining his argument. First, someone might conclude there is a God who is worthy of worship but does not want to be worshipped, that is God loves us in a benevolent manner but does not want our love. Or, as I would maintain, our task in this life is not primarily to know God as individuals but to take part in our collective history, including the relation between God and humanity. The disappointing thesis that God does want us to reciprocate the divine love clearly undermines Pascal's Wager. My collectivist response might seem to support it, however, because if we enter into relations with God collectively then individuals must participate in that collective, so maybe atheists are for no fault of their own excluded. I disagree because God would want all humans to be part of the collective entity that is ultimately saved, even if they turn out to be free-loaders. Hence, the collectivist response supports the thesis of post-mortem conversion. The doctrines of *Nulla Salus* and *Sole Fida* should be interpreted accordingly.

The second reply is that the good of reciprocal divine-human relations is so great even in this life that we should risk anything for it. I have a twofold response. First, the reply reflects the individualistic bias that I have rejected above. Second, it undervalues the humanist alternative to a religious life. We are not faced with a stark choice between religion and self-engrossed hedonism.

The third rejoinder is based on an amalgam of Wittgensteinian Fideism with Pascal's Wager. The idea is that a religious faith is a complex of explicit assertions, implicit beliefs, attitudes and emotions.[4] Therefore, the objection goes, we accept or reject it as a whole, not piecemeal. Acceptance is a risk, the 'leap of faith', but the risk, the objection goes, is justified by our attraction to the whole package. My rejoinder is not to condemn such Pascalian reasoning as to diagnose it as a proper reaction to a *partial* loss of innocence, one that ceases to take faith for granted but nonetheless is not a thorough critical reflection; for further reflection on faith shows that the whole complex of faith depends on worship and hence the existence of a worship-worthy God, which is not, therefore, just one detail in an all-embracing way of life. To think otherwise is to worship the faith rather than to worship God in faith. This is idolatrous and so condemned by that faith.

The 'heart' versus the 'head'

Pascal is famous for much besides the Wager, and one of his pertinent remarks is that 'the Heart has reasons of which Reason knows nothing'. I interpret this to mean that although we may reflect critically on some of our assertions (i.e. use reason) we do not and often cannot reflect critically on many of our tendencies to believe, including, I would say, the a priori and more generally what philosophers call 'intuition'. The use of the 'heart' metaphor suggests a connection between emotions and intuitions, as does the widespread use of the verb 'feel'. That our intuitions are swayed by our emotions is often taken as a reason to be suspicious of them. Commitments are an exception to this for we commit to what attracts. Hence, we should not totally condemn the influence of emotions on intuitions, but rather condemn the emotions only if they fail to be proportionate to the values they represent.

Loss of innocence and critical reflection

The epistemically innocent rely heavily on the 'heart', which in religious matters may well support faith, but loss of innocence leads to reliance, sometimes over-reliance, on the 'head', that is, critical reflection. This acts on our intuitions in four ways: undermining, explicating, endorsing or revealing recalcitrance. Critical reflection, also known as 'philosophizing', does good but also harm, and I am not condemning the unexamined life. Nonetheless, when epistemic innocence is lost we inevitably philosophize. The advantage of critical reflection is that it enables the self-correcting features of reason to operate for the individual as well as collectively. The disadvantage is that it can lead to the Fallacy Fallacy, as Bill Lycan calls it: the careless assumption that a piece of reasoning is fallacious because an obvious way of explicating it exhibits a fallacy. Clearly the alternative is that the reasoning is sound but the explication incorrect. Sometimes a philosophical explication is like vanillin (vanilla 'essence'). This is indeed a component of genuine vanilla but no substitute for a wonderful flavour.

When not exhibiting the Fallacy Fallacy the explication of intuitions might genuinely undermine them. For instance, there is an intuition that because the aesthetic (i.e. intrinsic) value of a work of art is subjective (i.e. assessed differently by different art-lovers) then that value is itself subjective (i.e. has no truth-value independent of the one judging). This intuition is undermined by explicating it as the following inference: the obvious explanation of the subjectivity of judgement is that the thing being judged is itself subjective. And, the inference goes, the obvious is the correct explanation. Further reflection tells us that sometimes the obvious explanation is best, sometimes it is not. And in this case, we may explain the subjectivity of the evaluations equally well as a case of different people noticing different aesthetically valuable characteristics without contradiction. (If you are dead to Rubens and I am dead to Rembrandt then both of our positive evaluations can be true.) So, explication fails to convert the case for subjectivity into an Inference to the Best Explanation, and the intuition is undermined.

At other times the intuition is endorsed but made redundant. It is now replaced by an explicit inference. An example is the intuitive incompatibility of *Nulla Salus* with a loving god, for the inference from a loving god to the negation of *Nulla Salus* may be explicated by arguing that the tension between the good of individuals and that of the community is resolved only if the harmed individuals either actually do consent to their own harm if that is required for the good of the whole, or should so consent. But no one should consent to exclusion from unitive love with God. In addition, this cannot be for the good of the whole. Hence God would not condemn any merely for unbelief.

The third case is when the intuition is endorsed and achieves the status of a priori insight. An example is the reflection on scientific method, revealing, I have suggested, the theorists' reliance on judgements of theoretical beauty or elegance. The result of explication is a sense that this is something we know – a priori.

Finally, there is the case of recalcitrance. Our enquiry might leave us where we started, with an intuition that is neither endorsed nor undermined by explication, but which we still have a disposition to believe. Philosophical arguments notoriously end up with just such a clash, but, in these cases, we have made progress by revealing the recalcitrant intuitions. Consequently, we should suspend judgement rather than disagree, unless, I say, there is scope for commitment.

'Heart' versus 'head' dilemmas

If we have lost epistemic innocence, intuition is no substitute for commitment. Intuition does, however, often play a role, forming one or both horns of an intellectual dilemma. This is then subject to philosophical explication, but where the intuition is recalcitrant the dilemma remains. For example, the preference for elegant theories is a recalcitrant intuition, one of the 'heart' but is opposed by another intuition, one of the 'head', that wherever possible beliefs should be checked empirically. Where the case against but not the case for is an explicit inference, then these dilemmas are of the 'head versus heart' kind, with the explicated reasoning being that of the 'head' reasons and the intuitive case the reasons of the 'heart'.

There are two reasons for trying to minimize 'head' versus 'heart' dilemmas, while being aware of the Fallacy Fallacy. The first is that critical reflection might in some cases show there to be no dilemma, because the grounds on one side of the debate might be undercut. The second is to avoid double dipping, for the reasons of the 'heart' combine the intuition that forms one horn of the intellectual dilemma with the emotional appeal that attracts us towards commitment. Critical reflection is required to distinguish these two aspects of intuition.

Two common examples of 'head' versus 'heart' dilemmas concern the Design Argument and the Argument from Evil. A natural, intuitive reaction to the order, complexity, beauty and wonder of the world is to take it as either divine or the work of the divine. An equally natural intuitive reaction to the horrors of life, extreme suffering, destruction, depravity and other evils is to assign to the divine a morally flawed character. Both theists and atheists are tempted to rely on the emotional appeal of their side of the argument when it suits them and make an appeal to cold reason otherwise. Hence few take seriously the idea that there is a god who acts well but is not one you would want to know. In my *Developmental Theism* (2007a), I suggest, however, that the primordial god was not God but chose to become loving and hence to become God, with an uppercase 'G', that is, worthy of worship. This is a speculation to which I return in Chapter 8. Here I note that if we rely only on the intuitive, the reasons of the 'heart', then we should conclude that there is indeed a god but a god who is no God.

Clifford and James

William Clifford

William Clifford famously proclaimed that it 'is wrong always, everywhere, and for anyone to believe anything on insufficient evidence' (1877). There are two moral issues concerning beliefs. The first is suggested by Clifford's story of the optimistic shipowner believing on insufficient evidence that the ship is seaworthy. This concerns the need to investigate thoroughly a topic on which false beliefs have harmful consequences. I agree, and before an intellectual dilemma is dealt with by commitment, due diligence is required to check that there is indeed a dilemma. The second issue is a more serious threat to my conditions for reasonable commitment. Out of respect for the value of truth, we should not believe anything in a capricious or whimsical fashion. The conditions that

I propose satisfy Clifford's requirement. For in an intellectual dilemma there is sufficient evidence for both positions that would be persuasive except for the contrary case. I invite readers to agree with Clifford that in an evidential vacuum with no good arguments on either side we should not, even if we can, commit. But faced with an intellectual dilemma we judge which of the pro tanto contrary cases outweighs the other. In making that judgement we also judge that there is sufficient evidence in Clifford's sense.

William James

James (1896) in response to Clifford laid down clear criteria for believing in situations in which there is insufficient evidence. If we interpret both Clifford and James as taking this to mean objectively insufficient evidence, these situations include intellectual dilemmas. For in dilemmas the judgement is subjective in the sense of not being in accordance with generally accepted rules. With that gloss, I reject Clifford's intellectual puritanism, and so need to examine James's criteria, which he clearly states. In Section I, he defines a genuine option as 'forced, living and momentous'. In Section IV, he states, 'Our passional nature not only lawfully may, but must, decide an option between propositions, whenever it is a genuine option that cannot by its nature be decided on intellectual grounds.'

A living option is defined as one with some appeal, however small. I propose a stronger necessary condition, namely, that the appeal be such as would be convincing apart from the case against. To believe is always to hold something true, and I fail to see how we can reasonably believe something for which the case – taking everything into consideration – is weak. On the theory of commitment that I propose, we simultaneously judge an option true and judge that the case for it defeats that against it. The idea of an option with some appeal might, however, relate to what Charles Peirce calls *musing* (1908). It is experimentally to imagine being a believer, trying out a belief system. James seems to be recommending such experiments in Section IX. Now, good philosophers and good students of religion enter imaginatively into a wide variety of positions and the criterion for this entering-in to be reasonable is indeed that they have some appeal, for we have no time for the others. But for genuine commitment more than imagination is required. I note, though, that musing is relevant to commitment in two ways. First, it can generate or strengthen relevant intuitions. Second, those who have experimented are in that respect in an epistemically superior position to those who have not. This does not, however, give the religious believers the right to dismiss the unbelievers, for many of them have experimented but have either never found or subsequently lost their faith.

James requires the option to be both forced and momentous. A forced choice seems to be one in which suspense of judgement has similar practical consequences to committing the opposite way. For example, given a three-way choice between atheism, agnosticism and theism, it might be said, although not by me, that agnosticism has the same practical consequences as atheism. In that case there would be a forced choice in James's sense. I grant that commitments require a forced choice but not the sort that James has in mind. If the sum of all our reasoning resulted in a choice between atheism and theism, then we should, I say, suspend judgement. The commitments that I defend instead involve a forced choice between an attractive belief and suspense of judgement.

My chief disagreement with James is that I require the Absolute Superiority Condition, to avoid pluralism. For, I repeat, to commit to a thesis is to commit to its truth. And if all that is required for reasonable commitment in the face of a dilemma is satisfaction of the Pragmatic Condition, then we are asserting that something is likely to be true precisely because it is useful, which not only is counter-intuitive and self-serving but also leads to a pluralism of commitments based on different pragmatic considerations.

The condition that the choice be momentous should be glossed as its being sufficiently important to overcome a proper aversion to dismissing those who hold the contrary position. With that gloss, I accept it. But without some such gloss there is no threshold of when a choice is momentous. An example might be a choice that arises for those of us who believe in the real presence of Christ in the Eucharist as to whether he always remains present so long as the consecrated bread and wine survive.[5] There are some practical consequences, such as the propriety of the ceremony of Benediction in which the host is venerated many hours after consecration. Let us assume that there is a genuine intellectual dilemma here. Is it momentous? That is, is it important enough to commit one way or the other in the face of the heart-felt contrary beliefs of Lutherans and conservative Catholics?

Another disagreement with James, and with moderate fideists such as Evans and Bishop, is my thesis that in committing we do not just judge the topic in dispute. We also judge what is reasonable in this case, thus avoiding the charge of blind faith. This second-order judgement is itself a topic of disagreement. But, just as the first-order judgement is constrained by the Pragmatic Condition if it is not to be arrogant, this second-order commitment has to meet some constraint. On my proposal, either those who consider my commitment unreasonable do not grant the rules I have laid down or they disagree with me about what is absolutely good. In the first case I challenge them to provide alternative criteria. In the latter, our disagreement has been located as one about the ranking of values, where we all grant disagreement occurs and that we have to disagree.

John Bishop's development

In his theory of doxastic ventures, as he calls them, Bishop (2002, 2007) endorses James's defence of passional choices provided they are ethically permissible. And perhaps we should make explicit that the Pragmatic Condition implies an ethical constraint. I have assumed that this condition requires that the commitment result in what is objectively good for us not merely what we desire. Now an act resulting in what is objectively good can fail to be ethically permissible only in one of two circumstances. The first is if it is a lesser good than that achieved by an alternative act. The second is if the act is contrary to an ethical rule, and in the case in question the ends do not justify the means. The first circumstance cannot occur with a commitment because the choice is between committing and suspense of judgement. In that case we only judge the consequence of the act good if it is better than the consequence of inaction. The second case occurs with a commitment only if it is insincere, as when a contrary belief is held. And I have assumed that an insincere commitment is defective, even if it is possible. So, an explicit requirement that the commitment be ethically permissible is redundant but harmless.

Schellenberg's conditions

In taking commitment to be active but belief passive, I agree with John Schellenberg (2005), provided faith is taken to involve intellectual commitment. He takes faith-that and belief-that to be incompatible, but I disagree, for you can do something deliberately that would happen anyway: breathing is a familiar example. Likewise, it is psychologically possible for someone to be nervous about whether they do believe and so make a redundant commitment. Such redundancy does not stop a commitment from being justified, so Schellenberg is not correct on this detail. Making allowance for this, we obtain the following interpretation of his requirement for justified faith (2005: Ch. 8).

> Faith that p is justified provided p is not justifiably disbelieved, and provided the Pragmatic Condition is satisfied.

The Pragmatic Condition is something that is common to all accounts of commitment. The chief difference between my account and Schellenberg's is that I require the extra Absolute Superiority Condition. That might seem to make his criterion laxer. As he applies it, though, Schellenberg is far stricter than I am, arguing that only a rather minimal religious commitment (Ultimism) is justifiable.[6] To clarify this, I note an ambiguity in the 'not justifiably disbelieved' requirement. It might be taken to mean either (1) the lax interpretation – that there is no contrary belief that is justifiably believed – or (2) the strict interpretation – that the absence of belief lacks justification. Note that I do not consider a third interpretation: (3) the strictest – that the absence of belief would be unreasonable, for given (3) the belief in question would be required by reason, which makes commitment redundant. The difference is that many beliefs held innocently can be reasonable even if they are not justifiable.

Using the lax or strict interpretation we obtain respectively the lax or strict Schellenberg requirement for believing that *p*. So, I take the real Schellenberg to be Strict, with Ultimism being such that absence of belief in it is not justifiable.

My case against Lax Schellenberg is, once again, the rejection of pluralism: we should not allow as reasonable rival commitments; hence commitment should not occur unless the only reasonable alternative is suspense of judgement, which is stricter than Lax Schellenberg. In fact, Lax Schellenberg is no constraint at all in the absence of any argument for or against. Strict Schellenberg is too strict, however, because it excludes commitment in the face of a dilemma, in which there is a justification both for belief and for suspense of judgement. My suspicion is that the Strict Schellenberg appeals to those who would like to be theists but are burdened with scruples.

Lara Buchak on faith

Buchak analyses the intellectual component of faith as choosing not to postpone commitment, even though postponing might give us time to collect additional evidence (2014: 54). This is perceptive in that the evidence gathering is often an excuse for procrastination. I doubt, though, whether all faith requires the choice not to postpone. Sometimes the need to commit is too urgent for postponing to be psychologically possible. Moreover, there can be the need for commitment even when no reasonable prospect exists for further relevant evidence. For instance, someone who has temporarily adopted religious practices will after a while have no reason for putting off a decision, and so no need for a Buchakian commitment to not gathering further evidence.

Buchak's insight can be incorporated into my account in one of two ways. We could say that the judgement that the choice is reasonable already includes the judgement that sufficient time has been spent gathering evidence. I prefer, however, to treat the decision not to postpone decision as a preliminary commitment not of an intellectual but a practical kind. This is my preferred response because the practical dilemma of whether to make up your mind now or seek further evidence often arises in circumstances where there is no intellectual dilemma.

Religious pluralism

The Absolute Superiority Condition is partly justified by the need to avoid pluralism, which requires further discussion because of the prevalence of religious pluralism. Now, no one should dispute that those with different relevant experiences (or different intellectual abilities) might reasonably hold opposing theses or hold them with differing degrees of confidence. For example, those who have had extraordinary religious experiences can reasonably be certain of what others should only hold with some doubt. I understand by pluralism, however, the stronger thesis that even those with no relevant difference in experience, ability or even wisdom can reasonably reach opposing conclusions. Pluralism follows unless we require high standards when considering what is reasonable. I have required high standards and, with one exception, I have rejected pluralism. The exception is that I sometimes judge as reasonable both commitment and suspense of judgement. In this section, I defend these high standards against any suggestion that religious pluralism is a further exception and compare my stringency with the views of three prominent philosophers of religion, Alvin Plantinga, Robert Audi and Richard Swinburne, in decreasing order of pluralist implication.

The case for high standards

I have characterized reason as our ordinary human ways of reasoning and being reasonable as relying on those ways to decide what is true. For the most part, we muddle through and for the most part 'near enough is good enough', but the circumstances of intellectual commitment are exceptional. They arise when epistemic innocence has been lost and where there is an intellectual dilemma. Moreover, the Pragmatic Condition is only satisfied if the topic is of importance. Hence commitments should satisfy high standards. I do not require the *highest* standards because that might suggest excessively time-consuming scrupulosity. (Compare the discussion of Buchak's account of commitment.) In particular the standards should, I have argued, be high enough to permit commitment only when there is a choice between commitment and suspense of judgement, for if we are faced with a three-way choice between a thesis (e.g. theism), its negation (atheism) and suspense of judgement (agnosticism) then fear of falsehood should result in suspense of judgement.

Against this, there is the acceptance of our contemporaries that when it comes to faith 'anything goes', and that it is silly to debate religious differences. This implies that our ordinary ways of reasoning do not succeed as well as I hope they do, because they fail to be decisive on religious topics. My response is to interpret the requirements of reason, which often take the form of prohibitions, as advice as to what you should do if you care about having true beliefs and avoiding false ones. On serious topics this advice should be followed as much as possible, rather than laying down limits in advance of the attempt. Hence, the conclusion that reason has limits when it comes to religious topics should be treated as a quasi-empirical result, based on bitter experience. The widespread acceptance of religious pluralism is, I submit, the result of reason seemingly having failed to resolve religious differences. On another occasion, I hope to re-examine these disputes and to establish that a generic, Nicene, Catholicism is the 'one true religion'. But that is not the topic of this work, which goes only as far as the commitment to worship God. The case for a series of commitments leading to worship shows we have not reached the supposed limits of reason.

Alvin Plantinga

I have interpreted Plantinga, and Reformed Epistemology more generally, as defending epistemically innocent religious convictions. His 'Aquinas Calvin' model of divine inspiration supports, however, the stronger claim that theism, and other Christian doctrines, should be believed by anyone whose reasoning is non-defective (Plantinga 1993). Relying on the doctrine of 'original sin', Plantinga claims that unaided humans suffer from a cognitive-affective disorder, but that as a result of Redemption the Holy Spirit heals us so that we are able to function properly, and come to believe the Christian revelation in an immediate, non-inferential manner. In that case, for any who have had that revelation proclaimed to them in a good enough fashion, there would be no genuine intellectual dilemma as to whether to accept it. (In addition, Plantinga argues that belief in Christian revelation counts as knowledge, but that is not my concern here.)

A preliminary point is that the Aquinas-Calvin model extends to any religion that teaches divine inspiration. Although Christian theology reserves the role of inspiration for the Spirit I know of no argument that only Trinitarians should believe in divine inspiration. Either, I say, the Aquinas-Calvin model is pluralist, or it is no substitute for commitment. The former holds if the sense of being inspired is taken to provide grounds for asserting the existence of God. That would be fine except the sense of being inspired is unreliable, for not only have some honest believers thought they were inspired to do highly eccentric things but, more incisively, vehement opponents have honestly appealed to inspiration: both Protestants and Roman Catholics claimed to have the Holy Spirit on their side.

What Plantinga has in mind, though, is the way inspiration ensures the reliability of our ways of reasoning about religious claims, whether or not we are aware of it. This is analogous to wearing glasses to correct for myopia – you might have forgotten that you are wearing them. Consequently, if what you commit to is in fact true then it amounts to knowledge. I have no quarrel with this, and it does provide one, somewhat weak, boot-strapping argument for theism, for being warranted if true confirms a belief (see Forrest 2006). Slightly sharpening one horn in this way does not defeat the dilemma. Hence, Plantinga's Aquinas-Calvin model does not remove the need to commit.

Robert Audi

Audi (2011) provides a detailed account of the continuum of faith, with doxastic faith (faith that) as the intellectually strongest, through to fiducial faith (trust that) and, at the limit, hope without faith (hope that). He defends the complete rationality of faith that God exists, not just minimal rationality, while reluctantly adopting pluralism not merely about what is minimally rational but about complete rationality, which I take to be much the same as what I call ordinary human ways of reasoning. The overall impression of Audi's insightful discussion is that rationality is hard to assess, and that each of us is in a somewhat privileged position assessing the rationality of our own beliefs given total experience. Hence, we might rationally disagree without being able to argue which, if either, of us is correct.

I differ from Audi in several respects. First, I take it that ordinary human ways of reasoning endorse Ockham's Razor, which he restricts to the task of describing what we already believe exists, not deciding what entities there are (2011: 283). That is a fairly minor point, however, and, although Audi uses it to cast doubt on naturalism, his reliance is not essential to his case for theism. More important, although he is concerned with the commitment aspects of faith, he does not concentrate on intellectual commitment, for which I have sought rules. In this regard his epistemology is holistic, that is, there are many relevant considerations both intellectual and practical and we lack clear simple rules for deciding what to judge true. My response is that, as with ethics, things are simpler than they might appear, because our judgements are too often complicated by not recognizing dilemmas. Thus, in the hostage situation there is no need for a refined capacity to decide about a difficult situation; instead, we should face up to the stark fact that whatever we do is wrong. Likewise, when I come to consider commitment to a worship-worthy God, there is no need for extraordinary skill at weighing up probable arguments; instead, we should face up to the dilemma that there are good pro tanto cases for and against, neither defeating the other.

My final point of difference with Audi concerns disagreement. To be sure, each of us is in a somewhat privileged position to decide if we have conformed to the requirements of reason. But that does not solve the problem of disagreement. Consider a case where judging the disagreement from a third person perspective we should perhaps be pluralist, because the different people have different evidence. One Greek accepts travellers' tales about a distant land nearer the equator than the insufferably hot deserts, but where the climate is delightful and the vegetation lush; another Greek dismisses this as fanciful and contrary to accepted theories. If they both know the travellers but differ in their assessments of their honesty, then we might judge that both were reasonable although only the first is correct. But now suppose the two Greeks were discussing the matter with each other: knowing that only one of them could be correct they should compromise, and suspend judgement. In this way, respect for others turns pluralism into a presumption in favour of suspense of judgement. My proposed conditions for commitment are in response to that presumption.

Richard Swinburne

Swinburne holds that any given thesis has a numerical probability relative to a given body of evidence. A belief is rational, in one of several senses, if it is more probable than its alternatives (2005: 5). As he understands it, though, *belief* is passive, so his conception of *faith* should be compared with commitment. To have faith in a creed made of several clauses is, he submits, to assign a not-too-low probability to each clause combined with the judgement that a way of life based on that creed is more likely to achieve salvation than rivals (2005: Ch. 4). Translating, and I admit distorting, his account to provide a general theory of commitment, Swinburne clearly requires that the Pragmatic Condition be satisfied. He is primarily concerned with *saving faith*, for which the Absolute Superiority Condition is obviously satisfied. My conditions are stricter, however, for Swinburne allows that saving faith can occur even if the probability assigned to each clause of a creed is less than 50 per cent. I maintain that in committing we judge the epistemic probability to be high enough to warrant assertion. Because we lack rules assigning these epistemic probabilities the difference is minor.

Swinburne's position is not explicitly pluralistic about faith because it requires faith to be a means to a goal superior to other ways of life. Nonetheless, there is a threat of pluralism. If we had a straightforward choice to accept or reject the Nicene Creed as a whole the belief that its truth is more conducive to salvation than rivals, combined with its being not too improbable, provide grounds for faith. Swinburne argues, convincingly I say, the superiority of the way of life involved in Christian faith to rivals (2005: Ch. 7). There are, however, many Christian rivals to the bare Nicene creed. We can add clauses such as justification by faith or the real presence of Jesus in the Eucharist, or we can delete clauses such as the belief in one, holy, catholic and apostolic church. The various Christian denominations sincerely assert the salvific importance of their creeds, and it is far from clear how we should choose unless we examine the creed clause by clause. As Swinburne emphasizes, however, the Christian way of life is based on a whole creed. The doctrine of the Trinity, for instance, is conducive to salvation largely because it (or maybe a Binity) is presupposed by the doctrine of the nature of Christ as true God and true man, which in turn is presupposed by Christian doctrine of Atonement. The holistic salvific implication of a creed combined with the weak requirement that each clause be fairly probable leads to the occurrence of rival creeds meeting Swinburne's criterion. I propose instead that we make a sequence of intellectual commitments and hence arrive at the asserted creed, whether more, less or just different from the Nicene.

This skerrick of pluralism might not matter except that we need to commit on more than religion. Suppose some future Council appends a preamble to the Creed committing to reason and humanism, on the grounds that the preamble plus Creed is conducive to salvation. Then a presuppositionist variant with the clause that reason has no authority over religion might be neither more nor less conducive to salvation. On Swinburne's principle we might rationally have faith in the presuppositionist variant. Instead, I say, when we commit to reason we do so for the sake of avoiding falsity when we seek to understand, not for the sake of salvation. In that context pluralism is abhorrent. Moreover, if we do rely upon a sequence of commitments as I suggest, then, using Swinburne's criteria, each could have a fairly low probability, and so the overall probability be so low that disbelief is inevitable for reasonable people. (This is the Problem of Reiterative Diminution, discussed in the section 'Heart' Versus 'Head' Dilemmas.)

Commitments and disagreement

It takes two to have a quarrel, but you can argue with yourself and the context of commitment is typically an internal debate over whether to 'let go' and assent to what attracts. Nonetheless the rules governing commitment should cohere with those governing disagreement, about which there has been much debate (see Feldman and Warfield 2010). This topic is reflexive in that philosophers disagree about disagreement. Some, whom following Adam Elga (2010: 175–6) I call the *conciliatory*, argue that respect for those who initially disagree should lead to suspense of judgement. Others, the *stubborn* insisting on the propriety of backing their own initial judgement.

Disagreement is relevant to commitment

Disagreement is relevant to commitment in two ways. First, commitment results in a disagreement with those who do not commit, and so being conciliatory is an obstacle to commitment. Second, the idea of commitment itself helps resolve the problem for the conciliatory that they should suspend judgement about the issue of disagreement, and so they have no objection to the stubborn. First, then, consider the obstacle, namely, the fear that the committed are too stubborn. There are only two ways of dismissing those you initially take to be your intellectual peers: either note your good fortune or deny that they really are your peers by asserting your superiority regarding the judgement in question. The former is incoherent. You may well note your past good fortune in having various true beliefs or the good fortune of others in having them. But how can you sincerely assert that your current belief is true as a matter of luck? Hence, those who stubbornly commit are apparently arrogant, dismissing others who have previously been treated as intellectual peers.

An obvious exception occurs with the commitment to worship God. For those of us who commit may attribute their giving in to the attraction of worship as due to divine guidance, and encourage others, even agnostics, to pray for this guidance. So, the committed are not being arrogant, just grateful for divine help. I say more. It is never arrogant to commit when faced with an intellectual dilemma, for arrogantly to dismiss one side of the debate is to deny there is a dilemma. Genuine arrogance, which we should seek to minimize, occurs when we disagree about whether it is reasonable to commit. Reducing arrogance is a good reason for philosophical inquiry, in order to find just where you disagree. For example, the first intellectual dilemma is whether or not to trust ordinary human reasoning. And I commit to trust in reasoning and expect opposition among my peers.

The sceptical response

To those sceptics whom I treat as peers, indeed as abler than myself, I argue that either their scepticism is insincere or it is limited. Insincere scepticism is illustrated by Hume himself who in the *Dialogues Concerning Natural Religion* has Cleanthes say to Philo, 'When the company breaks up: We shall then see, whether you go out at the door or the window' (Hume 1998: Part I). Limited scepticism is illustrated by those opponents of scientific realism who are nonetheless common-sense realists about familiar objects and events, such as Bas van Fraassen (1980). Neither group rejects reasoning: Hume has scruples about calling our reasoning reason, and instrumentalists pick and choose which bits of reasoning to rely on. I invite both groups to agree with me that it is reasonable to commit. Moreover, this example shows that I am not asserting intellectual superiority over those who do not commit: we can all agree on the case for and against, even if some of us have to take more time and effort understanding those cases than others.

The opponents whom I have to dismiss are those who insist it is not reasonable to commit. Historically, they cultivated suspense of judgement as a spiritual exercise, for example, the Greek sceptics and the Indian Jains. In that case the scepticism is self-refuting, because based on a prior commitment to a way of life, contrary to their policy of suspending judgement. Therefore, I find it easy to assert superiority over them in that respect.

The charge of arrogance

The charge of arrogance may well seem more serious when it comes to religious commitment. Here I invoke the Absolute Superiority Condition. I dismiss those who disagree with me about that condition, as lacking my insight – unless, that is, they come up with an alternative condition, which I shall duly examine. To others who accept the criterion but disagree with me about absolute values I say that this lies at the heart of those disagreements where we should not be willing to suspend judgement and have to live with disagreement, for it is familiar that values, or more accurately the ranking of different values, are disputed. This is shown by the conversational implication that the speaker has first-hand experience. Thus, if you say that the Mona Lisa is somewhat overrated we would expect you to have seen it, not to be relying on the judgement of someone whose artistic taste you respect.[7]

I say, therefore, that being stubborn rather than conciliatory is correct when it comes to values. Now, the problem posed by disagreement derives much of its force from the thought that your opponent is intellectually abler than you are. It is reassuring, then, to locate disagreements in the domain of values, where no one can claim authority because of their intellectual ability.

My hope, then, is that careful philosophical inquiry will put disagreements into four classes: those in which one party is clearly superior, those in which we should be conciliatory and suspend judgement, those in which we agree that both commitment and non-commitment are reasonable and those where we should be stubborn because we are forced to make a disputed judgement that commitment is reasonable. I hope that careful philosophical analysis can show that this last class concerns only judgements of value.

Commitment to the qualified conciliatory position

I advocate the conciliatory position, therefore, except where commitments are made in accordance with the rules I propose. This qualified conciliatory position is not refuted by the self-referential inconsistency of the unqualified position, a self-refutation acknowledged by Elga (2010: 182), for the commitment to being stubborn in the face of disagreement by peers only in the circumstances of reasonable commitment itself meets the three requirements for reasonable commitment. First, there are good pro tanto arguments for both the conciliatory and the stubborn positions. The testimony of others who disagree provides the obvious argument for being on the whole conciliatory. The argument for stubbornness is that we are assuming both sides have provided cases for their theses. But the case for a thesis is automatically a case for holding it, which implies being stubborn. The second, Pragmatic, condition is satisfied because minimizing disagreement decreases the occasions for strife in a community. In addition, conciliation encouraging the virtue of proper intellectual humility, which in turn removes some obstacles discovering the truth.

The Absolute Superiority Condition depends on how we rank the value of having true beliefs against the disvalue of false ones. We often praise the love of truth but my downbeat recommendation is rather to fear falsehood. If you love truth more than fear falsehood, then you should be a *besserwisser*, with an opinion on everything. If you rank them equally you still, absurdly, have the intellectual right to be a besserwisser, nor is this a case in which two values are incommensurable, for we are comparing success and failure for the same activity: aiming at the truth. (I say more: we should not assign positive value to truth at all but rather to understanding, for the mere accumulation of facts is of no intrinsic value.) Hence fear of falsehood should, in general, outrank love of truth. Therefore, the Absolute Superiority Condition is satisfied by a general policy of conciliation except in special circumstances, namely, those in which commitment itself satisfies the Absolute Superiority Condition.

These conditions for commitment provide a principled rather than an ad hoc exception to being conciliatory. This provides further support for the conditions for reasonable commitment, assuming that we grant the initial appeal of the conciliatory position.

I have been citing Elga because he is sensitive to the self-refutation of the unqualified conciliatory position. He insists that there is nothing ad hoc in stubbornly asserting the otherwise conciliatory position. I disagree. My case against him is that, as previously asserted, the conciliatory approach is not intuitive in the case of disagreements over values. Hence, once the simplicity of universal conciliation has been rejected, an intuitive, and not ad hoc, way of marking the exceptions is required. This is provided by the extraordinary circumstances of commitment in the face of an intellectual dilemma. In addition, the exceptions should include the area where we are intuitively comfortable with disagreement, namely, judgements of value. (Provided, that is, these meet the Pragmatic Criterion for commitment. As argued in Chapter 3, the Absolute Superiority Condition for value-judgements is satisfied trivially.) I grant though some residual discomfort about otherwise dismissing those who deny it is reasonable to commit.

I conclude, then, that the conditions for reasonable commitment are supported rather than undermined by consideration of the intuitive basis for the conciliatory position when faced with disagreement by peers.

A final point of comparison: Axiarchism again

Axiarchism may be stated as the principle that of two theories the one that exhibits the world as absolutely superior is the more probable. Hence, the Absolute Superiority Condition comes close to stating that it is as if axiarchism is correct. There are two differences, however. First, an axiarchist might reasonably believe in a theory that, apart from its absolute superiority is less probable, whereas I take absolute superiority to apply only when faced with a dilemma. Second, the axiarchist has no need of the Pragmatic Condition.

I judge axiarchism to be a plausible speculation but nothing more. I do not, for instance, treat it as a priori knowledge. Hence, to assert it would be a commitment. But the result of commitment to axiarchism is to abandon the Pragmatic Condition and abandoning that condition violates the condition itself.

Summary

The most striking comparison is with proposals such as James's that are too lax, permitting, it would seem, multiple rival commitments and thereby exacerbating the worry about why we should be right and all others wrong. To prevent such pluralism, I require there to be a choice between committing and not committing, rather than a choice between rival commitments. In addition, to prevent pluralism there is need for the Absolute Superiority Condition, or for some alternative that I do not know of.

The underlying reason for rejecting pluralism is the respect for the truth, more accurately fear of falsehood, which I urge commitment to as part of ordinary human ways of reasoning.

Commitment to Reason and to Scientific Realism

It is good to have an example of commitment from outside the religious context, to avoid the suspicion that I am being lax in order to defend cherished beliefs. And commitment to reason, that is, to the ordinary human ways of reasoning, provides just such an example. In addition, if required, it is a prerequisite for further commitments. I say 'if required' because it is not required by those sanguine epistemologists who retain their innocence about epistemology.

Qualified scientific realism follows from this commitment to reason. I argue, however that it is unreasonable further to commit to unqualified scientific realism, to physicalism or to naturalism. Finally, I argue that commitment to reason, which leads to scientific realism, provides a precedent for further commitments. More precisely, it is unreasonable to commit to reason but deny that further commitments are reasonable if they meet the three stated conditions.

Commitment to reason

In Chapter 3, I noted the circularity in committing to reason using the rules that are themselves reasonable in a way that goes beyond the core epistemology that is evident, and I would add indubitable. I argued that there is nothing vicious in this circularity and that alternatives such as reliance on divine guidance do not meet the standards of core epistemology. Although principled, Cliffordian, scepticism based on a general policy of suspending judgement does not meet those standards, there is no arguing against sceptics who repeatedly refuse to commit without thereby committing to a general policy of non-commitment. Now I fear for the safety of such sceptics even if we train them as children to 'go out at the door' not the window.[1] But broken bones are no refutation. So, I need to consider the option of non-commitment, even to reason itself.

The dilemma

The case for the reliability of our ordinary ways of reasoning is that they are intuitive; that is, they present themselves not as indubitable but as highly probable ways of discovering the truth. Absent counterargument, the sceptics can therefore be dismissed as insincere or because 'they ain't got no common'. On insincerity, I note that the practice of logicians of calling *invalid* any inference that is not necessarily truth-preserving can lead students to pretend-scepticism, a make-unbelieve.

Unfortunately, there is a counterargument, for reason partially undermines itself. That is, the ordinary human ways of reasoning set up a sceptical argument against their own reliability. We ask, 'Why should we humans be so fortunate that the way things are corresponds to the beliefs we tend to form?' Moreover, on matters of consequence we should check our conclusions, but there is no way we can compare our ways of reasoning with the truth to check how accurate reason is. That our ordinary ways of reasoning are self-correcting no doubt increases the probability that we get it right once we have learnt from past mistakes, but that self-correction does not imply this probability is high.

Our ancestors would not have survived without an impressive ability to predict threats and to find food. This shows something and shows it without resort to the theory of evolution itself. For suppose god had created billions of different genera of organisms of quite different kinds. Then, only the fittest would survive. This reliance on ancestral survival to answer the sceptic faces two problems, however. The first is that the radical sceptic, the sort who 'goes out at the window' half the time, would not accept the plausible enough idea of survival of the fittest as even true for the most part: Why might not some angel or extraterrestrial have used the earth as a laboratory conducting most peculiar experiments and with the less fit surviving? Ignoring these radical sceptics, we note that reason has been tested and judged accurate only in a limited range of circumstances, those that have practical consequences. Reason extrapolates from these cases to all others, but the self-correcting character of reason warns against the over-enthusiastic use of the extrapolation from the circumstances in which evidence was gathered to rather different circumstances. Hence, the Vaihingers among us can ask why we trust reason to conclude anything more than that it is as if the best explanation is true for all practical purposes. Why go further and say the best explanation is likely to be true, that in Peter Lipton's phrase 'the loveliest is the likeliest'? (Lipton 2004).

There is, then, an intellectual dilemma, and the resort to further reasoning to resolve it is circular. It should be clear that the Absolute Superiority Condition is satisfied by a commitment to reason, for it should be clear that it is a great good to discover the way the world actually is, and not just have the dubious advantages of technology. I say 'should be clear', because pure mathematicians and theoretical physicists go to such trouble to point out that their arcane discoveries may well have practical benefits. That suggests they worry that the general populace does not value purely theoretical knowledge. No doubt their worry is well founded, but that is just one of the many defects of our system of education.

The gravity of the commitment

I should not need to stress that the reason to which we commit is the capacity to arrive at objective truth, not some miserable pluralist substitute, such as what is 'true for me', whatever that means. I grant, however, that truth is relative to a conceptual scheme, but that scheme is universal and rather sparse, namely, that which cannot be conceived of otherwise. But a conceptual scheme is neither the same as a person's innocent beliefs nor the stuff of pomo-babble.

The self-refutation of pragmatism

The Pragmatic Condition is that we should not commit on matters of no practical consequence. Initially it would seem that our theories can have no practical consequences that their as-if versions do not have. I claim, however, that the discovery of the way the world is has advantages over merely discovering how it is for all technical purposes. The wrong way to argue for this is to note that the motivation for useful discoveries is often a desire for understanding independent of all technical purpose, for that might just show that sometimes it is useful to encourage unreasonable commitment to motivate research.

The right way to show the practical benefits of avoiding the as-if versions of most theories is itself based on an as-if theory, namely, quasi-pantheism. It would be crass to restrict the practical benefits of a commitment to things of monetary value, or technical achievements more generally, and I have included our *attitudes* among the consequences of a commitment. Among these are the attitudes of wonder, awe and humility occasioned by the discoveries of modern science. I call this quasi-pantheism because it is as if the cosmos is divine, which is nonetheless compatible with a naturalistic rejection of any object of worship. It is also, I hasten to add, compatible with taking the universe to be the divine body, to be adored as such. Therefore, the Pragmatic Condition is satisfied, provided, as I shall argue, reason leads to scientific realism. This may be contrasted with the instrumentalist or as-if interpretation of the sciences, which does not lead to the same degree of awe and wonder, being restricted to the real but lesser admiration for 'the starry sky above', or the beauty of plants and animals. Even the starry sky above derives much of its sublimity from the knowledge of the vastness. A thorough instrumentalist would undercut this by saying that is only as if the stars are so very distant; they are just lights in the sky.

A corollary of the above is that perhaps we should commit to ordinary ways of reasoning, such as reliance upon Inference to the Best Explanation, only when the positive benefit of discovering the truth is sufficient to outweigh any harm. It is not clear, though, whether we are to assess the benefits of our ways of reasoning considered as a whole, or case by case. Only if it is to be considered case by case does the corollary follow. This might have some consequences that are important although beyond the scope of this work. Consider the idea of presuming someone innocent unless shown guilty beyond reasonable doubt. This applies both in a court of law and in the court of gossip. It can be justified on the grounds that the Inference to the Best Explanation that condemns on circumstantial evidence should only be committed to if the overall consequences are beneficial.

Qualified scientific realism

Reason has given us science. And initially we understand science realistically. When the theory mentions quarks, we suppose the quarks are real, not just that it is as if there are quarks. Reason is, however, self-correcting, and we should adjust in the face of the arguments against scientific realism, notably Newton-Smith's Pessimistic Induction (1981: 14) and van Fraassen's Threat of the Unknown Hypothesis (1980: Ch. 2). In this section I consider these arguments and present a qualified scientific realism intended to be proof against them. I take this to require no commitment in addition to that to reason. Not only is the topic of intrinsic important, the self-correction of reason required to arrive at a defensible scientific realism provides precedents of caution for the application of reason elsewhere.

Unqualified scientific realism

Reason is self-correcting in that it takes objections into consideration. Prior to the objections, the reasoning that leads to scientific theories also leads to the conclusion that, apart from its speculative frontier, the overwhelming majority of theses of the physical and biological sciences are literally true. For instance, there exist subatomic particles; again, all organisms on Earth have a common ancestor. The exception of the speculative frontier of science may be expressed by saying that the scientific realist should accept *only* well-confirmed scientific theories. And the unqualified scientific realist accepts *all* well-confirmed theories, even those that posit unobservable things, among which I include things not currently observable. I say a theory is well confirmed if it: (1) is *a priori* plausible, (2) has many and varied successful predictions, (3) admits plausible speculative explanations of anomalies and (4) does significantly better than available rivals regarding (1), (2) and (3) taken together. Unqualified Scientific Realism, then, is belief in all the well-confirmed scientific theories.

The extensive philosophical discussion of scientific realism seems to lead to a stand-off. Anjan Chakravartty (2017) notes 'van Fraassen's ... intimation [is] that neither realism nor antirealism (in his case, empiricism) is ruled out by plausible canons of rationality'. He goes on,

> Each is sustained by a different conception of how much epistemic risk one should take in forming beliefs on the basis of one's evidence. An intriguing question then emerges as to whether disputes surrounding realism and antirealism are resolvable in principle, or whether, ultimately, internally consistent and coherent formulations of these positions should be regarded as irreconcilable but nonetheless permissible interpretations of scientific knowledge.

My diagnosis is that reason leads to *qualified* scientific realism and that opposition to this reflects lack of commitment to reason. The appropriate degree of risk is based on reason's self-correcting tendencies. These self-corrections are manifested as objections to unqualified scientific realism, and so the appropriate risk is achieved provided we qualify scientific realism to meet the objections. There are two familiar objections, the Threat of the Unknown Hypothesis and the Pessimistic Induction, as well as the Humanist Objection, which is not usually made explicit.

The Pessimistic Induction

The Pessimistic Induction, as Newton-Smith calls it, is based on the past record of confident science being overthrown in a revolution. The standard example is Newtonian mechanics, superseded by Special and General Relativity and by Quantum Theory. Another standard example is the electron as posited by Thompson, which was assumed to be a little solid particle, rather unlike the mysterious electrons of current physics. Newtonian mechanics was well confirmed, and yet we now treat it in an instrumentalist fashion as an accurate prediction-device within certain limits. Much the same can be said of the Thompson electron. The unqualified scientific realist would have thought – and did think – that Newton had discovered genuine, universal, laws of nature that forces exist and that electrons are particles in the sense of small material objects. We should, the argument goes, not repeat those mistakes. Fair enough! But reason self-corrects by minimal adjustment. Hence, the appropriate degree of risk is achieved by making qualifications that if they had been in place would not have led to the judgement that we had been incautious. Anything more than that is an overreaction to past lack of caution, an overreaction that on reflection we should judge unreasonable and over-cautious.

There are a number of lessons. The first is fallibilism: we should never have been so sure of Newton's theory. So maybe to count as *knowledge* in the strict sense, science must dissociate itself from the metaphysics of scientific realism. But I am concerned with knowledge only in a loose sense of meeting the legal criterion of beyond reasonable doubt, not certainty. The second lesson is that we never had evidence that the old theories were *fundamental*. Although it might turn out some day that we discover a fundamental theory and know we have discovered it, this was not the case then nor the case today.

Given fallibilism we might say that the overthrow of Newton's theory was just bad luck, without there being anything wrong with scientific realism. My judgement, though, is that it does show us something about the appropriate degree of risk: we should have been more cautious. We can consider various ways of weakening a theory while retaining its predictions, and so increasing its probability. A policy of caution is to decide what theory we would accept apart from the Pessimistic Induction and accept instead a somewhat weaker theory. This policy reflects the way we initially tend to overestimate the probability of a well-confirmed theory. One important way of weakening a scientific theory is no longer to assume the laws we have discovered are universal.

To be sure, it is intuitive that the whole of our universe is governed by laws that are universal and in some sense necessary. But these would be the fundamental laws that are yet to be discovered. In various different circumstances these universal laws yield derived and local laws. Even chemistry, which can seem the most secure, prosaic even, of sciences, may well hold only in our domain of our universe, or in our universe in the Multiverse, a domain where the fundamental constants are just right for life as we know it. Most other selections of these constants, occurring in other domains, will result in no chemistry at all, but some variations might provide interesting but alien chemistry.

Therefore, we should weaken the theory while retaining its empirical confirmation, by restricting it. Not only does Newtonian mechanics fail spectacularly at speeds near that of light and in strong gravitational fields, we have learnt the folly of extrapolating prematurely to very low temperatures and very high densities.

Another way of weakening a theory while retaining its empirical confirmation is to separate the science from its interpretation. When a theory mentions a *particle* all we need for the science is that there is a localized something-or-other. We do not have to take it to be a 'little, gritty granule'. Likewise, the forces of Newtonian mechanics should be understood as tendencies to accelerate, opting for neutrality as to what if anything grounds the tendencies. (This is compatible with interpreting General Relativity as showing that these tendencies are grounded in the curvature of space-time, and that acceleration is relative to a frame that is only locally salient.)

The third way of weakening theories in order to arrive at a qualified scientific realism is to use the verisimilitude qualification where appropriate. One idea here, based on David Lewis's theory of possible worlds, is to say that a theory has verisimilitude if the nearest possible world in which the theory is true resembles the actual one more than the nearest possible world in which some other theory is true. I do not think this is helpful because resemblance admits of many respects and weighing them up is too subjective. A more plausible verisimilitude qualification is that various numbers occurring in a theory (the 'constants' of the theory) should be given an error margin of plus or minus a per cent or so. Laplace was worried, for instance, that the square in Newton's law of gravity might be replaced by a power very near to two. On the supposition that Newton's theory was fundamental this might seem a silly worry, but I have already noted the folly of prematurely assuming we have a fundamental theory. When we weaken theories in the above ways, the original unweakened theory then has the status of an interesting speculation, which we should not believe true.

The Threat of the Unknown Hypothesis

This is the objection, pressed by van Fraassen, that Inference to the Best Explanation is a misnomer: it should be called 'inference to the best available explanation'. Hence scientific realism is threatened by the possibility of an as yet undiscovered hypothesis superior to the ones we have considered. For example, immediately after the Michelson Morley experiments failed to detect an aether wind, the best available explanation would have been the Lorentz Fitzgerald theory of the effect of motion on the temporal and spatial extension of objects. But a better explanation was the Minkowski Einstein unification of time with space. The empiricists' disdain for generating a multitude of empirically equivalent theories, or their even greater disdain for purely metaphysical speculation, tends to discourage due diligence. On the contrary, we should meet the Threat of the Unknown Hypothesis by employing both scientists and metaphysicians to survey the widest possible range of hypotheses. 'Let a hundred flowers bloom; let a hundred schools of thought contend!' I submit, then, that the self-correcting tendencies of reason lead to a due diligence requirement. We should not be realists about a given theory unless we have seriously considered rivals. Let me be clear: we have a duty to speculate. But even if we exercise due diligence, there is a measure of luck. It was not so much a dereliction of metaphysical duty but the prestige of Euclid that would have prevented Newton from coming up with General Relativity.

Once we have generated alternative theories, scientific realists need to decide between them. Hence, we have the next caveat: if the observations are theory-laden, then the presupposed theory in question should be itself well confirmed, nor of course should we permit the circularity in which observation O both presupposes theory T and is its chief empirical prediction. There is a related caveat: if the observation O presupposes theory T that is supported by the observation O*, presupposing theory T*, then exceptional confirmation is required for T*, and even more for a longer chain of presupposed theories.

The requirement that we consider competing hypotheses provides a further reason to consider verisimilitude as discussed above. For instance, Laplace was right to worry that the square in Newton's inverse square law might be replaced a power of two plus or minus some very small quantity.

To reduce the threat of unknown hypotheses it is wise to divide the scientific theories as much as possible. It will not do to argue that physics, say, has many well-confirmed predictions, and therefore we should believe it true. We must divide and divide, so that we assess something as specific as the quark theory of atomic nuclei. That is because the conjunction of highly probable hypotheses might turn out to be rather improbable. Consequently, the qualified scientific realist will not affirm that all well-confirmed scientific hypotheses are true, but only that the vast majority of them, provided they meet the other requirements of caution.

The Humanist Objection

Academics in some humanities and some arty types despise us geeks who are fascinated by fossils or the Higgs boson. This would no doubt motivate them not to commit to scientific realism, if that was a commitment rather than a consequence of committing to reason. There is, however an objection to scientific realism that may be extracted from geek-aversion. It is not clear when we commit to reason that we should commit to its use even when the overall consequences are bad, or whether we should be more selective. The joy in understanding that we geeks experience is a good consequence of scientific realism, but if the enthusiasm for science generated by realism distracts from, or even leads to the rejection of, that which humanists celebrate then its overall consequences are bad, and we should, the objection goes, not be realists. Note that this argument concerns the attitude that scientific realism engenders not the perils of a technology growing like cancer.

I note this Humanist Objection but have good reason to ignore it, for it does not undermine my use of scientific realism as a source of caveats or qualifications to believing in theories, nor does it undermine the commitment to reason. Rather it is based on a prejudice about the commitments of scientific realists. Hence, there is no need to deal with this objection before considering the existence of god. And when we grant that the existence of god is fairly probable given humanism, and even more when we commit to worship, then this puts science in its place and counters the Humanist Objection. Dialecticians might thus like to see theism as the synthesis of science and humanism.

Qualified scientific realism

The response to objections to unqualified scientific realism serves two purposes. First, they result in qualified scientific realism, which is a consequence of the commitment to reason. Second, the lessons are of general application and similar caution is required, I submit, when reasoning on other topics. Consider again the conditions for a theory to be well confirmed. It must (1) be *a priori* plausible,

(2) have many and varied successful predictions, (3) admit plausible speculative explanations of anomalies and (4) do significantly better than available rivals regarding (1), (2) and (3) taken together. First, we need to emphasize that the theories are not proposed as fundamental. Next, we need to add the due diligence qualification so that as broad a range of rival theories are considered as possible. In addition, the theory should be divided as much as possible into a series of theses, and we should only accept those that are individually well confirmed. In particular we should do our best to separate out various unwarranted metaphysical assumptions about, say, the nature of particles, from the modest requirement that the 'particles' of our physical theories be localized something-or-others of unspecified nature. Moreover, the theories being considered need be neither fundamental nor universal, and they will allow for approximation, making them weaker, and so more probable than, universal, precise theories.

Overall, the lesson we learn from the discussion of scientific realism is that we should first examine our naive conclusion and then consider ways of exercising caution, based on examples of past overconfidence.

Rejecting unqualified scientific realism, physicalism and naturalism

To get a rise out of scientists I recommend two tropes. The first is to describe their scientific beliefs as 'mere theory'. The second is to suggest that science rests like religion on faith. In response to the second scientists might go Popperian and extol the virtue of falsification, affirming, without self-irony, how willing they are to revise their theories. Not only does that put new life into the Pessimistic Induction but it supports the first trope, for a 'bold conjecture' is indeed 'mere theory'. The proper response, I say, is to express the qualified scientific realist position that most scientific theses, suitably qualified, are not 'mere' theories but truths, and that this results from the application of reason. I then concede that we may need to commit to reason, which is in many ways like committing to a religion.

Qualified scientific realism requires no commitment once we accept reason as the guide to truth. Nonetheless those impressed by the sciences might be tempted to commit further. In this section I consider three such commitments and reject them as unreasonable. The first is to unqualified scientific realism, the second is to physicalism and the third is to naturalism.

Against commitment to unqualified scientific realism

One reaction to the Pessimistic Induction might be to insist we have made progress. Yes, it will be conceded we declared victory too soon. But now we have scientific theories that are better confirmed and so a degree of caution that would have been appropriate a hundred or so years ago is now unduly sceptical. Hence, we need not qualify scientific realism.

This illustrates an intellectual dilemma that often occurs when we have failed in the past and do not adjust our policy to prevent failure in the future. The 'true believers' lament bad luck; their critics demand that we learn from history. (An example that comes to mind is the remnant of old-school socialists.) The Absolute Superiority Condition might be satisfied for commitment to unqualified scientific realism in the same fashion as for commitment to reason, because of the great good of knowing the laws of nature and other scientific facts. The problem is the Pragmatic Condition. There is enough in a qualified scientific realism to support the as-if pantheism of awe at the cosmos. To go further and commit to unqualified scientific realism only results in a slight increase in this respect. On the other hand, there is the concern, which Descartes had, that mistakes can multiply, like one rotten apple infecting all those in the basket. Explicitly, there is a good reason why science requires very high standards, namely, that it is collective and diachronic activity: no one thinker could check everything that is assumed in a given research program. So, if we are too lax as to what enters the corpus of science, mistakes might spread, as Descartes feared. In addition, further progress will be hindered because the research programs have false presuppositions. Hence a commitment to unqualified scientific realism should be discouraged as harmful to the progress of science. It is better to distinguish what is beyond all reasonable doubt from what is speculative, and so cheerfully grant that research programs, at the cutting edge of scientific progress, are speculative but worth funding.

Naturalism and physicalism

Naturalism is the thesis that in some sense reality can be completely described by a scientific description. Physicalism is the thesis that in some sense reality can be completely described by a physical description. The phrase 'in some sense' is being used to characterize both naturalism and physicalism, and further clarification is required. At its weakest, these are statements of supervenience: there is no possible difference without a scientifically described difference, and there is no possible difference without a physical difference. In terms of metaphysically possible worlds this amounts to denying that there are two worlds that exactly resemble in all scientific/physical respects but differ in some other respect.[2] The supervenience theses imply that philosophers' 'zombies' – molecule for molecule replicas of ordinary human beings but lacking consciousness – are judged impossible. If we grant with David Chalmers (1996) that zombies are conceivable then that supervenience theses tells us that we can conceive that which is not even possible.

Understood this way, there might be a genuine intellectual dilemma concerning both naturalism and physicalism. On the one hand, zombies are intuitively impossible; on the other hand, they are conceivable, and conceivability is a guide to possibility. But there is no reasonable commitment to either physicalism or naturalism in this weak sense, for I fail to see how it could be absolutely good or bad whether supervenience in this sense holds. To be sure these two theses follow from commitments to naturalism in a stronger sense, which I shall discuss and reject. I judge, therefore, that although both physicalism and naturalism in this weak sense are plausible enough metaphysical speculations, we should not commit. Moreover, they do not threaten religious beliefs. For instance, you might hold that we have immortal immaterial souls not describable by science. (I do not.) But that is quite compatible with both physicalism and naturalism in this weak sense, for maybe it would be wrong of god not to create an immortal soul for a body capable of supporting one for a while. And maybe god necessarily does not do what is wrong, being free only to choose between good acts of creation. If so, it follows that beings like us but without immortal immaterial souls are impossible. Hence our ensoulment supervenes on our thoroughly material and mortal bodies. Likewise, if god is a necessary being, then atheism is believing the impossible, and so god supervenes on anything whatever and so on anything physical.

The weak explication of physicalism captures something of philosophical interest. Naturalism is, however, clearly intended to be incompatible with an immaterial god and with immortal immaterial souls. So, we need to strengthen the 'in some sense' clause. The most plausible strengthening adds to the thesis of supervenience a dependence clause. In this way, we obtain a statement of naturalism that says that everything depends for its existence on that which can be described scientifically. The corresponding strengthening of physicalism has a consequence that I consider highly implausible, namely, that mathematical truths depend on the physical. So, I concentrate on naturalism, stipulating that mathematics is part of science, even when not empirical. (Readers can adapt my discussion to physicalism if they do not believe there are mathematical truths.)

By *dependence* I mean something rather like those cases of causation in which the cause necessitates the effect.[3] The difference is that the dependent entity is necessitated of metaphysical rather than monic necessity. Just as causes explain their effects, the dependent entity's existence is explained by that on which it depends. Again, just as we can bring about the effect by bringing about the cause but not vice versa, we can bring about the dependent in bringing about that on which it depends. For instance, if the mental depends on the physical the latter explains the former, and we can bring about a mental state in bringing about the physical one, say by electric stimulation of the brain. One difference between dependence and causation is that we typically treat the identity of a thing under two different descriptions as compatible with dependence. So, the identification of mental states with brain processes is compatible with saying that the mental depends on the physical.

Naturalism as intended by its proponents may be explicated, then, as the thesis that everything depends on that which can be described scientifically. What, then, is the case for naturalism understood this way? The case has, I say, atheism as a premise. We seek a fairly simple way of understanding the universe. Under the supposition of atheism, the argument goes, the only feasible way of understanding the universe is the nomic. That is, understanding must be in terms of the laws of nature, which science seeks to discover. In Chapter 2 I granted that this had much to commend it as a way of understanding, but this only supports naturalism if there is no way of understanding that is at least as good. But theism understood as the existence of a god also provides a simple powerful theory of everything – or so I shall argue. So rather than naturalism supporting atheism it requires atheism to support it. Moreover, something weaker than theism casts doubt on naturalism, namely, the prevalence of mystical experiences or the more diffuse sense of something transcendent, like *Heaven* in Chinese thought.

Against commitment to naturalism

A persuasive case for naturalism presupposes atheism, but maybe some naturalists *commit* to naturalism. This could be described as an intellectual faith in science, which is trusted to explain the world around us. The naturalists' trust in science is that it will explain all that can be explained, and so there is no need for alternative explanations. Such naturalistic commitment is far more than the confidence that science will continue to have explanatory successes, for these naturalists are *committed* to there being nothing outside the scientific domain, which is subject to the general criticism of committing to completion, discussed in Chapter 3. Between that and the confidence that science has more to explain, is, however, the intermediary position of quasi-pantheism, based on awe at the beauty revealed by science. Maybe someone could reasonably be committed to quasi-pantheism, but that does not imply naturalism, for quasi-pantheism not to be compatible with religious commitments, this awe must be tied to the metaphysical thesis that the laws of nature are necessary in a sense that precludes their being ordained by a god (Fales 1990). That is not an established fact but a speculation, one which may be compared with the theists' conviction that god is necessary. In neither case does the proposed necessity explain anything. But in both cases, it reconciles us to not being able to explain.

I deny that naturalism is a corollary of quasi-pantheism, for I consider plausible the position, which I attribute to Rāmānuja (Lipner 1984) and, more recently, Grace Jantzen (1998), that the Universe is the divine body. Or if that is not enough, I recommend to fellow science-enthusiasts Personal Pantheism, which not merely treats the Universe as the divine body but denies the need for any sort of immaterial divine soul (Forrest 2016). In that case, although the laws are not metaphysically necessary they are the result of god's choosing what to become, and the Universe as a whole is a necessary being because identical to god. What this shows is that the good of quasi-pantheism is not promoted by naturalism, although it is compatible with it.

No doubt some find naturalism attractive because they consider it a way of rejecting religion, but that too would be commitment to completion, namely, to there being no better religion than that naturalists have considered.

Reason, scientific realism and non-scientific commitments

(Qualified) scientific realism presupposes reason, which makes explicit its intuitive appeal. So that appeal in no way adds to the case for scientific realism. It is the other way around: just as a successful prediction implied by a theory decrease somewhat any doubt we have, the intuitive appeal of scientific realism should help remove any lingering hesitation about the propriety of commitment to reason. And commitment to reason is a precedent for further commitments, including what I call humanist commitments, to be discussed in the next chapter, and to the commitment to worship commended in Chapter 8. In this section I anticipate objections to this precedent.

The objection from manifest superiority

It might be objected that science is so manifestly superior to religion in its evidential support that it provides no precedent for religious commitments. The obvious reply to this objection is not, I fear, the correct one. The obvious reply is that the manifest superiority of science lies only in its use as the guide to predictions or technology, but not in science realistically interpreted. Thus, it would be silly to worry about the aerodynamics that supports the initially counter-intuitive occurrence of heavier-than-air flight, for we know it has worked, and any well-confirmed theory may be predicted to hold, at least for the immediate future hereabouts. This objection understates the superiority of science. In spite of various philosophical sceptics, the scientific realist position that, for example, all many-celled animals have common ancestry is intellectually more secure than, say, the orthodox Christian doctrine of the divinity of Jesus. That is because scientific realism is not a commitment: it follows from one, the trust in reason, which trust is also required by a Christian even before any specifically religious commitment is made. Hence, Christianity requires commitment additional to that supporting scientific realism. For example, it requires our ordinary human ways of reasoning to infer that the man Jesus existed, was crucified and proclaimed as risen by his disciples. Hence religious faith is added on to trust in reasoning as an extra commitment. The intellectual superiority of scientific realism over religion is precisely due to its requiring fewer commitments, rather than a more secure commitment.

It is not, then, because the commitment required is more secure that science is epistemically superior to religion but because, even interpreted realistically, it requires fewer commitments. One commitment, though, is much like another and so the commitment to ordinary human ways of reasoning does act as a precedent for further commitments.

The objection from long chains of commitments

My reply to the last objection was that scientific realism depends on the first of the sequence of commitments that make up a religious faith, and that this commitment is no more or less reasonable than the others in the sequence.

But this reply leaves me open to an objection that goes back to Hume (1975) concerning long chains of reasoning and has been discussed by Robert Fogelin (2009: 32) as the Problem of Reiterative Diminution. If each inference in the chain is probable rather than certain, then as the chain lengthens the degrees of doubt compound, undermining the argument as a whole.

My reply is based on the dual nature of commitment in the face of an intellectual dilemma: a conclusion is drawn but also a judgement made as to which horn of the dilemma is sharper, that is, which is the better case. Those making the commitment thus make a chain of inferences each one of which has, they judge, high epistemic probability, and they need therefore only be worried about long rather than the medium-length chains that I shall be considering. The objection would hold if, unreasonably, we committed to a hypothesis that was about 50 per cent probable. There is a proviso, however: the various judgements as to which case is the stronger in the various dilemmas should cohere. So, we should not, for instance, rely upon a chain of commitments in which we sometimes employ metaphysical speculation to buttress a case but at other times express scepticism about metaphysics.

Objections from modularity

'Everyone knows' – those weasel words – that we reason differently on different topics, using different modules. Moreover, the weasels can cite reputable papers in cognitive science (e.g. Spelke and Kinzler 2007). Who am I to disagree? This could be used as an objection to the relevance of scientific realism to religious commitment. A second objection is that if there is no single way of reasoning, how can we be committed to it? The first of these objections coheres well with the suspicion of scientific reasoning that some religious groups exhibit, as well as the widespread view that religion is for each person to decide – on what seems to me a whim. The second objection might be congenial to those Wittgensteinians who consider rival world views, including religions, to be incommensurable forms of life.

In reply to both objections I say that the reasoning that I am committed to may well come in modules, but it also includes the way we negotiate between modules when they interact. Many try to keep their beliefs in compartments, corresponding perhaps to the reasoning modules, but that decision is contrary to our ordinary ways of reasoning. Consider, for instance, Stephen Jay Gould (1999) with his NOMA (Non-overlapping Magisteria) thesis that science and religion concern different areas of human concerns. He is, rightly I say, criticized by Richard Dawkins (2006) on the grounds that religion proposes miracles. Now I have a different understanding of the miracles from Dawkins and, like C. S. Lewis (1947), I consider miracles to be, in my terminology, preternatural rather than supernatural. That is, they exploit the laws of nature in ways we cannot yet comprehend rather than breaking them. But that does not affect the criticism, for either I am wrong or, as I believe, miracles are preternatural. In the former case, there are law-breaking miracles. Hence a religious topic, that of miracles, forces a revision to how we interpret science. Or, if miracles are preternatural then scientific discoveries can limit what miracles might occur. For instance, the common practice of praying for rain would be absurd if it was already determined by the laws of nature and the fixed past that it will not rain this year.

This is just one example of where the domains overlap. Another is the Argument from Evil. If, as I believe, God cannot now break the laws that god set up, then on a day to day basis we can understand why there are many evils that God does not prevent – God cannot. To be sure, we must still ask why there is this kind of natural order, but that is another question. This appeal to the natural order is threatened by quantum theory, which seems to show that all sorts of strange occurrence are possible, however improbable. In this case, then, an advance in science threatens something I rely on to answer the Argument from Evil. My reply is to speculate that for God to bring about the highly improbable causes divine suffering. But here my point is to agree with Dawkins. NOMA might be a useful legal fiction, but it exaggerates the clarity of the boundaries between intellectual compartments.

Humanist Commitment

I commend various humanist commitments prior to any religious commitments:

1. There are absolute values, that is, things or situations that are objectively valuable in themselves, as opposed to merely being good for some person or persons or some other thing.
2. Likewise, some things are absolutely better than others.

I call 1 and 2 combined 'the *Not All Relative* thesis'.

3. Someone making a commitment, either practical or theoretical, in the circumstances of a dilemma is free to make a significant choice between different alternatives in a way that incurs moral responsibility. I call this 'the *Moral Dignity* thesis'.
4. Human beings have an absolute highest good, which is to love and to understand. I call this 'the *Telos* thesis'.
5. All persons are of positive value as individuals; that is, their existence is absolutely good, and it is false that some persons are intrinsically more valuable than others. I call this 'the *Egalitarian* thesis'.

In addition, at the end of this chapter I consider a further commitment, to absolute ethical rules. I argue that it is not reasonable to commit to them, but unless we worship God we have an ethical obligation to commit. This is potentially, then, a different kind of dilemma from the purely intellectual ones I have been considering. The desire to avoid that dilemma is a motive for commitment to worship, similar to but not quite the same as the Kantian argument for belief in God.

In this chapter I first clarify humanism, distinguishing the generic version from secular humanism. I argue against committing to secular humanism but justify as reasonable the commitment to generic humanism. This leads to speculations about agency that, among other things, answer objections.

On humanism

Although humanism has a negative anti-religious aspect that I oppose, it also has a positive aspect that is, I say, presupposed by theism, and so requires a prior commitment before committing to the worship of God. That is because the case for there being a god of any kind seems rather weak without humanism. The order of precedence implies that no humanist commitment is acceptable if incompatible with (qualified) scientific realism, and that no religious commitment is acceptable if it is incompatible with the combination of (generic) humanism and (qualified) scientific realism.

Comments on the humanist theses

The Not All Relative thesis might seem strange, because I imagine many humanists are proud to be the measure of all things, as to whether they are good or bad. To be sure, I am stipulating the content of humanism, and so how acceptable it is to self-ascribed humanists is not crucial. Nonetheless, I invite readers to judge that any humanism worth committing to will treat the welfare of humanity as an objectively valuable goal.

Moral Dignity is a rather strong statement of human freedom because it requires significant choices, excluding the totally implausible hypothesis that the physical is determined but we are free, in and only in the privacy of our souls, to concur or otherwise. It also excludes a hypothetical Nanny God scenario in which we can freely do wrong but God ensures no lasting harm results: shooting victims make miraculous recoveries and so on. It should not be controversial that if we are free to choose between alternatives we can choose between significant ones.

Although the Telos thesis is contrary to the 'anti-essentialist' thesis that it is a mistake to prescribe how human beings should live their lives, it does not imply any specific lifestyle for women or men, which is the usual target of anti-essentialists.

The Egalitarian thesis also requires comment. It does not imply that somehow deep down all persons are morally good. This strangely popular idea has neither intuitive appeal nor supporting argument – likewise the opposite thesis of innate depravity.[1] (The evidence of mystic experiences is decidedly ambiguous on the character of the deep Self, if there even is such a thing.) It is evident that we have both good and bad tendencies and, both individually and collectively, are capable both of great good and great evil. Third, and most important, by an *individual* I mean something that is distinct from others of its kind and that persists. This does not require a mysterious principle of individuation, the thisness or haecceity. Contained in this commitment is the good of persistence as that individual.

Perhaps readers will explicate the content of humanism differently, and some of the above may not even require commitment, but others are important examples of commitments that I would recommend but not call faith. In my proposed program of sequential commitment, humanism is, as I have said, prior to commitment to a, by definition, worship-worthy, God. For the case for there being a god will depend on Not All Relative, and the case for the central commitment that god is God will depend on Moral Dignity. Having committed to this, the Telos thesis is then plausible and may not require further commitment.

On the order of commitment

The order of commitment – humanism before religion – is important because of the pragmatic requirement that commitments do no harm. For the Telos thesis, whether treated as corollary or an independent commitment, then acts as a constraint on any, further, religious commitments. I am, therefore, advocating religion within the bounds of humanism. In particular commitment to the existence of god depends on humanism and so cannot rationally survive its rejection.

To illustrate this priority of positive humanism over theism, consider the story in Genesis of Abraham's willingness to sacrifice his son, Isaac, and please abstract from any scholarship about this being a way of saying that human sacrifice was replaced by animal sacrifice. Further imagine that Abraham's faith was based on the sequence of commitments here being advocated. Then he should not sacrifice his son, because he should argue that (a) his humanism is more secure intellectually than his commitment to the thesis that his god is the worship-worthy God and that (b) a god who asks for human sacrifice is not worthy of worship.

The coherence of humanism

We might pick and choose between the various humanist assertions listed above, but they cohere in that they support and are supported by a sense of human worth and dignity. Hence the case for commitment to them one by one is also a case for commitment to the whole package.

Humanism and secular humanism

The central humanist thesis is probably the fourth. As the 2002 Amsterdam Declaration (IHEU 2002) puts it,

> *Humanism is ethical.* It affirms the worth … of the individual and the right of every human being to the greatest possible freedom compatible with the rights of others. (Emphasis in original)

I interpret this as egalitarian in spirit because, in situations of scarce resources, the worth, dignity and autonomy of an individual would count for little if others are regarded as worthier or more dignified. Even so, this statement of the values underlying humanism seems rather weak. For most of those who proudly call themselves humanists are secular humanists, and the spirit of secular humanism is Promethean. It is that we humans are more valuable than the other things we know of, and presumably, of equal value to any extraterrestrials there might be. Thus, the secular humanist is a human supremacist. The Promethean and anti-religious assertions of secular humanism follow, I suggest, from the refusal to make due allowance for the dark side of humanity, our manifest unholiness. I express this secular humanist thesis thus:

6. *Unaided Progress:* Although human beings have flaws and failings there is nothing to stop continued progress by our unaided efforts, towards achieving the highest goods of love and understanding.

A corollary is that to achieve these things we need consider neither god nor an afterlife, which even if they exist are considered distractions. Hence one of the central tenets of secular humanism is as follows:

7. *No Religion:* We should live as if there is neither god nor an afterlife.

Humanism, then, is the acceptance of theses (1) to (5), and secular humanism the acceptance of (1) to (7), or so I stipulate.

Against committing to secular humanism

Many secular humanists assert that theism is contrary to reason. I shall argue in Chapters 7 and 8 that given the humanist commitment it is atheism that is unreasonable, leaving a dilemma: either suspend judgement or commit to God.

The secular humanist principle No Religion does not follow from suspense of judgement. Instead the agnostic might well offer prayers conditional on the existence of God. But here I am assessing a *commitment* to Unaided Progress and No Religion. The latter might or might not satisfy the Pragmatic Condition. For I guess an argument can be made for living as if there is no God (or afterlife) even if you believe there is one, but conversely there might be a Pascal's Wager argument for living as if there is a God (or afterlife) even if you believe there is none. The Absolute Superiority Condition is not, however, satisfied: there is nothing absolutely superior about living as if there is neither God nor afterlife. So here we have a situation in which by my criteria we should not commit to secular humanism. I challenge dissenters to provide an alternative condition that permits commitment to secular humanism but does not permit pluralism.

Humanism, environmentalism, naturalism and theism

There are tensions between humanism and environmentalism, between humanism and naturalism and between humanism and theism. The first two tensions prompt the question, 'What is so special about humans?' Not All Relative emphasizes ways in which we are special. Without it the superiority would be subjective, reducing humanism to the unsurprising thesis that humans think humans rather fine. The third tension prompts a further question, 'On the hypothesis that there is a god, are we god's equals?' If we are, then there is no god worthy of worship, and so there is no God. There is a difference in power and knowledge between us and god, but no true humanist should take that to be relevant if, as I assume, human beings are deemed equally worthy regardless of *their* differences in power and knowledge. Moreover because of our technology we are all too rapidly becoming god-like both in power and in knowledge.

Complaints against secular humanism

I now consider these tensions in greater detail and show they provide some valid complaints against, and hence reduction in the probability of, *secular* humanism but not against the combination of humanism with the worship of God. First, although humanists may well accord a degree of worth to individual animals that are sufficiently like us, the vast majority of species, and the ecosystems they form are not individuals. Hence, environmentalists should complain that humanism neglects something of enormous value. In a rather similar way naturalists see the human as just one part of the vast and wonderful universe governed by laws of nature and judge our sense of our own importance as purely subjective. Theists typically think of the humanist as guilty of arrogance, trying to put us in God's place. Naturalists may well be quasi-pantheists, and their awe at the universe and its laws likewise suggests the arrogance of humanists. Conversely, humanists may think of both theists and naturalists as undermining human grandeur.

The wrong way to reply to these objections is to invoke the fallacy of pejorative comparison, the mistake of thinking that something lacks a property because others have it to a higher degree (e.g. 'You think Kuala Lumpur is hot? Try living in Chennai!'). To avoid the fallacy, we might be tempted to say that the existence of something, maybe God, more valuable than human does not lessen our value. That applies to aesthetic values: the joy of the lesser is not diminished by the existence of the greater. But ethical values compete for scarce resources of attention, time and money. If the Blob Fish is more valuable than the Derwent Sea Star and equal effort is required to save them and we can only save one of these species, then we should save the Blob Fish. Likewise, if humans are more valuable than other animals then resources for saving the Blob Fish may have to be reallocated to helping the homeless. And the existence of God demands some reallocation of time, because the rituals of adoration that support the basic act of worship (submitting your will to God's) take up time that could be spent helping our fellow human beings.

These tensions are problematic for humanism because, intuitively, the value of the environment is great enough to divert some resources away from human welfare, and if God exists, likewise it is appropriate to divert resources to, say, building places of worship. There is also a serious problem that theists have to grapple with, namely, that the great value of God seems to imply that it is good to be *totally* concerned with the things of God – it was said of St Dominic that seldom spoke unless it was with God or about God – but this we judge to be obsessive.

Intuitively, effort and other scarce resources should be distributed by someone between nature, humanity and God (if there is a God) in proportions that reflect that person's character, but in which none of the three is dismissed as unworthy of attention. A speculation that gets the balance right between God and nature goes beyond quasi-theism to the thesis that the natural world is the divine body. (I say that human beings are exceptions to this – the unholy holes in the holy whole.)

The reverence to God, who is of surpassing value, therefore underpins the environmentalist intuition of the value of the non-human world.

Again, the central Abrahamic doctrine, which is not restricted to Abrahamic religions, is that God wants to be part of a community with humans, and so we should value each individual human even though we lack the moral purity, the holiness, characteristic of God. For it was God's decision not to be the whole of reality. To those obsessed with the things of God, we may retort that this God commands us to attend to our fellows and that the whole natural order is to be reverenced as the divine body.

Quasi-pantheism cannot be substituted for treating the universe as the divine body if we are seeking to underpin our intuitive valuations. For it implies a merely subjective assignment of worth to nature, which is insufficient to balance the objective superiority of human beings over animals, which I take to be part of humanism.

I conclude that the tension between environmental and humanist values provides a further reason why secular humanist commitment fails to satisfy the Absolute Superiority Condition, for it is incompatible with the speculative theism required to reconcile humanism with our intuitive valuation of nature. Therefore, a non-theistic humanist should be agnostic, rather than atheist, and commit only to humanism generally not secular humanism.

Commitment to absolute values

For each of the humanist theses (1) to (3) there is a case for and a case against. The case against absolute values may be adapted from John Mackie's case against objective ethics (1977: Ch. 1). He relies on two arguments: the Argument from Relativity and the Argument from Queerness.

The Argument from Relativity

Mackie's explicit target is ethics, and I could concede a great deal to him while submitting that many judgements of the absolutely good are not culture-dependent in the way that ethical rules, especially those concerning sex, seem to be. In that case, I could go on to submit that ethical rules are objective but relative, because they are the application of culture-independent objective values to specific cultures with their institutions, which should themselves, however, be judged as better or worse in an objective fashion.[2] For instance, it is decidedly 'queer' to say that slavery is wrong relative to our culture and institutions but permissible relative to others, unless we add the rider that in this respect our culture is objectively superior to slave-based ones. In the last section of this chapter, I shall consider whether this objectivist but relativist theory of ethics is adequate and submit that it is contrary to a fairly firm intuition about the imperious character of ethics. For that reason, I advocate a version of the Divine Command Theory. But my point is that, when assessing Mackie's argument, I could concede a great deal.

Perhaps his point was that in ethics there is much more disagreement that we would expect if the judgements were of something objective. If so then, I argue, the same complaint cannot be made about judgements of what is good, and the extent of disagreement in ethics itself may lie in the Principle of Least Moral Effort, namely, that we tend to adapt our ethical judgements so that we can seem virtuous to ourselves on introspection.[3]

Initially it might appear that we do disagree a great deal about values generally – the good – not just about ethics – the right – but this disagreement is not about what is good so much as about what is better. That is, we tend to agree about a list of good things but tend to disagree as to how we rank them. For instance, we all agree that suffering, including physical pain, is bad, and most of us agree that artistic creation is a good thing, with some of its products good to see or hear. Likewise, most of us agree that is good to understand. Where we disagree is how much suffering is worth putting up with for a life spent as an artist or in pursuit of understanding. I explicate the intuition that disagreement about values supports subjectivism as based upon the premise that reasonable people would have a capacity to make fairly accurate judgements about value when it is objective. Conceding this premise, I draw the conclusion that in many cases there is no objective weighing up of values. So, the value of the artistic life, like Vincent van Gogh's, is incommensurable with that of a pleasant but bland life. That is, it is neither better nor worse nor equal. In other words, values are partially not linearly ordered. Although this restricts the scope of Not All Relative, it is consistent with it: the ordering is objective but partial.

The Argument from Queerness

The Argument from Queerness has intuitive force against realism about intrinsic values treated as properties incapable of further analysis – they would be rather peculiar. But if we seek to extend it to an argument against objectivism about values rather than realism about values interpreted as unanalysable properties, then its force is much less. Here we may compare values with truth. The truth of some assertion is intuitively analysed as an extrinsic property, namely, being related by the truth-making relation to reality. Likewise, we may analyse the objective value of what is loved or hated as the love or hate *fitting* reality. Beauty and goodness differ somewhat in that goodness is value all-things-considered, whereas beauty concerns a limited range of known features. (It would be absurd to criticize a painting because of how repulsive it looks in ultraviolet light to bees.) Some truths are like beauty in this regard, others, such as universal generalizations, are like goodness.

The Argument from Queerness, as applied to objective values rather than peculiar intrinsic value-properties, collapses, therefore, into an appeal to Ockham's Razor: without objectivism about values, we require only truth-making, but I need to extend this to the generic relation of *fitting*: the telos, purpose or function of our mental states (including both beliefs and desires) is to fit what is external to us. The application of Mackie's arguments to absolute values is, then, nothing more than an appeal to a razor argument, and not an especially sharp one.

The case for absolute values

The case *for* absolute values has been made by Raymond Gaita (2000, 2004) using examples, and by Tim Mulgan (2015) using argument. The absolute value of human beings is central to Gaita's humanism. He describes the love of a nun working with abject patients whose value as human beings was sincerely asserted by the psychiatrists in a way that he judged somewhat condescending. By contrast, in the nun's case, 'the purity of the love proved the reality of what it revealed' (2000: 21).

Mulgan's argument is that when faced with difficult moral choices subjectivism provides inadequate motivation. We hold that moral truths are not merely interesting theoretical truths but should motivate us to do the right thing even when that is hard. This provides a case against subjectivism.

Commitment to absolute values

I am not sure that there is a genuine dilemma here, for I am inclined to judge that the case for absolute value defeats the case against. But if it is a dilemma, then commitment to absolute values meets the Pragmatic Condition, for as Mulgan points out, objectivism motivates us when it is difficult to do what is right. That the Absolute Value Condition holds for absolute values is not so obvious. If there were no absolute values, then the world would be absolutely worse in some respects, lacking absolute goods, such as absolute beauty and absolutely better in others, lacking absolute evils such as suffering. This sets up a further, emotionally charged, dilemma. We can judge the beauty not worth the suffering and then, just as easily, change our mind, without any balancing off of the goods and evils. Commitment to the good outweighing the evil results in a moderate optimism, which is healthy. So, the Pragmatic Condition is satisfied by that commitment.

To sum up, The Absolute Superiority Condition is satisfied provided good does outweighs evil, a moderate optimism to which we may commit. For if so, then it is better that it is objectively so. I conclude that either there is no need to commit to absolute values, or we may do so by making this further, moderately optimistic, commitment.

The horrendous suffering objection

Overwhelmed by the amount, variety and intensity of suffering, you might protest that there is no dilemma because evil definitely outweighs good, and hence the Absolute Superiority Condition is not satisfied by the commitment to absolute values. I reply in two ways. First, this objection ignores the possibility of an afterlife, something yet to be decided on. Second, the earnest character of the protest presupposes the absolute evil of suffering and hence shows no commitment is required to there being absolute values.

Moral Dignity

This humanist thesis is not merely disputed, but the dispute threatens to get bogged down in the overwhelming literature on Compatibilism. As I understand it, this is the thesis that the sort of freedom presupposed by praise or blame for what we have done with our lives is not a topic of metaphysical dispute, being consistent even with the thesis that all behaviour is determined by the laws of nature and the state of the universe before we were born. I shall argue that Moral Dignity is incompatible with Compatibilism but that determinism is no threat.

The Principle of Alternative Possibilities

The Principle of Alternative Possibilities (PAP) states that moral responsibility implies the freedom to choose between alternative possibilities. Because Moral Dignity combines the requirement of alternative possibilities with moral responsibility it enjoys the intellectual virtue of parsimony if PAP holds. For in that case the combination relies only on the firm intuition that we are (sometimes) morally responsible and does not require the further premise that we are free to choose between alternatives, which, if it is indeed an independent assumption, would merely enjoy the status of a fairly plausible metaphysical thesis. PAP is intuitive but this intuition is threatened by Harry Frankfurt's proposed counterexamples (Frankfurt 1969).

In these examples someone, the 'demon', has the power to affect your brain to ensure that you, the 'subject', act wrongly. The 'demon' might be Frankfurt's evil neurosurgeon, but the details do not matter. Demons have a problem: if they merely tempt the subjects to do wrong not only might their wicked plans be foiled but the subjects have the glory of resisting temptation. If, however, the demons use their powers to force the subjects to do wrong, then the subjects are not free and do not incur the guilt that delights demons. A Frankfurt demon goes between the horns of this dilemma, waiting until just before a final decision by the subject is made to do wrong or not. Then if the subject is about to do wrong the demon relaxes and does not intervene. The subject was free and guilty. If the subject is about to decide otherwise then the demon intervenes to ensure that the subject does wrong, and there was no freedom. The upshot is that the outcome is inevitably a wrong act, so there were no alternative responsibilities, but in many cases the subject was morally responsible.

As Robert Kane has pointed out, Frankfurt examples are persuasive only if the freedom required for moral responsibility is compatible with someone, in this case the demon, foreknowing the outcome. Such foreknowledge is problematic if the outcome is not determined (Kane 1985: 51). Hence, Frankfurt examples do not refute PAP, unless we assume determinism, which I see no reason to. The intuitive support for PAP is not undermined, therefore, and Moral Dignity retains its parsimony.

The mention of foreknowledge reminds us of the theological dispute over whether *useable* divine foreknowledge is compatible with human moral responsibility.[4] Such compatibility is part of the Molinist position, which I reject in Chapter 7. A Molinist god is much like good version of a Frankfurt demon, deciding which world to create guided by knowledge of how creatures would choose. Here it suffices that we have firmer intuitions about blame than praise, perhaps because of the importance of criminal law. Hence, we should settle the Frankfurt argument first.[5]

Moral Dignity and practical dilemmas

Moral Dignity concerns *significant* choices. Contrast with Buridan's ass, if instead of starving it chooses one rather than another identical bale of hay. The ass's choice may well exhibit a lack of determinism, but its only importance is the challenge to show that the freedom we value differs from the ass's. My slightly speculative theory of freedom is based on Susan Wolf's (1990). Her idea is that we are free if we act or could have acted for reasons ultimately derived from love of 'the True and the Good'. I suggest something similar: we act freely when we act because it seems to us that the chosen outcome is one such that none is better. Choices in which the alternatives are of equal value, such as that Buridan's ass are free but of no significance. In cases in which the chosen act seems the best then the act is determined by reason. An example would be choice of the ass to eat a bale of hay rather than starve, if there is only one bale.

The interesting case, however, is that of an agent faced with a dilemma. Both courses of action are reasonable and, we may suppose, motivated by love of 'the True and the Good'. Or as I would put it, they are both such that, it seems, none is better and yet they are not of equal value, illustrating the partial ordering of values. This is the case that as a humanist I say confers the greatest dignity on us, our choice affects how the world will be like the ripples on a pond into which a stone is thrown: even though the effects diminish in quantity with time they increase in extent. It is this type of freedom that Jean Paul Sartre (1973) illustrated with his example of the pupil who has to decide between looking after his mother and joining the Free French in England.

Moral Dignity: The intellectual dilemma

Our sense of the significance of a choice when faced with a dilemma is undermined if the outcome is determined. But it is also undermined if the choice is random: How would Sartre's student have reacted to the advice to toss a coin?[6]

There is, then, an intellectual dilemma concerning our freedom in the circumstances of a dilemma, whether practical or intellectual. On the one hand, there is the case for freedom when faced with a dilemma, occasioned by regret about not having done what we could have. This arises because we have had to choose one way rather than another, narrowing down the vast range of possible lives that we might have thought about as adolescents. The intuition in question is the rejection of the comforting thought that the way we live our lives is not something we can control, being either determined or random. The case for this comforting thought and so against human freedom is often based on determinism, and the threat of determinism will be dealt with below. For the moment, I shall suppose that the laws of nature and the past do not jointly constrain human acts. That leaves two arguments against human freedom. The first is the intuitive appeal of the Principle of Sufficient Reason. Combined with the premise that a genuinely free act by a human being would be inexplicable, it is concluded that we are not free. In reply, I distinguish a stronger from a weaker version of the Principle of Sufficient Reason. The weaker asserts that for every event (or every contingency) there is a reason that, but for any opposing reasons, would sufficiently explain the event's occurrence.[7] The stronger asserts that for every event (or contingency) there is a reason for its occurrence and no reason for its non-occurrence. My response, then, to the argument against human freedom is that it requires the stronger and hence less probable version of the Principle of Sufficient Reason. Accepting the weaker version, I grant that genuine human freedom never occurs in the absence of reasons for acting that make the action comprehensible. There are, then, three cases to consider. In the first, there is only one act reasonable in the circumstances and so, if it is not performed, the act is not free but exhibits a degree of insanity. The second is the Buridan's ass situation in which there are no reasons inclining the agent one way or the other. In such cases, assuming the ass does not starve – a martyr to reason – there is no freedom but instead a random choice is made. The last case occurs when the agent has a practical dilemma in which there are incommensurable reasons for acting in different ways. In that case either of the decisions is comprehensible, and so only the stronger version of the Principle of Sufficient Reason is violated. I call this radical freedom. The first case would be compatible with determinism by the laws and earlier events.

The second and third cases might both be correlated with random brain processes, but only in the second is the behaviour itself random. Consideration of the Principle of Sufficient Reason leads, then, to a conclusion that I judge independently plausible, that freedom is unconstrained by reasons only in the circumstances of a dilemma, where I call it radical freedom.

If the only argument against radical freedom was based on the universality of the strong version of the Principle of Sufficient Reason I doubt there would even be a dilemma, but the argument from the strong version may be modified. The idea is that we intuitively demand explanations and exceptions are to be kept to a minimum: mysteries are not to be multiplied. Hence, the argument goes, it is bad enough that we have to grant there are random events, but to avoid multiplying mysteries we should construe apparent cases of radical freedom as in fact cases of randomness. So, when we think we have the dignity of radical freedom, we are no better off than Buridan's ass.

There is then a dilemma concerning radical freedom, and it is, I say, reasonable to commit. First, the Pragmatic Condition is satisfied because the belief that you are not free can undermine your effort. The thesis that freedom is absolutely better than the alternative is not obvious, however. For freely doing what is good is better than doing it without freedom, but freely doing what is bad is worse than doing it without freedom. A special case is the value of loving freely rather than being coerced and the disvalue of hating freely. In this case I judge that freely loving is the more significant. Moreover, I doubt that hating, as opposed to merely not loving, is ever free. Here I appeal to the asymmetry between good and evil: the good attracts us in a way that evil does not. Instead evil threatens to swallow us up; it is something we need deliverance from. A so-called evil person is a slave to evil and not free. I conclude that the dilemma meets the conditions laid down.

The remaining humanist theses

The other two humanist theses to which I urge commitment, if required, are as follows:

> The Telos thesis: Human beings have an absolute highest good, which is to love and to understand.
>
> And the Egalitarian thesis: All persons are of positive value as individuals, that is their existence is absolutely good, and it is false that some persons are intrinsically more valuable than others.

Commitment to these theses

These theses are themselves judgements of absolute value, so the Absolute Superiority Condition for commitment is trivial (see Chapter 3). The intellectual dilemma is one that holds for most such judgements. The case 'against' is a razor argument: do not multiply judgements. The case 'for' is the emotional appeal of the proposed evaluation. Although on many matters our attitudes are irrelevant to the truth, objectivists about values should concede to emotivists that there is a connection between loving something and judging it good. As Aquinas notes, whatever we desire, we desire 'under the aspect of good' (Summa Theologica, l, II.i, Q1, 6). Hence, what we desire seems good. We then make the fallible but nonetheless fairly reliable inference from 'seems' to 'is'. The Pragmatic Condition is satisfied because these two humanist theses hold in check our self-serving tendency to justify self-indulgence at the expense of others. The grounds for these self-serving judgements are either (1) that others are not our concern or (2) that they are inferior or (3) that traditional moral teaching is to be despised.

A corollary of humanism

Let me make explicit something mentioned in passing above. A humanist might well hold that divine persons are not intrinsically more valuable than human ones; that is, their well-being does not matter more than our own. More explicitly a given joy or sorrow is of the same concern for a divine or human person. This might seem startling but I see no objection to it.

Agency and the Multiverse speculation

The humanist commitments support the thesis that agency is not reducible to non-agency causation. In particular, acts that are not random are correlated with physical processes that are. Therefore, they establish a precedent, an intellectual niche, for a cosmic agent, a being who is an agent like us but not restricted in knowledge and power the way we are. In earlier works (Forrest 1996, 2007a) I used this approach without conceding enough to those atheists who reject the humanist theses.[8] So here I make it clear that my case against atheism in the next chapter depends on the humanist commitments of this one. Nonetheless, by providing a speculation about agency, the basic idea of an intellectual niche for a cosmic agent can be shown more probable than it otherwise would be. I do this using the Multiverse hypothesis in its Delayed Collapse version, developed in Chapter 2.

Van Inwagen's argument

I begin by considering an objection to the case for human freedom. Peter van Inwagen (1975) has argued that if the laws of nature are deterministic then a free action must affect the past, which is absurd. To be sure there is little evidence that the laws *are* deterministic. The objection is nonetheless worth answering in case they turn out to be. To do so, I shall rely on universe termination. But first consider the standard Many Worlds Interpretation, according to which all possible outcomes of an observation occur in various universes. We may adapt this to agency by supposing that someone in a dilemma splits into a successor who chose one way and a successor who chose the other. Each of the successors has acted in accordance with the reasons judged of greater weight. Hence, both are responsible for the outcome in their respective universes. That would hold even if the individual universes are governed by deterministic laws. For the agent has chosen which universes to inhabit.

This reconciliation of free actions with determinism is vulnerable, however, to Robert Adams's Moral Objection to David Lewis's Modal Realism (see Lewis 1986: §2.6). Whatever difficult decision you make in the face of a dilemma in this world, perhaps after much inner struggle, you may be assured that your counterpart makes the other choice, thus undermining the gravity of your choice. Why bother struggling? For instance, let us consider again the variant of the Hostage Dilemma, in which the negotiator is given the choice to kill the baby or to commit suicide or watch all ten hostages die, and the negotiator heroically commits suicide. Yet the overall situation is no better than if the negotiator had made another choice. For the hero, the baby-killer and the passive watcher all exist, in various universes.

Another way to argue the inadequacy of this reconciliation of free will with determinism is that it assimilates freedom to chance. Consider two asses, Buridan's and Balaam's. The former is an asinine ass with no free will; the latter is not merely eloquent but capable of choosing just as we are. Each is exposed to two equidistant bales of hay. Unfortunately, one contains weeds that are bitter, and the other contains weeds that are known by asses to cause stomach ache. Buridan's ass chooses at random, but Balaam's faces a dilemma and deliberates. On the standard Many Worlds theory the result is the same, both asses undergo fission, with bitterness or pain as the outcomes. Balaam's ass seems no different to Buridan's.

Universe termination, and the associated Delayed Collapse Interpretation of quantum theory, is open neither to Adams's objection nor to its donkey variant. It is as if the hero, the baby-killer and the passive watcher struggle to see who will survive and only one does. Now, I concede that this does not remove the mystery of freedom, but it does integrate it with the natural world. I shall also show how consciousness fits in – all in a speculative fashion, to be sure.

Universe termination

For the remainder of this section and the whole of the next I speculate further in a way readers might like to skip – on a first reading, as optimistic authors say. To avoid saying that physical stuff comes into existence, we may suppose that all possible universes exist, spread out in their four dimensions, three of space and one of space-like time. A universe endures in Time until it is terminated by, for instance, the choice by agent y to be F, where, in some universes, y is not F. In the case of bodily acts, F is typically that the agent's body takes a certain shape. For instance, after some deliberation some of us raise our hands at a meeting to indicate that we affirm a motion. This is a matter of bringing about the body shape, thus terminating those universes in which the arm is not raised.

Both the interpretation of quantum theory and the account of bodily acts require that the agents be spread across many universes. For if I decide to raise my left hand then there are many different ways of doing so, and my proprioceptive awareness does not distinguish between subtly different ways. So, the non-terminated universes differ slightly in that respect.

To avoid fission, at a given moment T of Time, counterparts that differ introspectively at T must, however, have been terminated at or before T. Because agents are spread out, we may take the situation that is actual for that agent at Time T to be indeterminate between the situations occurring in the many universes that are not as yet terminated.

Situation and history

Agency is reflexive ('de se') in that I decide to raise *my* left hand and in doing so raise P.F.'s hand because I am P.F. My being P.F. is not part of the content of the act (see Perry 1979). What makes the hand-raising mine is the way the act is situated. Now, of course the situation involves a lot of brain-detail, but it may also be described as the agent's history (up to the present). By that I do not mean a fragment of autobiography, which is the narrative, but a sequence of nested parts of the Multiverse, X_T, indexed by moments of Time, where if T^* is later than T then X_{T^*} is part of X_T.[9] A sufficient condition for a universe to be terminated is that it is not part of some agent's history. This condition is not a necessary one. If it were then all the agents' histories would coincide with the universal history, with the sequence of nested parts of the multiverse consisting of those not terminated at a certain moment of Time.

For this speculation, it is required that the terminated universes exist in the tenseless sense. Hence, universe x terminates before universe y just in case the temporal span of x is a proper part of that of y. The proposed speculation is therefore a version of the Growing Block theory of Time, according to which the past exists in this tenseless sense.[10]

The stage of universal history at time T is specified by the sum of the non-terminated universes, U_T. It divides space-time into a past which is fairly determinate at the macroscopic level, and a much less determinate future, with the present as a transition zone. (Here I say that a question has a determinate answer if it is the same in all the universes not terminated.) A stage X_T of the history of agent X provides determinate answers only near X's body. In particular, we may suppose that various details of other brains are not specified. For a cosmic agent X, however, we would expect near coincidence of the X_T and the U_T.

Random events such as the famous electron passing through a given slit also have their individual histories, specified by the physics. For instance, if we suppose the electron cannot go faster than the speed of light, then its history does not specify it being very near the given slit just before it arrives. For if it did it would be determined that it went through that slit.

Digression

David Stove used to liken philosophy to eating spaghetti: you try to take a mouthful and fork up half the plate! The proposed speculation could grow into a whole metaphysics. I now provide some more details that many may, therefore, choose to ignore. They serve to forestall objections and explain the superiority of universe termination over branching universe theories such as Storrs McCall's (1994) or that of Rachel Briggs and Graeme Forbes (2012).

Passage of time

By the specious present I mean the interval of which a person is directly aware. Presumably it varies, and in extraordinary states it could be very long. The rate at which time *seems* to pass may be measured by the span in seconds of the specious present: the longer it is the slower the apparent passage. Dynamic theories of time assert that in some objective sense time itself passes, and that the apparent rate provides a somewhat inaccurate clock. On my proposed account, objective passage is measured by the spatio-temporal thickness of the boundary between the macroscopically determinate (the past) and the largely indeterminate (the future). The thicker this boundary the faster the rate at which time passes with respect to Time.

The Morgenbesser problem

Consider a genuinely random event with probability 50 per cent. It could be which slit the electron goes through, but suppose it manifests as the toss of a coin. I do not like betting, but someone induces me to bet by offering me better than even odds. I bet on heads; the coin lands tails. Then, as Sidney Morgenbesser points out, I might not only regret making the bet but fatuously say that if only I had bet on tails I would have won. But if I had made a different bet, it is objected, the hypothetical situation in which the coin was tossed would not be the actual one, and, because the coin-tossing was random, what actually happened does not tell us what would have happened in this hypothetical situation.

This is a serious problem for the branching universe theories of McCall and of Briggs and Forbes. It would be as serious for my speculation if I took random events merely to divide into two the sum of all universes not yet terminated. The division is, however, of the sum of all the universes *not yet terminated by the agent's history*, a sum that included many universes terminated by universal history. Therefore, there is the requisite independence of prediction and predicted event.

Relativity and non-linear Time?

It might seem arbitrary which of the two acts separated in a space-like fashion comes first. Suppose some astronauts are moving at near the speed of light relative to us. The astronauts decide to play their hundredth game of Monopoly as do some Earth-bound tragics. Then, according to Special or General Relativity, which decision is the earlier depends on whose frame of reference is being considered. In response to this, I grant that time, with a lower-case 't' is relative to a frame: different frames result in different coordinates. But Time is quite another thing. The proposal that the present divides space-time into the determinate and indeterminate sets up an imprecise but absolute division of events before and after the astronauts' game. This would be contrary to the laws of nature only if the successive divisions into past and future were nomically necessary. That these divisions are somewhat imprecise and, perhaps, not even flat shows that they are unlikely to be specified by the laws of nature alone. They may have something to do with the cosmic clock that the expanding universe provides (see Shallis 1986; Forrest 2008). Or maybe it is something to do with quantum entanglement.

It has been suggested that Time itself might be non-linear.[11] This results in a slightly simpler theory in which the sequence U_T is not required and its role played by the X_T for various agents or observers. The gain in simplicity is slight, however, for we still have various ways of dividing the sum of universes. And the cost is that we have to abandon the idea of an absolute reality in favour of what is real for various individuals. On the version of the Growing Block I am proposing, absolute reality is what is the case now and consists of all the universes together with facts about which the order in which some are terminated. Intuitively, we should not say that something is real for you but not me.

Propensities and objective chances

The probability of a random event is specified by the proportion of universes in which it occurs. These probabilities are *conditional* in that they are relative to which universes are being considered. If we take the proportion to be of universes in U_T, that is the universes not terminated at T, then the probability in question would seem to be an *objective chance*. If we take the proportion to be of the universes in the history of event X at some time T, X_T, then the probability would seem to be a *propensity*. Here I am following Hugh Mellor's distinction, but my purpose is not so much to analyse various concepts of probability as to show that the proposed speculation provides the metaphysics required for a nuanced theory of chance such as Mellor's (1971).

Initially the idea of a proportion of universes might seem to make sense only if there are only finitely many of them. The mathematics required to extend the idea would require a digression within a digression.[12]

A theory of consciousness

Universe termination enables us to integrate agency with the scientific world view, showing how certain events that would be described as merely random in the physics can be described as acts that affect the future, even if each universe is governed by deterministic laws. To complete the metaphysical synthesis of science with humanism, we need a theory of consciousness. Therefore, I sketch a speculation, which I call Agency Functionalism. It is a bit of a mongrel, with Donald Davidson's Anomalous Monism (1980) and Homuncular Functionalism (Lycan 1987) among its ancestors.

Functionalism

Functionalism is the thesis that at a suitably fine level of classification mental states may be characterized by their functional roles. For instance, itches and aches are quite distinct species of physical suffering, and we could explain the difference to someone who had never had either by noting their roles in a whole causal network of mental states leading to typical behavioural outcomes. One obvious difference is that we tend to scratch itches but rub aches.[13]

Agency Functionalism

By Agency Functionalism I mean functionalism with three additional principles, the first of which I attribute to Graham Oddie, combined with an agency theory of personhood.

> *Oddie's Principle*: The lower the physical probability of a process correlated with an act, the greater the sense of difficulty in performing it.

Given the universe termination speculation we may generalize and say that the greater the proportion of universes terminated by an act, the greater the sense of difficulty in performing it. This principle is illustrated by akrasia – weakness of will. If someone judges that an act should be performed but out of weakness of will does not do it, then that act was, physically speaking, improbable. If people systematically exercise considerable strength of will and suffer only rarely from akrasia, then the proportion of akratic failures to act would be lower than the physical probabilities would suggest, but systematically correlated: the lower the probability the more akratic outcomes. The same holds for the proportion of irrational acts by rational people. If the rational act is less physically probable than the irrational one then there is a temptation to perform it, but assuming the temptation is resisted fairly often the irrational acts will occur less often than the physical probabilities suggest.

The other two principles of Agency Functionalism are as follows:

> *The Anticipation Principle*: The agent knows the possible actions by being in a state indeterminate between those in which the agent performs the various possible acts.

The Reasons for Acting Principle:[14] The way a mental state seems on
    introspection would provide a reason to perform an act in agreement with
    the functional role of that state.[15]

The concept of a reason for acting is multiply ambiguous. First, we can
distinguish motivation from justification or explanation (Pearson 2018: Ch. 4).
I stipulate that I am considering reasons as motivations. Second, the reason
might be taken either as a mental state, being aware of something, or that of
which there is awareness. I stipulate that we are considering the former. Hence,
my reason for voting for the Greenish Red party is the belief that they will
govern better than other parties, not their governing better, which may or may
not be the case.

    This principle excludes, for example, a pain, as characterized functionally,
seeming pleasurable on introspection. It does not, however, exclude a pleasure
due to pain, such as eating food spiced with chilli.

Personhood

Next, we need a theory of what it is to be a full person, with the dignity assigned to
personhood by humanism. There are four stages on the way to full personhood.
First, there is sentience or consciousness, which I take to be widespread. Second,
there is the requisite unity for many bits of sentience to form a mind. Third,
there is the requirement that the mind have a sense of self. Finally, there is the
way the self at different times forms a person.

Minds

A sufficient condition for there to be a mind is, I submit, (1) proprioception or
body awareness, that is the sense of having a body arranged in a certain shape,
and (2) interaction (via sensation and behaviour) with the world by various
parts of that of which there is such proprioceptive awareness. Presumably the
illusion of a body and of interaction would also suffice, but that is not my present
concern.

The sense of self

For a sense of self, we require not merely the integration of various conscious
events into a mind, we require the capacity to reflect on that mind, noting

tendencies to behave and acting by endorsing the tendency or otherwise. Because I do not endorse the parochial restriction of awareness to brains, the sense of self cannot be due to an identity of self with brain. A more general theory is required. I submit that a sense of self is due to the negative character of the integration of certain bits of sentience into my mind. Explicitly, various other bits of sentience, those I think of as belonging to other minds, are not integrated. Proprioception provides just what is required in this way. To take a rather distressing example, inextricably conjoined twins provide a puzzle case, and we might well doubt whether there are two selves or one.

Rejecting the Simple View

I hold, then, the unoriginal theory of selfhood as the awareness of the unity of various bits of sentience or mental states. Hence, I reject the venerable Simple View, as Roderick Chisholm names it (1976), that the person endures as a temporally indivisible whole, or else has a part (a soul) that thus endures. Likewise, I deny the existence of a special property, a 'thisness', that the stages share (Swinburne 1984; Chisholm 1991). I have already rejected radical dualism in Chapter 2, and we should reject all these answers based on souls, thisnesses or brute identity, because, although themselves intuitive, they fail to support the intuitive importance of the biography of humans (and maybe some other animals). This failure is shown by the following story of inappropriate rebirth in Heaven. Reproba is informed by a predestining Calvinist god that she is to be damned, while her brother Electus is to be saved. She lives virtuously, he does not. After death, someone with her memories and character enjoys a heavenly reward, while someone with Electus's depraved character and memory is damned. He complains that he is Electus and was promised salvation. The god replies, 'No, Reprobata, you have been damned as I predestined but I have swapped your bodies and your minds.'[16] If we abandon these swap-vulnerable accounts of personal identity based on endurance without temporal parts, we need to consider ways of unifying the mental states occurring at different times.

Agency and personhood

Once we reject the Simple View or other theories based on an enduring temporally indivisible conferrer of identity, then the theory we provide of personal identity, and the intuitions used to support this theory, may well reflect what we value about ourselves (Johnston 1989; White 1989). A humanist should therefore prefer an account of personal identity based on a sequence of actions, with later ones presupposing the habits and memories resulting from of earlier ones. This agency theory of identity over time is influenced by John MacMurray (1957), and even by Sartre (1973).

I take it that there is value in persistence as the same person. I then note that the agency theory of personal identity leaves scope for the idea of degrees of unity, and the greater the unity the more value is attached to it. Degrees of unity arise because the relations uniting mental states at one time or stages over time can vary both in number and directness. This explains moral character because to act out of character is to lessen the degree of diachronic unity. There is, therefore, a practical dilemma if we judge an act good, but it is out of character: the value of the good act is balanced against the value of a high degree of unity. The value of preserving character applies even to divine acts, except for the first. Therefore, if initially god chooses to act for aesthetic reasons then at the second act god has the character of an aesthete.

I propose, then, a theory of both the synchronic and diachronic unity required for personhood. The idea is that two mental states are 'glued together' in a way that ensures they belong to the same person if their combination is a reason for acting. In that case I say the two states are agency related. For example, if I am persuaded of the wisdom of the Greenish Red party's policies there is an enduring mental state of believing these policies wise. If I subsequently vote for the Greenish Reds, the combination of the enduring belief in their wisdom and the short-lived intention to vote for the wisest party is a single state that provides the reason for voting for the Greenish Reds. Hence the enduring belief and the short-lived intention are agency related.

The various agency-relations between mental states bind them directly or, more often, indirectly, into a single person. The resulting theory of what it is to be a person may be stated more formally as follows:

The Agency Characterization:

1. A person is a *complete* sum of *agency-related* (occurrent or dispositional) mental states, where two states are agency related if their joint functional role may be interpreted as a reason for acting.
2. By a complete R-related sum x, I mean a sum x of R-related parts, such that (a) nothing disjoint from the sum x is R-related to any part of x and (b) there is no proper part y of x satisfying (a).

We have an intuition – not an especially strong one to be sure – that personhood is a metaphysically significant category, not just a morally significant one. Earlier in this chapter I provided an objective account of the history of an act as consisting of some but not other universes. Hence the history that constitutes a person is a sequence of sums of universes with each sum a part of all the earlier ones. Thus, personhood can be described in terms of fundamental metaphysics, preserving the intuition about significance.

For this agency characterization to be plausible, we must include among the reasons for an act many states that we are not currently introspecting. We must also say that two states separated in time can play a joint functional role. It is more controversial whether we should allow states we *cannot* introspect merely by asking ourselves a question, I suspect we should. For instance, my reason for voting for the Greenish Red party might be that they will govern better than the other parties, together with a now totally forgotten insult by the Reddish Greens' candidate.

The effect of freedom on this process of the formation of a person is that although the reasons might be beliefs about something that does not exist, a reason for acting must be one that makes reasonable the actual action that occurred, not some other action. Hence, when we choose, we choose which states are unified into a person, which is reminiscent of Sartre.

Bodily and psychological continuity are relevant to personhood, I submit, because we should recognize the goodness of the persistence of our bodies and our personalities, so we have reason to maintain them. Hence the default action is to preserve both body and personality. To act in ways that do not preserve ourselves in these senses is either insane or heroic, and such heroism is the stuff of martyrdom or conversion, depending on whether the body or the personality is sacrificed.

Global Agency Functionalism

The fourth and final principle is more ambitious. Adjoined to the first three it results in *Global* Agency Functionalism. It is as follows:

> *The Ubiquity Thesis*: Every real change, that is, every universe-termination is an act.

The Ubiquity Thesis is more ambitious but in a way less speculative than the other principles. For it would be parochial to restrict something so fundamental as consciousness to brains. Brains are associated with minds not because of some fundamental law but because brains are very good at representing the world around an organism, thus providing the circumstances for the unification of mental states required for personhood. Previously (1996, 2007a) I have submitted that the way to avoid parochialism is to adopt the thesis that there is awareness of everything, but generalizing from functional roles better supports the more specific thesis that the fact of awareness is associated with agency and hence universe termination. The Ubiquity Thesis permits persons embodied in ways quite unlike our own brain-centred organisms, or other humanoids, *provided* their conscious acts are unified. Otherwise there is, to borrow Kant's term, just a *manifold* of thoughts, sensations and acts.

Some examples of non-humanoid persons could be god and the angels, and god is the topic of the next chapter. Another example is the homunculus. The idea of homunculi is that various sub-systems of a brain have a partial autonomy. So, for instance, the visual processing system first generates fragments of a visual field and then builds up a detailed picture that best explains these fragments. Here it is *as if* the visual processing system is a homunculus, hypothesizing a visual field containing these fragments. Using the Ubiquity Thesis, we may strike out the 'as-if' qualification. Each human being really is a community of conscious agents. Likewise, the half scientific ideas of the Freudian subconscious and Jungian unconscious may well correspond to conscious agents lurking within, to which we have limited access. Heady stuff!

Final causes

When Aquinas asserts that god is good by analogy (in Aristotle's *pros hen* sense) a first reading suggests that all he is saying is that god's effects are good or, perhaps, like those of a good and powerful agent. This results in a difficult version of the Problem of Evil, because the effects of the act of creation are more like those of an aesthetically motived artist of indifferent morals. In addition, it seems to rob god of any personhood, whether one or three, because to say the effects are good would be true of axiarchism without a personal god. And given the identification of god with goodness, we should be even more suspicious of Aquinas, who sounds to contemporary ears like a puzzlingly pious Platonist atheist. An alternative reading, however, is to take Aquinas, and Aristotle before him, to be anthropomorphizing all causation. In that case the force of the claim that we speak of god by analogy is merely to deny that we know what is like to be god. That is acceptable, because even if the introspected character (the 'qualia') of mental states supervene on their functional roles, those of the divine mind are sufficiently different from ours to warrant ignorance about what it is like to be god (see Alston 1985). This anthropomorphizing of causation coheres with the role of 'final' causes, the *tele* of events or processes, what they are *for*. To be sure, in his Fourth Way Aquinas argues that the tele of apparently inanimate processes suggests a divine agent, which presupposes a more modern understanding of physical causation as not essentially guided by tele, and so requiring an external source of tele. Regardless of the interpretation of Aquinas, the idea that real changes are universe-terminations permits the treatment of all change as action.

Comparison with Process Philosophy

Final causation has also been an important thesis in Process Philosophy. Now, I am not a process philosopher, more a *poputchik* – a fellow traveller. So, I have some criticisms. The first concerns a pervasive feature of Process thought, dipolarity, the idea that things may be described in two apparently conflicting ways. Whitehead takes every process to start as a result of efficient causation, evolve internally for while in accordance with final causation and then be an efficient cause, before or when it ceases. A priori, this is a fairly plausible. At least it is fairly plausible if we take the final causes to be reasons for acting. For I find the idea of a final cause without agency counter-intuitive. Unfortunately, although final causation (teleology) coheres well with biology where it is hard to avoid an as-if teleology, physics at the nuclear level has no preferred temporal direction, if by time we mean the fourth dimension of space-time. This prevents us taking literally the causal description of nuclear events such as a photon causing an electron and a positron. Whiteheadians therefore adopt the top-down metaphysics that seeks to explain the very small in terms of the medium sized or even in terms of the whole universe. Again, this is not implausible *a priori* and the account of real change as universe termination is a top-down approach. Physics, however, has succeeded by describing the very small in ways that do not mention the larger systems they are part of. I conclude that process philosophers have located final causes in the wrong place, namely within the individual spatio-temporal universes rather than acts on the whole Multiverse.

Should we commit to absolute ethics?

Humanism requires commitment to objective value, and hence to morality in a broad sense. Consider, for instance the decision to save a drowning child, which will make you cold and wet, get your clothes muddy and make you late for a lecture. Given the objective values, the decision is obvious, and even having to deliberate is a moral defect. So, *morality* in the broad sense is clearly entailed by objective values. By *ethics*, though, I mean something narrower, namely, rules about what you ought or ought not to do. Previously when considering the widely proclaimed cultural relativity of ethical rules I noted how peculiar it would be to say that slavery was permissible in many societies without noting that at least in that respect those societies are inferior to ours. This supports the objectivist but relativist theory that ethical rules are relative to a culture, but some cultures are in some respects absolutely better than others. Should we nonetheless commit to absolute ethical rules, asserting that specified acts are wrong for everyone regardless of culture or other circumstances? To answer this, we need to consider the following problem with grounding ethical rules on absolute values.

The pro tanto problem

Because, for instance, pain is absolutely bad, we have a pro tanto reason to relieve it. This explains the corresponding pro tanto ethical rule: relieve pain! But here is the problem: either our ethics contains no rules for comparing different pro tanto obligations, or it is mysterious why these rules hold rather than variants. Suppose I am hiding someone whom I know to be innocent, but who the police are convinced is guilty of plotting a heinous terrorist act. Unless I deceive the police, they will find and torture the person I promised to protect. There is a pro tanto obligation not to lie and a pro tanto obligation to keep the promise. If these conflict, because silence will divulge the secret, we have a dilemma. Now some dilemmas are such that whatever you do is wrong, but a system of ethical rules does not serve its purpose of promoting the good if there are too many such dilemmas. So, what do you do? I say that in this case it is not wrong to lie, and it is wrong not to lie. Kant notoriously told us not to lie, something the Oxford Brethren would have endorsed. We might complicate the absolute ethical rule, stating that it is wrong to deceive anyone who has not forfeited the right to know. Then we list circumstances in which you do not have the right to know. That does not help explain why it is, in the circumstances, absolutely wrong to lie. It would be less mysterious to develop a moral theory that rests content with pro tanto rules.

Some case is needed then if we are to believe in an absolute ethics that goes beyond pro tanto rules based on absolute values. This case is the phenomenologically imperious character of the rules. Their natural expression is 'Thou shalt not!' And that is the basis of R.M. Hare's analysis of ethical rules as universal prescriptions (1952). The phenomenology excludes, although Hare's theory does not, the obvious response to commands, 'Don't order me around!' Or to the voice of conscience, 'Stop nagging!' The other way of bringing out the imperious character of ethical rules is to contrast them with mere mores, such as wearing clothes in public or grammatical conventions, like the defunct injunction not to split infinitives. Intuitively they differ in kind. One difference is that we agree that it is reasonable to be both ashamed and guilty if you do wrong, but going against the mores should only result in embarrassment. Another difference is that absolute ethical rules bind us all, even god, at all times – something denied by the Divine Command Theory of ethics, according to which god was not bound by the rules when commanding them.

In this section I argue that commitment to absolute ethical rules is unreasonable, but might nonetheless be judged as morally obligatory by non-theists. I also argue that a version of the Divine Command Theory provides a plausible enough substitute for absolute ethical rules, so that theists do not need that unreasonable commitment. Before I do so I make a concession to ethical absolutists.

A concession

I am reluctant to dismiss innocent beliefs, and I can well understand how a sound upbringing might result in an innocent acceptance of absolute ethics. This innocence about ethics interacts in various ways with the case for a worship-worthy God. For a start, a god who creates our world but allows much animal suffering prior to human evolution is probably taking the ends to justify the means. On many ethical theories, this will be problematic and so the creator would be condemned as unethical and hence not worthy of worship. That seems to be the force of Dostoevsky's criticism put into the mouth of Ivan Karamazov. For the end of a loving heavenly society does not, it could be judged, justify the means of allowing the torment of a child. On the other hand, on those theories such as Utilitarianism in which the ends do justify the means we would say that god is being ethical, but an utilitarian god is not worthy of worship.[17] Either way, then, absolute ethics looks like bad news for religion.

The prevalence of innocent absolutism might help solve two puzzles. First, the appeal of Christianity not merely to repentant sinners – that is the advertised deal – but to those of us who persist in our sins. The sinfulness of Christians can be explained but not excused, because a rigorously ethical upbringing, often the product of parental religious belief, tends to result in innocent absolutism and hence a heightened sensitivity to the Problem of Evil, leading to atheism or agnosticism, leaving those of us with laxer ethical standards remaining as believers. The second is the incomprehension of many as to why thinking theists, among whom I flatter myself to be included, do not take the Argument from Evil as decisive. The answer is that we are not ethical absolutists.

Having made these concessions, I now inveigh against an all too common inconsistency in those whose upbringing secures their innocent ethical absolutism but, under intellectual pressure, cease to treat ethics as objective. They should not press the Argument from Evil against theists on the grounds that the theists, unlike themselves, should be ethical absolutists. For that is an example of the fallacy of religiously orthodox atheism, that of crying foul whenever the thinking theist adopts a less rigid or conservative position than the atheist had been brought up to believe. ('That's what the nuns taught me.')

In our culture, the prevalence of relativism and the implicit appreciation of Mackie's Argument from Queerness has resulted in a widespread loss of epistemic innocence about ethics. And I am assuming just such a loss when considering commitment to ethical absolutism.

Mackie's argument endorsed

The case for Ethical Absolutism is the phenomenology, the sense that ethical rules command us. The case against is Mackie's Argument from Queerness as applied to ethical rules. For just as absolute values are sui generis and mysterious, absolute prohibitions attached to various kinds of act are likewise sui generis and mysterious, and so vulnerable to Ockham's Razor. The two mysteries are assimilated by the non-ethical morality in which harms and benefits provide the reasons for acting, but absolute ethical rules introduce a different way in which beliefs motivate. Now we cannot live without values, and I have made the case for committing to their absolute character in spite of the Razor. But the case of absolute ethical rules is distinct from that of values and morality more generally and the Argument from Queerness establishes a pro tanto case against these rules, setting up the intellectual dilemma.

The reason why we should not commit to ethical absolutism

The reason for non-commitment is that those ethical rules that may reasonably be taken to satisfy the Absolute Superiority Condition fail to satisfy the Pragmatic Condition. There are, to be sure, many general moral principles whose content is good and beautiful, such as the Golden Rule, 'Do as you would be done by', or the Law of Love, 'You shall love the Lord your God with all your heart and mind and strength, and love your neighbour as yourself!' But these are not ethical rules. Pro tanto ethics is messy and lacks the elegance we find in the laws of nature, and so do not satisfy the Absolute Superiority Condition. The only ethical rule that does satisfy it is Act Utilitarianism, 'Maximise expected utility!' But that, I say, fails the Pragmatic Criterion. For we have a fairly firm ethical intuition that the ends do not always justify the means. Now utilitarians sneer at those reluctant to 'get their hands dirty', for instance, by detaining children without trial for various reasons. They thus assimilate our intuitive dislike of justifying means by the ends to an aversion to cleaning out some foul decay. This attempt to silence our intuition has, I say, been decisively refuted by Bernard Williams, (in Smart and Williams 1973: 247) who points out that in such 'dirty hands' examples we do not have a case of utilitarianism trumping other intuitions, but rather a moral dilemma in which whatever we do is wrong and, I would add, whatever we do we should feel guilt. (Williams prefers talk of compunction to guilt, but that subtlety eludes me.) Consider again the Hostage Problem. Following Williams, if utilitarianism was correct, then the negotiator would be irrational if he felt guilt (compunction) for killing the baby to save the other hostages. But here it is non-guilt that is irrational, because wrong has been done. Another example is killing a wounded, slowly dying, soldier on the battlefield because circumstances do not permit medical treatment. To avoid that dilemma all soldiers should carry morphine, but that certainly was not the case and probably still is not. Utilitarians would say this was permissible euthanasia, and that the non-utilitarian allows the poor wounded soldier to die slowly in agony out of a priggish regard for ethical rules. But that is not the correct diagnosis, and so this example does not support utilitarianism. The correct diagnosis is that, faced with someone dying in pain, if you cannot provide suitable pain relief then you are in a dilemma: whatever you do is wrong. You will probably do the wrong thing by speeding up death, rather than doing the wrong thing by not alleviating unnecessary pain. But, I repeat, whatever you do is wrong.

The problem of 'dirty hands', then, does not support utilitarian theories so there is an intuitive case against the only ethical rule that might satisfy the Absolute Superiority Condition. Moreover, commitment to Utilitarianism fails the Pragmatic Condition. For we humans have self-serving tendencies, and the need for ethical rules in addition to loving (God and) your neighbour derives from our parlous state. The above-mentioned Principle of Least Moral Effort describes our tendency not just to act wickedly but then to kid ourselves we are good people. These self-serving tendencies interfere with any genuinely impartial examination of the long-term consequences, even in circumstances where they could be assessed. For example, consider the dropping of the atomic bombs on Japan in 1945. It was justified on the grounds that it saved more lives than were lost. But you don't have to be a postmodernist to deconstruct that judgement as tacitly putting American combatants above Japanese civilians. The moral is that we cannot trust ourselves to be utilitarians, and if we do take the ends to justify the means it must be with a heavy heart, as in an insoluble moral dilemma.

A dilemma for atheists

I reject commitment to absolute ethics as unreasonable, but this sets up a further dilemma, namely, that what is not reasonable is in this case morally obligatory. For as Simon Blackburn points out (1993) we seem to have a moral obligation to attach some sort of objectivity to ethics. But if we acknowledge this moral obligation at all it might seem to require ethical absolutism, not half-measures. In response, I deny that anything unreasonable is obligatory. Instead, I offer a version of the Divine Command Theory that comes close to Ethical Absolutism. But for atheists I think the dilemma is a genuine one. Perhaps their most plausible response is not to deny that 'ought' implies 'reasonable', but treat the Absolute Value Condition for commitment as a necessary part of a sufficient condition, rather than a necessary condition. Given the tentative character of the Absolute Value Condition I concede therefore that atheists might reasonably reject my conditions for reasonable commitment not as too lax but as too stringent. Hence, they might reasonably, but, I say, incorrectly, judge it reasonable to commit to Ethical Absolutism and so, perhaps, to a strengthened Argument from Evil that makes it unreasonable to believe in a God worthy of worship.

A Divine Command Theory

The Divine Command Theory explains the imperious character of ethical rules by attributing them to god. It is not a version of ethical absolutism because on it god performs the act of establishing the ethical rules without being bound by those rules. That does not, however, prevent god being subsequently bound, which would make god worthy of trust and hence worship as God. So, we can provide a near absolute theory of ethics. Mackie's Argument from Queerness is then irrelevant because the force of the ethical rules is that they were commanded by god for the general good. To be sure, the absolutist will pose a version of the question to Euthyphro, 'Do ethical rules hold universally only because god commanded them; or does god command them universally because they hold absolutely?' This elicits an absolutist intuition, but not one that is so firm as to defeat the Argument from Queerness, which the Divine Command Theory resists.

There are two versions of the Divine Command Theory that should be avoided. The first, which is abhorrent, is that god is in no way constrained when ordaining the ethical rules, and so might command the destruction of your enemies and their families, as recorded in Joshua 6–8. On the contrary, I am assuming commitment to absolute values and disvalues, which constrain the divine acts. Moreover, the commands of such a god would not be ethical rules. The other version to avoid is the idea that conscience is the voice of God, commanding us to act or not act. This cannot be correct, because people sometimes perform heinous acts in good conscience.

How then might god ordain ethical rules that subsequently have universal force, binding even their divine author? I assume that at all times god is constrained by the absolute values. So, god never performs an act such that an alternative has better consequences. This does not imply that god performs the very best act, because there might be many acts that are optimal in the sense of none being better. At some moment of Time, maybe the first, god judges that there being universally binding laws will have good consequences and so ordains wisely chosen ones. This is done by restricting world-histories to exclude any in which, although the laws are broken, the consequences are better than not breaking them. Hence de facto utilitarianism holds. For instance, if it really is wrong for the negotiator to kill the baby to save the other hostages, then that is because god has excluded all those world-histories in which killing the baby had better consequences. If this is a genuine dilemma then god has also excluded those in which watching as all hostages are killed has better consequences. Hence the consequences in the two cases are incommensurable. This is not counter-intuitive, for apart from this speculation we have no way of judging the long-term consequences of particular acts. This assumes that in one way or another god has the power of self-limitation, something I shall need to assume in any case to meet the Argument from Evil. My preferred speculation is that this restriction on possible world-histories is achieved by the universe termination that I have relied on to explain agency.

To sum up, I propose a kenotic Divine Command Theory. Initially there is a god who is not God but for our sakes becomes God by ensuring that even divine acts are in conformity with the ethical rules. These rules, whose discovery is not trivial, hold because the possible ways history can develop are constrained so that de facto the rules satisfy the utilitarian constraint. If god chooses uncomplicated absolute rules then moral dilemmas will be fairly common, which is an evil. On the other hand, rather complicated rules would not only be contrary to god's love of elegance but hard to follow. We should expect only a few straightforward absolute rules, capable of universal understanding, with the rest of morality being important but not governed by absolute rules.

Summary

Innocent humanists and innocent ethical absolutists may well be opposed to theism. But I am considering those who have either never been innocent or have lost innocence. It is reasonable for them to commit to humanism but not reasonable to adopt the usual anti-religious humanist theses. Because the worship of God requires commitment it is not unreasonable, however, for a humanist to be agnostic. Any commitment to Ethical Absolutism is, I judge, unreasonable, partly because there is a substitute, a version of the Divine Command Theory, that satisfies our intuitions almost as well and does much better at replying to Mackie's Argument from Queerness – as Mackie acknowledged. Because of this substitute, theists should not be ethical absolutists. I concluded that it is unreasonable for non-theists to commit to ethical absolutism but reasonable to believe it is reasonable to commit. And if they do so, then Ethical Absolutism would so strengthen the Argument from Evil as perhaps to incline non-theist humanists to atheism rather than agnosticism. So, within the scope of commitments to reason and to humanism I reach the conclusion that atheism is not reasonable, but it is reasonable to suppose it is.

Humanism and the Cosmic Agent

By God I mean a being worthy of worship, while god is a being who is powerful and knowledgeable enough to be worthy of worship if good enough. Hence a creator is god but not obviously God. I stipulate that a theist is someone who believes there is a god, an atheist someone who denies there is a god and an agnostic someone who suspends judgement. This leaves scope for theists to deny that God exists. In the next chapter I argue that worshipping God is subject to a dilemma. Now one requirement for worship is having sufficient power, and in this chapter I argue from the humanist commitment to the conclusion that there is a cosmic agent, god, a personal being who set up the natural order and who is powerful enough to be worshipped provided the other requirements are met.

There are many differing conceptions of god, and correspondingly different styles of argument for theism. For the purpose of discussing commitment to God any fairly good case for god suffices, and there is no shortage of arguments (see *Walls and Dougherty 2018*). My case is distinctive only in that I am arguing for god as a cosmic agent whose earlier acts constrain later ones, by forming the divine character.

Speculating about cosmic agency

I begin then by making a case for god, who in some sense created the universe.

The primordial agent

My speculative conception of this creator is as a primordial cosmic agent. Here I continue to contrast the sequence of universe terminations that constitutes Time with time in the sense of the fourth dimension of the relativistic manifold. There is, I speculate, at least one moment of Time before time, that is before there is a natural order that ensures the distinction between the (macroscopically) determine region of space-time, the past, and the indeterminate region, the future.

In the previous chapter I characterized a person as a sum of stages, each with a self, related by the history of agency. And I argued that on pain of parochialism we should grant the Ubiquity Thesis that agency is not restricted to brains or brain-analogues. Brains are special only in that their processes play functional roles that are conducive to the survival of the organism that hosts the brain, and do so by representing the world around them.

Now, I take the passage of time to be an increase in the domain of what is determinate. Moreover, some ways of becoming determinate are more likely than others. This implies that various features of the universe play causal roles. These roles should then be associated with conscious states that render the change rational. Where conscious states are unified to form minds, the free choices of those minds affect which of the universes terminate.

There might be many ways in which such minds arise in addition to organisms having brains. But one plausible hypothesis is that there is, or at least once was, a cosmic mind, that is unrestricted unified awareness. This is a mind with power that is not restricted to this or that location. A cosmic mind requires or at least is rendered more probable by the idea of awareness of the whole Universe by proprioception.[1] The cosmic agent would be aware of all that is determinate, that is, shared by the universes, and aware of all ways of increasing determinacy. So, an act of this agent is the transition from the less to the more determinate.

On the Delayed Collapse Interpretation of quantum theory, when an agent acts, then there is initial indeterminacy between the outcomes. Associated with this, by the Anticipation Principle, the agent is aware of several determinate possibilities between which there is indeterminacy. In the human case these are represented by brain processes, so the possibilities are the ways these brain processes appear. Hence, we choose between the possibilities as they appear to us. In the case of cosmic agent, the same would hold, but the ways the *whole Multiverse* might be after a termination appear to the agent, not just some *brain processes*. Initially there is no past of which to be aware, so the first act is one based purely on the possibilities and cannot reflect a pre-existing history of agency. Later acts involve choices between what is still indeterminate, but the choice is made by an agent that is aware of all that is determinate, which will include the whole of time past. Here there is a contrast with us, humans, who have a rather limited *specious present*, by which we mean the duration of time which is now being directly experienced. Such a restriction would not be plausible for a cosmic agent, for whom the specious present would include the whole of the past.

To call this cosmic agent 'god' we might have to suppose that in the beginning there was nothing but god. In that case we should identify the sum of the universes that have not yet been terminated with the divine body. So, in the beginning this body was the sum of all possible universes. There is no reason to object to this identification if required.[2]

The divine unity

I shall now develop the hypothesis of god as cosmic agent, along the lines of previous work (Forrest 1996, 2007a). The case for such a god as creator will then be straightforward. I begin with an obvious objection: For there to be a cosmic agent there has first to be a cosmic self. But the divine awareness is of the whole Multiverse, and so there is a self only if that awareness is suitably unified. In addition, there should be awareness of this unity. This problem is made worse by the way theists should explain the laws of nature in terms of a primordial choice. (Otherwise they forfeit much of the explanatory power of theism.) So, the initial state is one of all metaphysically possible universes, with varying laws. How could the awareness of them and of the array of more determinate possibilities have the requisite unity?

To answer this, I rely on the Hyperverse, the version of Multiverse in which all the universes are parts of a large or even infinite dimensional hyper-space-time.[3] There is an equivalence relation of being separated by a finite amount, so it is conceivable that the Hyperverse is the sum of components that are infinitely separated, and hence not connected to each other. It follows from the requirement of unity that then there would be different gods aware of the different components (cf. Leslie 2002). If, however, there is only one component then there is (initially) just the one god. I assume the latter, not out of any confidence, but because we could ignore the gods that are not of our component. They will not affect us, nor we them. There is room enough within the one hyper-space-time for a great array of universes with differing space-time geometries.

Next, suppose a thesis that is *a priori* plausible but, as yet, lacking empirical support. It is that all physical variety supervenes on geometric variety, more precisely that there are no two universes that are geometrically exact duplicates but physically different. If that Supervenience on Geometry thesis is correct, then the hyper-space-time gives unity to the initial manifold of universes, which is all that is required for the initial unity of the cosmic mind. Even if the pleasing Supervenience on Geometry thesis is false, there can be a continuous variation of the furniture of the universes within the one Multiverse. So initially the array of all possible physical universes can be included as parts of the one connected system. This supports the thesis that – initially at least – there is just the one cosmic mind aware of all the universes. The Multiverse is then analogous to a sculptor's block of marble: the carving is the process of universe termination.

There is a problem, though, concerning self-awareness. In the human case the sense of self is associated with a sense of what is not self and of the boundary between the two. An infant lacking that sense of a boundary might be considered to have a mind but not to be a self. I agree but selfhood is not required for agency, for a sense of what is good overall suffices in place of any sense of what is good for me. Initially, then, it may be that the cosmic agent is a selfless agent, not in the morally admirable sense of agents who treat the well-being of others as providing as much reason for acting as their own good, but in the sense of an agent lacking the self/other distinction required for that morally admirable type of selflessness. Likewise, divine personhood might be incomplete if the history of acts contains no reference to external factors that mark the boundaries of self. This might affect whether we describe god as being a person even before there are non-divine agents – unless, that is, we accept the Christian doctrine of a multiplicity of divine persons. But this consideration does not affect the case for god, and the idea that a worship-worthy God requires personhood is not relevant here because there can be no worship without the agents to worship, whose existence ensures the self/other distinction required for complete divine personhood. (For this reason, I deny that the body of God is now the whole Multiverse – other agents are unholy holes in the holy whole.)

Primordial divine acts

On the proposed speculation, the divine acts terminate many of the universes. If, as I have suggested, the Multiverse, that is the array of universes, is, as it were, glued together to form a connected whole, the Hyperverse, then we may think of this termination as sculpture, with universes cut away. Part of this process is to set up the natural order, which includes time, that is, time as we know it. By the primordial act or acts I mean those that precede in Time the beginning of time. Because there are absolute values (something to which I am assuming commitment) these primordial acts are explained by the divine knowledge of possibilities and the values they have when and if made actual. One primordial act that I shall not consider here because it pertains to the details of Christian doctrine would be the generation of the Trinity, say, by a fission of the one god into three divine persons. This leaves several candidate acts: establishing the geometry of space and the natural order more generally, commanding the ethical rules, providing initial conditions and ensuring general providence.

The natural order consists of constraints on the geometry of space-time, some laws of nature, a system of kinds and the termination of those universes that have no comprehensible order.[4] The terminated incomprehensible universes will include those in which because of their complexity, ordinary inductive extrapolation succeeds up to a certain time, say 2032, but then fails spectacularly, as well as universes in which Ockham's Razor is violated so that there are entities that do not affect ordinary matter in any way. To terminate incomprehensible universes underpins our reliance on reason. In both the case of laws of nature and of ethical rules, we need only to consider rather fundamental laws or rules because the way they work out will vary in different universes or, indeed, in different domains of our universe. This act of creation terminates universes for which the laws of nature do not hold and those for which keeping the ethical rules has (knowably) worse consequences than breaking them. The god will act in this way out of regard for what is good even though not yet bound by ethical rules.

This initial act is in response to a dilemma: variety is of value, but the imposition of a uniform set of laws and rules is good if there is one set better than the remainder. To choose varied fundamental laws of nature would be to undergo fission by disrupting the prior continuity of the Multiverse, whereby we can pass by small degrees from one universe to another, for between universes governed by different laws there will be incomprehensible ones without the right sort laws for them to survive the divine act of termination. Note that I am only concerned here with uniform *fundamental* laws; we can vary the 'constants' in the laws continuously, and even by sending Planck's constant to zero and the speed of light to infinity leave classical mechanics holding in some universes.

The laws of nature, perhaps when combined with initial conditions, ensure that we have time, that is time as we know it, with the whole of space-time divided, fuzzily, into a macroscopically determinate past and a macroscopically indeterminate future – with the present being the (fuzzy) boundary.

Initial conditions?

If the laws are time-reversible, then a choice of initial conditions might be required to ensure time as we experience it. For instance, the initial conditions might ensure that the universe, from our perspective, contracts down to a dense state, a Crunch and then expands in a Big Bang. This could result in time passing the other way on the far side of the Crunch/Bang, so that the determinate region, that which creatures experience as the past extends both sides of the Crunch/Bang. For those on the other side, our Bang will be described as their Crunch.

Another kind of initial condition is for the cosmic agent to determine the macroscopic details of the whole history of the universe up to some stage. This would require an absence of free creatures up to this stage. For instance, it has been suggested that there have already been an infinite number of cycles starting with a Bang ending with a Crunch, but that, before this cycle, the universe has been unsuited to life (see Lauris Baum and Paul Frampton 2007). Then, the cosmic agent could easily have specified in detail all the previous cycles leaving this one to develop in part under the influence of non-divine agents.

There is one situation in which initial conditions become problematic, namely, that in which throughout an infinite past there have been non-divine agents. For instance, there could be a cyclic universe with each cycle containing chemistry much as we know it with life evolving on rare and special planets (Steinhardt and Turok 2004, 2007). In that case, an initial condition consisting of an initial segment of history would rob the agents in that segment of their freedom. My response is that there is no need whatever for initial conditions. Imposing the natural order but otherwise leaving a vast multiplicity of universes will leave, in addition to inhabitable universes like our own, ones without any proper passage of time and ones otherwise unsuited to life. There seems to be no reason to exclude these.

Providence

The final component that we might expect in a primordial act is providential control. Here I distinguish general from particular providence and argue against including the latter in the primordial act. The former is the termination of all universes without a supremely worthwhile end state, even if on purely utilitarian grounds they might be acceptable because of intermediary flourishing. The latter concerns the response to events that are not determined, such as free acts. The cosmic agent could indeed specify a response in advance, like an answering service, by terminating those universes in which a certain creaturely act occurs and the divine response is not providential. There are, however, several reasons not to assume god builds these conditional responses into a primordial act. The chief of these is that these responses will typically be in the face of practical dilemmas, and it does not seem reasonable to settle dilemmas purely hypothetically. Readers will not have forgotten that I am speculating so the best response, I think, is to suspend judgement at this stage as to whether particular providence is pro-active or re-active, noting the case for the latter.

Alternative conceptions of god

Pantheism?

To better understand the cosmic agent, I shall compare some other conceptions of god. First my proposal is compatible with but does not imply a qualified pantheism, for in one sense an agent's body is that which the agent directly controls and is directly aware of. To be sure, in another sense our bodies are the animals who we are if we abstract from the mental activity they are associated with. In the former sense, we may say that god's body consists of those parts of the Universe god has control over. Prior to other, non-divine, agents, it follows that the divine body is everything actual, namely, the whole array of universes that have not yet been terminated. Hence, the primordial god is embodied in the Universe. On the further speculation that there are no non-physical minds or souls it follows that we may identify god with the divine body, as suggested above. In that case pantheism was true before there were non-divine agents. That we human beings are agents is a humanist commitment. That god does not have power over my acts is a requirement for the sort of freedom I am also committed to. Hence, pantheism is not now correct. It may well become correct again in the future. As of now we are the holes.

Two rejected conceptions of god

I reject two popular conceptions at opposite ends of the conservative/radical spectrum. The classical conception of God is of a timeless first cause that is only *as if* personal but does not provide an adequate object of worship. At the other extreme, the process theologians' god encourages and inspires but has no providential control over the outcome of human history. This is sufficiently anthropomorphic for us to love and respect, but probably not powerful enough to worship.

Satisfactory conceptions of a god are as an agent with sufficient power and knowledge for us to trust totally if the divine character is trustworthy. As far as Christian doctrines go, the metaphysical discussion of different conceptions hardly matters, provided they are compatible with a worship-worthy God and the doctrine of the Trinity.[5] Although our conception of a god is of little doctrinal importance, it affects the cases for and against god's existence. Roughly speaking, the positive case for existence is stronger if we do not arbitrarily limit the powers ascribed to god, whereas the Argument from Evil against God's existence is likewise stronger if we do not arbitrarily limit the powers ascribed to God. Intellectually, the easiest way of reconciling these two conflicting arguments is to suppose that initially god is not good enough to be God. I have speculated previously (2007a) that god not only comes to love creation, thereby coming to be God, but also restricts the divine power, ordaining unbreakable laws. In this way, god ceases to be all-powerful but retains enough power for providential control over human history.

Predestination and its rivals

Concerning the initial, or, as most would say, persisting, divine state there are three positions, differing in the role ascribed to human freedom. Predestinarians follow Aquinas and Calvin in holding that at all times god knows and causes the whole of history down to every last detail, past, present and future. Assuming this implies universal predestination to Heaven it is a cheerful doctrine, but it renders creation static – a four-dimensional work of art, with no narrative meaning. Moreover, it strengthens the Argument from Evil by making god responsible for all the suffering that occurs for no good reason. Rejecting Predestinarianism has led many, including myself, to prefer Open Theism, defended by Clark Pinnock (2001), William Hasker (1998, 2004) and others. The characteristic thesis of Open Theism is that the future is not real, and so there is nothing in the future for god to know in strict sense, except in so far as it is determined by laws. Consequently, we humans can be, on occasion, radically free, and god neither causes nor knows what we shall do.

An alternative to both Predestinarianism and Open Theism is Molinism, defended by, among others, Thomas Flint (1998). Molinists hold that god has *middle knowledge*. That is, god foreknew what free creatures would choose if created, and hence takes no risks. Some might complain that a Molinist god is too manipulative to be worshipped (Anderson 2014), but my objection is that the capacity for middle knowledge lacks precedent in our humanist commitments, namely, radical freedom and absolute values. Therefore, on Ockhamist grounds the case for a god whose power is like ours except unlimited is stronger than the case for a god with special unprecedented powers, such as Molinists propose. Against this, it could be objected that god is a perfect being, with some maximal combination of possible attributes it is good to have, and middle knowledge would be such an attribute. My response to that objection is that, without a human precedent, middle knowledge is only conceivable in much the same way that time travel is conceivable, with no good reason to believe it is possible. When arguing for the existence of god, I shall, therefore be guided by Ockhamist considerations, only attributing to god power and knowledge like that of humans but unrestricted.

A necessary being

Although I reject the classical conception of god, the idea that god is a necessary being is worth further consideration. I am relying on the Delayed Collapse Interpretation with its process of universe termination. The simplest version is that in which all metaphysically possible universes exist at a first moment of Time.[6] This Multiverse containing all possibilities is a plausible candidate for a necessary being. Assuming the mental supervenes on the physical then god's initial existence is also necessary.

A first cause?

By a first cause we might mean an ultimate explanation. For the reasons given in Chapter 2, I do not think the cosmic agent is first cause in that sense. But we might also be considering the initial process of causation, one which begins *history*, understood as an extended causal process. In that case, the initial divine act is a first cause and the primordial acts of god partially explain all those that follow, in the same way that of history provides partial explanations.

Does god choose the best?

Leibniz famously held that god chose the best of all possible worlds, which Plantinga calls Leibniz's Lapse, his point being that to choose the best of all acts of creation might well involve leaving various events indeterminate, to be decided subsequently by free creatures. Nonetheless, William Rowe (2004) has argued that if there is a god this god must indeed choose the best of all worlds and so is not free. I amend his position to the thesis that god would act in the best possible way. As I understand it, Rowe holds that the existence of the classical omni-God (an all-powerful all-knowing God who is morally perfect) is inconsistent with there being no best possible divine act.[7] If the absence of a best is due to there being a sequence of possible acts each with a better one, then I agree, but I note that commitment to God does not require that there is such an omni-God because, I speculate, god started out as all-powerful and all-knowing and was moved by what is good in utilitarian fashion, that is, because it is good. So initially god did not act out of moral perfection but became virtuous, I say, only by an act that ensures that future divine acts performed for the sake of a good ends coincide with ones constrained by the universal moral laws. But god likewise, I submit, ordains a natural order that restricts the initial divine power and so is no longer all-powerful.

More pertinent to the proposed conception of god as acting out of knowledge of the good is a decision problem inspired by Rowe. How does god decide which act to perform if there is no best? Here there are three cases to consider. The first is the above-mentioned scenario of a sequence of better and better possible acts. I fail to see how god could choose which to perform, and we have no human precedent for this case. Let us suppose, then, that faced with that sort of choice god fails to act. The next case is that of indifference, the situation faced by Buridan's ass. Maybe god could choose at random in this case, but I shall not make any such assumption.[8] The third case is the one that concerns me, that in which god is faced with possibilities that exhibit incommensurable values, as it might be a choice between elegant comprehensible laws of nature, on the one hand, and avoiding creatures ever having dysfunctional pain, on the other hand. This, of course, concerns the Problem of Evil, but here I am thinking of the decision problem. Initially god is faced with a dilemma and it is, I grant, a mystery that an agent can choose in the face of a dilemma, but that mystery is one that humanism accepts. There is no further mystery in saying that god, when faced with a dilemma, makes a choice for which there is good pro tanto reason but also a good pro tanto reason for deciding otherwise. In making this choice god would acquire a character and so will in future prefer aesthetic goods over non-suffering and hence prefer a good for creatures of sharing the divine aesthetic joy rather than ensuring they have pleasant lives.

Finally, consider the circumstances where god does not act because either it is arbitrary which of two equally good acts to perform or because there is an infinite sequence of better and better acts. The speculation I am relying on, with god terminating various universes, implies that in those circumstances the universes are not terminated. So, the result of divine indecision is not a void but indeterminacy. By establishing the natural order with time as we know it this indeterminacy shrinks with the passage of time. A corollary of this case for indeterminacy is that there is not even a pro tanto reason to infer predestination from theism unless you hold the heroic Leibnizian thesis that there is a best of all possible worlds and ours is it.

The case for a cosmic agent

The case for either axiarchism or theism

The first cause is an initial act of a cosmic agent who acts like a good utilitarian moved by the absolute value of things. This hypothesis has several advantages over its rivals. It synthesizes the various suggestions as to the ultimate explanation, repairing the defects in each one. Thus, positing a plenitude of universes as an initial necessary state requires a selector if we are to avoid various problems noted in Chapter 2. For instance, there would be many possible systems of laws of nature that mimic ours empirically but are horrendously complicated. Both axiarchism and theism explain why these do not occur. Another advantage that theism and axiarchism share over naturalism is that they provide a more thorough explanation of why the natural order is suited to life than the many worlds explanation of fine-tuning, for fine-tuning requires there to be fundamental laws that, with suitable tuning, are life-friendly. The superior explanatory power of theism in this respect does not depend on a prior demonstration of the contingency of the laws of nature (a thesis that, I grant, non-theists might well have doubts about), for necessity does not entail explanatory power or intelligibility. If it did, then we would only have to hypothesize that some fact was necessary to provide a hypothetical explanation of it, which is absurd. The theistic explanation is superior over those rivals that do not hold that life was selected for, and, in particular, over the hypothesis that the laws of nature are the ultimate explanation, for that hypothesis does not exclude simpler laws unsuited to life. The advantage of theism in this respect is subject to two promissory notes, however. The first is that a thorough investigation of simpler or more elegant laws than the actual ones would show them unsuited to life. Because we have not yet made this investigation, I make do with the argument that if our laws require such delicate fine-tuning to be suitable for life it is unlikely that simpler ones would be up to the task.

The other promissory note is that we shall not have to posit alien possibilities. This is a problem for all those who are realists about possibilities that do not depend on what is actual. That includes not just non-theist modal realists such as David Lewis but all theists who in one way or another follow Leibniz in thinking of god choosing from among possibilities. The problem is that a description of our universe includes not just its geometry but various properties such as mass, electric charge and quark 'colour'. Because these properties occur in the actual universe we should expect quite different, perhaps inconceivable, properties to occur in other possible universes. These are called 'alien' properties and their possibility 'alien' possibilities, and they violate Ockham's Razor. My promissory note is that physics supervenes on geometry, and hence the array of possible universes is just the array of possible geometries, all of which can be contained in one hyper-space-time. It is as if god sculpts from a block of uniformly white marble without there being colours in it. This has the further advantage that it enables us to understand the divine awareness of the Universe, that is, the Multiverse, as proprioception. Granted these promissory notes, theism and axiarchism have a clear advantage of those rivals that lack a selection from among possibilities. Otherwise I would judge this round of the contest to be a draw.

Theism and axiarchism also explain the beauty of nature in ways that go beyond the laws themselves, for the hard truth about god is that, initially at least, a beautiful world with much pain is preferred to an ugly one full of sensuous delight. Then again, theism explains the imperious character of the moral law as ordained by god to bind all beings. Because I have been emphasizing the character of god as like an artist, a sculptor of the hyper-space-time, god's interest in ethics might seem perplexing. But the divine preference for some values over others does not render those others of no significance. Moreover, human flourishing is not just a matter of a pain-free disease-free happy life, and the struggle exhibited individually and collectively to achieve some noble goal has value, a value which is in the broad sense aesthetic. Not only should we value beautiful things, we should in the same spirit value beautiful lives, and the ethical rules are an aid to a beautiful life. The problem with ethics is discovering the right rules, and obedience to the wrong ones is a great source of misery. Hopefully, we recognize the right rules intuitively when they are proclaimed to us.

The advantage of theism over axiarchism

Axiarchism and theism would enable us to understand equally well except that, I say, there are incommensurable values, that is, cases in which X is neither better nor worse than Y, and yet X and Y are not of equal value. For example, I claim that aesthetic value and the absence of suffering are incommensurable. As in the previous chapter, I consider an artist, say, Vincent van Gogh, whose life has much joy in beauty but is blemished by much suffering. Ignoring an afterlife, we wonder whether van Gogh's life is better than a bland but pleasant one. If all values are commensurable, then there must be some degree of suffering that makes them roughly equal. Suppose van Gogh was in that position. Can we say that if he had suffered from gout the extra suffering would make the difference? That is not plausible. Moreover, in the previous chapter I examined the intuitive appeal of Mackie's Argument from Relativity as applied to values, with (some) incommensurability as a corollary. Because, therefore, there is no one best possible act of creation, neither the agency explanation provided by theism nor the axiarchist explanation is complete. Therefore, the intuitively appealing Principle of Sufficient Reason has exceptions, if stated in the version that demands all truths be comprehensible. The best way of understanding that we have is therefore one that makes a principled exception, picking out a certain class of truths as lacking explanation. Now as part of the humanist commitment to our capacity to make free choices in the face of dilemmas, we have already picked out a class of exceptions, namely, such choices. Having granted one class of exceptions it is best not to have to add further classes, so the best way of weakening the Principle of Sufficient Reason is to say that when an agent is faced with a dilemma both acts that might be performed have merely pro tanto sufficient reasons. Making this one exception permits as a valid but incomplete way of understanding the provision of a causal history, a narrative, in which some of the causal links are decisions made in the face of dilemmas. Such causal explanations are both central to the discipline of history and to the personal narrative that provides much of our sense of 'who we are'. Theism by providing such a causal history exhibits its superiority to axiarchism when it comes to exceptions to the Principle of Sufficient Reason. That in no way prevents the axiarchist understanding of some necessary truths, including the existence of the primordial god embodied in the Multiverse.

The Problem of Religion

The final advantage of theism over religious scepticism is that reflective sceptics should not just dismiss religion as outmoded but owe us an explanation of the origin of religion, and of its importance in human history. The Problem of Religion for atheists, as we may call it, is in some ways like the Problem of Evil for omni-God. In both cases there is no shortage of proposed solutions. Combining them results in the sort of defence to which the proper response is, 'Is that the best you can do?' That is, the defence suffices to show that the thesis being defended is not totally refuted so much as lowered in probability by an amount that is hard to judge. A corollary is that, when assessing the history of religions, we should be open to the interpretation of that history as a record of the, often distorted, human–divine relations, based on the need for divine assistance and the command to worship.

To support my judgement that the atheists can only offer somewhat unsatisfactory responses to the Problem of Religion, I consider four responses that may be gleaned from the literature: Religion as Primitive, Religion as Insane, Religion as Oversensitivity and Religion as Functional.

Religion as primitive?

The Enlightenment did some good, but it also resulted in that hubris of Western Civilization, the delusion of smooth progress. Along with the egregious historical error of identifying the Middle with the Dark Ages, this results in the dismissal of premodern beliefs as childish. There is a grain of truth in this: if you belong to a small community, whether a tribe of hunter-gatherers, an isolated village or a religious sect, there is less scope for the corrective of dissenting views. But if there ever was a time when adults more generally thought in primitive ways it was a hundred thousand years ago.

Religion as insane?

Sigmund Freud (1959) and Julian Jaynes (1976) have in different ways linked the origin of religion with insanity. Abstracting away from their intriguing but implausible details, we should note that hearing voices, obsession with rituals, self-destructive asceticism and delusions of grandeur can be used to explain the actions and words of shamans, prophets and popular saints. Here I press the analogy between the Problem of Evil and the Problem of Religion. Free will is widely appealed to when responding to the latter, but its most plausible application is to the restricted class of evils that result from human acts. Likewise, the diagnosis of much religious behaviour as insane is plausible only as an explication of the religion of minor deities, titans, angels, demons, efrites, ghosts and ghouls. This sort of religion shades off via salacious tales of gods and goddesses to folk tales trivialized as fairy stories. Call it folk religion. It is usually tolerated by the priests of the contrasting high religion, although condemned by some Hebrew prophets, the iconoclasts of the eighth and ninth centuries, and Calvinists. To extend the Religion as Insanity thesis from folk to high religion is analogous to explaining natural evils as due to the supernatural influence of Satan – is that the best you can do?

Religion as hypervigilance?

Justin Barrett (2004), who is, however, not an atheist, explains religion as due to a hyperactive agency detection device (HADD). The idea is that at a time when the chief threats were predators there was survival value in interpreting situations in terms of agency, even if nine times out of ten they were not. Positing one or more high gods is indeed an explanation by means of agency. But in the context of the humanist commitment, resort to agency in explanation is neither outmoded nor hyperactive. What HADD explains is animism, the idea that 'all things are full of gods'. We have discovered that nature is not enchanted like that, a discovery that, I say, prepares the way for the re-enchantment of nature as the divine body. Animism is close to folk religion, and a combination of Religion as Insanity and the Religion as HADD offers, I judge, a satisfactory – and destructive – explanation of folk religion.

Religion as functional?

A common idea among sociologists and cultural anthropologists is that religion can be explained because of its role or function in society. Cultural anthropology tends towards subjectivism about values, which is a shame since it should make clear the distinction between mores or customs, genuine ethical rules and morality more generally. One of the ways in which a society maintains cohesion is by foisting upon us a custom, say, a food taboo, as an ethical rule. If that rule helps the society flourish, then, I submit, it is part of culture-dependent ethics. Otherwise it is purely subjective. Cultural anthropology should but does not, I say, make clear which rules are universal in that they help any good enough human society to flourish. Putting that criticism to one side, I grant that society often relies upon religious sanctions to maintain these ethical rules. In return, the religious institutions are supported by the society in question. This corrupt relationship between religion and the dominant social order needs exposing ('demystifying').

The aspects of religion that clearly perform social functions are those that encourage self-sacrifice for our own tribe and the slaughter of others, as shown by the religious fanatic. These aspects include the idea of an all-perceiving god you cannot hide from, with rewards and punishments hereafter. Likewise, the threat of damnation for unbelief serves the function of buttressing the religion against doubt. The application of this functional account to the characteristic doctrines of Christianity is far from clear, however. Moreover, if Christianity did arise to serve a social function it is hard to see why it thrived in spite of state opposition for several centuries. It was perceived as a threat to the dominant religion's function in supporting society, not as aiding it. Christians should take seriously the idea that their religion came to support the stability of society once it became the dominant religion and that has tended to corrupt it. But we don't need Émile Durkheim (1912) to tell us that.

In addition to the thesis that religion functions to preserve a social structure, Durkheim speculates that the idea of worship develops from the sense of depending upon and needing to obey the society to which you belong. In a way we may say that, according to him, worship was originally of the community. (That is an idolatry that lies at the heart of Fascism.) I do not find the details of this speculation plausible, partly because Australian Aboriginal religion, one of Durkheim's sources, has sacred places and sacred archetypal events, and associated animal species, which involve not so much archetypal societies as archetypal social roles. And there is recognition of the sacred character of the sacred places and archetypes of other Aboriginal peoples speaking other languages. What I think Durkheim's speculation supports is the thesis that god or gods we worship often reflect what we depend on. For hunter-gatherers it may well be the community, but they also venerate the totemic animals.[9] For agrarians it is the cycles of the seasons and the other requirements of fertility.

Alternatively, the gods reflect the values that are highly regarded in a society, such as military prowess. Such a study of the various influences on religion is important, but it does not explain away the history of religions. Rather it helps us concentrate on those features that stand out as not so easily explained in this way. For instance, after Israel split into a northern and a southern kingdom, various prophets in the northern kingdom denounced idolatry and proclaimed an ethically demanding religion that required social justice. The study of religion reveals similar disruptions in other places and at other times, for instance, the short-lived religious reform of the Pharaoh Ikhnaton. In this way, the history of religions coheres rather better with the thesis that we humans have an instinctive need for worship and an intuitive but fallible sense of the divine, than with the Enlightenment view that, apart perhaps from an attenuated deism, religion is a rather silly hangover from a more primitive age.

Because of its advantages, I judge that theism wins on the balance of probabilities, and, if my promises about future science are kept, it wins beyond all reasonable doubt. But before reaching that conclusion we need to consider the case against theism, notably the Argument from Evil.

The case against a cosmic agent

The Argument from Evil has some force against the existence of god, although not as much as it has against the proclamation that god is God. So, in the next chapter I shall consider it in greater detail. Here I discuss the issue rather abstractly. Antecedently, we judge that a god acting out of recognition of values would have found some way to achieve all the familiar good things without so much pain and other suffering. It is hard to be confident about that judgement, though, and there are three relevant considerations.

Primordial utilitarianism

Prior to ordaining the ethical rules, we should think of god as a good utilitarian, for whom the ends justify the means. We trust human utilitarians only if they are humble enough to recognize their limits as predictors of consequences. Otherwise we accuse them of playing god. In philosophy seminars, we often assume a god-like knowledge, which makes moral monsters out of utilitarians, for instance, torturing innocent children for the greater good. The primordial acts of god are in that respect like those considered in the seminar. Moreover, I have already submitted that god is motivated largely by aesthetic considerations, at least in the broad sense. And utilitarians should not unselfishly ignore their own benefit, including the joy of contemplating what is beautiful. Therefore, it is not so surprising that god has created in a way that involves great suffering.

We can form some idea of god's purpose from our experience of the world around us: there are opportunities for moral heroism, for compassion, for repentance, for progress and, more generally, for individuals to flourish because they belong to flourishing communities for the sake of which they are prepared to sacrifice their own wills. We might nonetheless ask why god would permit such a high propensity for dysfunctional suffering, even given that the primordial acts of god are not constrained by ethics. The answer, I think, is that humanity has damaged creation and god, like a stern parent, demands that we repair the damage. All this coheres with primordial utilitarianism.

In his 2003 Gifford Lectures, Peter van Inwagen seeks to show that the Argument from Evil fails. One of his premises, when considering animal pain prior to the evolution of human beings, is that, for all we know, 'every world God could have made that contains higher-level sentient creatures either contains patterns of suffering morally equivalent to those of the actual world, *or else is massively irregular*' (van Inwagen 2008: 119, my emphasis). A less harsh plan would be irregular and that is a grave defect (2008: 120–5). I can think of two reasons why irregularity would be a defect. First, if we suppose that god intended us to have our actual reasoning powers then that god would be deceiving us if in fact there are these irregularities. The second is that irregularity is intrinsically defective. I reject the first reason because the less harsh package could include reasoning powers that exhibit sensitivity to just when god is likely to intervene miraculously. This leaves the second reason, and, I say, the intrinsic defect is aesthetic. I conclude that van Inwagen's case against the Argument from Evil succeeds only if we suppose that, for all we know, god is a utilitarian, with high aesthetic motivation. This is just as I am speculating holds for the primordial god.

Indeterminacy as the default

The second consideration is that if god has no reason to choose a given history god might well leave it indeterminate, allowing subsequent events, especially creaturely choices, to decide. The Argument from Evil would have greater force if god had determined every precise detail of history.

Preternaturalism

The third consideration is that if god terminates all the universes in which certain rather simple laws fail, then god's power is limited to intervene *preternaturally* rather than *supernaturally*. By that I mean that god acts in history doing wonderful things but only within the scope provided by the laws of nature. The nature of reports of miracles at Lourdes tends to support this, with many remissions from cancer, or in an earlier age tuberculosis. In an apocryphal infancy narrative, Jesus is described as working the silly supernatural miracle of making clay birds and bringing them to life. This contrasts with miracles reported either in the canonical Gospels or the less extravagant apocrypha. The conclusion to be drawn is that if you ask why prayers are not answered the answer is not that you lack faith but that often god cannot intervene.

Against the restriction to preternatural acts, the Quantum Problem of Evil might be posed, namely, that quantum theory does not exclude as supernatural such events as restoring a lost hand but just makes them extremely unlikely. My response is to appeal to Oddie's Principle: an act will be difficult to perform and so occasion suffering if it is such as would, apart from considerations of agency, be improbable. It follows on utilitarian grounds that god will not perform highly improbable acts lightly because of the divine suffering involved.[10]

But would you want to know this god?

These three considerations greatly reduce the force of the Argument from Evil as applied to a god who we have not yet judged worthy to be called 'God'. But they cast doubt on whether god is God, for a human utilitarian who was given divine knowledge would be a moral monster, sacrificing the few for the sake of the many. And for all we know god was similarly ruthless. Maybe the whole of creation was just part of a gambit intended to win back Satan to god's friendship, with our lives, our joys and our suffering, just a by-product.

Life after death

We might rail at a utilitarian god, creating us for some unfathomable purpose or, even worse, tolerating our existence as by-product. But a god who creates out of awareness of what is good would want all of creation to be happy and fulfilled, although maybe allowing some to freely damn themselves. Because so many are, for no fault of their own, unhappy and unfulfilled in this life, we may draw the conclusion that if there is a god there is an afterlife, perhaps of finite extent. There are also considerations of justice that a utilitarian would recognize as of some value. Therefore, it is plausible that the wrongs we have done to others results in afterlife punishment unless those others forgive us. Again, god would judge it fitting that there be appropriate shame and glory, which require an afterlife in which the truth about our lives is revealed. All this holds even if god is not God and even if god never wants to have any dealings with humanity or individual human beings. In addition, if god is God then an afterlife is required as a condition of trust in God in the face of suffering.

The afterlife can seem problematic for those of us who reject the idea of an immortal soul. We require, therefore, a metaphysical speculation that shows how an afterlife can occur without unduly complicating the laws of nature. For then we know there is some way in which god can ensure an afterlife and so if there are good reasons to ensure it, it will be done some way or another. Previously I have provided a speculation based on the Multiverse (Forrest 2007b), using the very small but positive probability of surviving to suggest that the Universe undergoes fission with the dead surviving on side branches. I now think that this was mistaken: because the branching or fission of the Universe would be highly improbable on naturalistic grounds, it follows from Oddie's Principle that an agent would be able to stay in existence on a side branch only at the cost of some suffering, plausibly the sense of exercising 'will power'. The innocent should not undergo further suffering in this way.

In this work, then, I rely on the idea that at death we are absorbed, becoming parts of god, without retaining the capacity for independent action, and so ceasing to be individuals. This has two consequences. One is that subsequently the process could be reversed leading to the resurrection of the dead. The other, less happy, consequence is that the less aligned your will is to god's the less pleasant it will be to be thus absorbed, providing the basis for the doctrine of Purgatory.

Afterlife in the Multiverse, without fission

I develop the idea of absorption into god in two ways, first using an alternative Multiverse speculation, conceding that there is no fission. Instead I suppose that the universe termination following observation and action results in a distribution of universes in which the vast majority are as observed or intended but there are outliers. This is like the situation for a normal distribution

(Gaussian bell curve) in which a very small proportion can differ from the mean by many standard deviations. (About one on a billion deviates by six or more standard deviations.) That is because quantum theory is somewhat fuzzy, and we should therefore grant that quantum measurements as described in theory are idealizations of actual observations that merely establish a very high probability of the observed result. To undergo fission into two branches the distribution of universes would be bimodal, with two distinct humps like a Bactrian camel. I am assuming this never happens but maybe it is just highly improbable, in which case I resort to Oddie's Principle to exclude it from consideration. The survival of the dead occurs, then, in the 'tail' consisting of a small proportion of universes. Hence, when we say someone is dead in fact they are alive to some exceeding small degree. Because this is such a small degree, further terminations are almost entirely controlled by the way most of the universes appear, either to god or to the creatures who are alive in the ordinary sense. Therefore, the dead can neither act nor observe in the active sense and so, it would seem, become parts of god. At some future time the tail could become the hump (of a Dromedary camel!) if the termination of the vast majority of universes occurs. Then the dead would have risen again. In setting up the natural order in this way god can either put in place some mechanism to ensure such a general resurrection or make it contingent on our collective salvation.

Afterlife in the divine specious present

The idea of absorption into god can be developed in a different way by considering the specious present, that interval of time that is directly experienced. In the human case the specious present is usually no more than a minute.[11] What about the divine specious present? Two hypotheses come to mind: either it contains past, present and future or it contains the past and present only, in which case the divine specious present grows as time passes. The former coheres with the classical conception of god as unchanging, the latter with Open Theism according to which God does not know the future, presumably because there is no future to know before it happens. In either case the lives of the dead are known to God as present, and not just remembered. My speculation is that this divine knowledge consists of the very same experiences the dead had while alive. That raises the question of what makes these experiences those of a non-divine being while that being was alive. What divides them from the rest of experience? I am assuming that we reject the thesis of an immaterial Self or soul that unifies our experiences and that our sense of selfhood either is identical to or depends upon the relations that hold between the experiences. I grant that this No Self assumption is controversial, but I am here just using it as a speculation.

Given these speculative assumptions, the sense of self that we humans have, and the unity of consciousness that lasts for no more than a minute, depends on an individual human's experiences being related to each other by integrating relations, but it also depends on being integrated neither with experiences of other individuals nor with those of any non-human. As time passes, additional integrating relations hold and this affects the way the whole manifold of experience is divided into individual minds. One consequence is that the mental unity associated with a human being lasts only for the specious present. Another consequence is that if additional integrating relations could be added later then the whole life of a human being could be re-integrated, resulting in someone whose specious present is a whole lifetime of experiences.

If we combine the two speculations we might say that future termination of universes will result in the annihilation of the relations that bind these lives into the one divine consciousness, converting them back into the god-like specious present of individual non-divine minds related by love rather than psychological integration. Even if we reject the Multiverse, absorption into the divine specious present coheres well with Growing Block theory of Time. The 'block' in question is a region of space-time for which there is macroscopic determinacy.

Divine hiddenness

This is a serious problem with the idea that there is a God who loves us and wants to know us. Why do so many good and wise human beings seek but fail to find God? The utilitarian primordial god might well intend that we collectively come to have knowledge of the divine, but not be in any great hurry. The Problem of Divine Hiddenness will, however, be taken seriously when considering the worship of god as God.

On the classical argument from Evil: Omni-god and God

The classical Argument from Evil claims God's existence is inconsistent with the evil we find in the world around us. It is common to say that Alvin Plantinga (1965, 1974) has shown this argument to be fallacious because of the mere possibility of free will. Interest then turns to the Evidential Argument from Evil, based on the judgement that the evils around us are highly improbable on the hypothesis of a good, powerful and knowledgeable god (Rowe 1979, 1986, 1996).

I concede there are evils that are most unlikely on the assumption of an omnipotent, omniscient and morally perfect God. This is a refutation unless, when we bracket off the evils, the probability of there being omni-God is near 100 per cent.[12] Readers might disagree but although there is a good case for a creator of some sort, the case for omni-God does not seem strong enough to have the high probability required to resist the Argument from Evil. My response is to reject omni-God, asserting that god is not now omnipotent and can only intervene in preternatural ways that do not break the laws of nature.[13] Consequently much evil is either permitted for the sake of something good or even caused by god as the means to a good end.

I suggest two speculations about this divine respect for the natural order: either god cannot break the laws or it causes god suffering to do so. In the former case god is (no longer) omnipotent; in the second god is not morally perfect, for a morally perfect being would suffer rather than take the ends to justify the means. Furthermore, an omnipotent God should prevent human freedom resulting in acts that harm others. Suppose someone refuses to accept a spouse's genuine apology and as a result of the consequent marriage breakdown the children suffer. Not even an omnipotent god could ensure the apology was freely accepted, but divine intervention could ensure that the marriage did not subsequently break down. A morally perfect god would intervene to achieve this happy result. This shows the limitations of the free will defence when it comes to omni-God.

I conclude that there is no omni-God. But the god whose existence is part of the explanation of the Universe is all-powerful. I reconcile the past existence of an omnipotent god with the current moral perfection of God by the kenotic speculation that god starts as omnipotent and omniscient but acts well only as implied by the intrinsic attraction of what is good (Forrest 2007a).[14] This god then abdicates omnipotence by setting up a natural order that cannot subsequently be broken. The choice is also made to love creation not just in the limited sense of deriving aesthetic joy from it but in the agapeic sense of making the divine well-being to some extent contingent upon creatures flourishing, and eventually coming to share in the divine life. This love is moral perfection, a perfection god did not initially have.

On agnosticism and atheism

Humanist agnosticism

In Chapter 5, I argued that any intellectual case for naturalism depends on a prior atheism, and that no one can reasonably commit to naturalism without that case. Likewise, when I argued against committing to secularism, I postponed my final assessment of atheism and agnosticism until after a consideration of the problems of Evil and Divine Hiddenness. The case for belief in god is, I judge rather strong, but that for a worship-worthy God less so. I see no point in committing to a god or gods outside the context of commitment to God. So, if you choose not to commit to God either you find the case for a god persuasive or not. In that latter case, agnosticism should be a *provisional* response, for a committed agnosticism would offend against the requirement of not committing to completion. I respect non-committed agnosticism, however. In the context of the commitments of humanism, I invite readers to judge the case for a god or gods to be at least strong enough to exclude atheists. Hence, a non-theist humanist should be agnostic. I concede that non-humanist atheist naturalism is reasonable – rather sad though!

Humanist atheism?

It might be objected that a non-theist humanist might *commit* to atheism. I doubt if much needs to be said in reply in addition to the earlier rejection of commitment to secularism and naturalism. The Pragmatic Condition for atheism is hard to assess. Belief in some kinds of god does harm, belief in others does good. I imagine many atheist commitments are motivated by hatred, either of God, a god or religion. The first is perverse. The second requires more detail about the god in question. The last is understandable, and it could lead to atheism by means of a commitment to this-worldliness based on a rejection of an afterlife, which in turn is required if there is a god because of the horrors of this life for many. This reaction is, I say, too individualistic, ignoring the importance for Christians along with secular humanists to bring about what I call a demi-paradise. I differ from secular humanists because I hold that this demi-paradise can only be brought about as the Kingdom of God, but that is not because we humans can be slack and leave it up to God. Rather the task requires both human effort and divine help.

Suppose, though, the atheist insists the Pragmatic Condition is satisfied by atheism, because, it is said, religion distracts from the task of making this life better ('opiate of the people', 'pie in the sky when you die'). There still remains the absolute goodness requirement. How could it be good that there is no god? It is silly to say it is good because we humans would then be the greatest things in the universe, for being less than the greatest does not make something less good. Moreover, it seems rather likely that somewhere in the vast, perhaps infinite, life-friendly universe of ours there are extraterrestrials who by human standards are greater than us. Hence, to proclaim that humanity is the greatest requires not just atheism but an unreasonable commitment against extraterrestrials (and angels).

Atheists are likely to reject the Absolute Value Condition. I do, however, insist that something more is required for intellectual commitment than a pragmatic choice in the face of an intellectual dilemma. Committed atheists owe us an account of this something more. Otherwise, the proper position for non-theist humanists remains provisional agnosticism.

Commitment to God

In this chapter I make the case for commitment to a worship-worthy God, based on the, albeit inconclusive, case for there being a god, provided in the previous chapter.

The case for God

I have speculated that the primordial god is not worthy of worship and so not God, but that the primordial divine acts have changed the divine nature.[1] Regardless of this speculation there are three questions that have to be answered:

1. Is god (still) powerful enough to be God?
2. Is god (now) good enough to be God?
3. Does God want to be worshipped?

The Problem of Divine Hiddenness pertains to the last of these. Most of this chapter is taken up, however, by an undermining of the Argument from Evil, which pertains to the second. In this section, though, I present the case for worship, taking for granted the case made in the previous chapter that god exists.

The case for God, ignoring revelation

First, there is a case that can be made without any resort to purported revelation. The freedom we humans have to influence events is considerable, although localized. That shows that the natural order does not constrain too much for agents generally, and god in particular to intervene. I fail to see any consideration that would put limits on divine knowledge, except perhaps knowledge of the minds of non-divine agents. This suggests that divine preternatural powers are extensive. Moreover, even though god seems to have delegated much power over the universe to creatures, it is good to have retained enough power to ensure a good outcome no matter what goes wrong, contrary to the process theologians' idea of a cosmic friend. It is plausible, then, that god has retained enough power to be God.

The question of whether god is good and so worthy of trust depends on whether the moral order that god has set up is, like the natural order, binding on god's future acts. There are two reasons, apart from revelation, for holding that it does. The first is the intuitive pull of the Euthyphro question, as ordinarily posed. Are the ethical rules commanded by god because they are obligatory, or are they obligatory because commanded by god? If the latter, then god could command heinous deeds for the greater good, like telling Abraham to sacrifice his son Isaac, and these deeds would be obligatory. Now theists should explain the imperious character of the ethical rules as due to divine commands, but it is hard to resist the idea that even god is (now) constrained by them. Therefore, in the story Abraham should have denied that the god who commanded him was God.[2] The second reason for holding that the ethical rules bind even god follows from the proposed mechanism for establishing these rules, namely, terminating all universes in which breaking the rules is for the greater good, for then god, acting for the good, will thereby do what is right.

The case from revelation

This case for a worship-worthy God is rather weak, though, unless we supplement it with the empirical evidence, namely, the history of (purported) human-divine relations. Because the Problem of Religion is a serious one for atheists we should examine this history without anti-religious prejudice. Now, the history of religion can be assessed as a story of the gradual revelation that there is an ethically righteous and just God, concerned for our well-being, who loves us and wants to be loved, which is one of the reasons for god's kenotic act of being bound by the natural and moral order. Alternatively, it can be assessed as nothing but failed attempts to relate to the divine. Much religion, especially folk religion, is indeed unedifying or infantile. But there is a seam of prophetic inspiration, notably in the Old Testament, which calls us not only to worship but to love God. This provides empirical confirmation. For on the hypothesis of god's existence, the otherwise surprising content of (purported) revelation is more probable than if some naturalistic explanation holds such as the murky psychological forces that generate myths.

The case for the existence of God, even with its empirical confirmation, is a pro tanto one. The case 'against', which includes the Argument from Evil, would, I think, defeat the case for God except that it may be partially undermined by the thesis that God has a plan that involves our good collectively not just as individuals. That this undermining is only partial provides the other half of the dilemma.

Divine Deception?

The first objection is that I posed a false dichotomy, by contrasting 'murky psychological forces', or other naturalistic explanation, with truthful divine revelation as the two possible explanations of purported revelation. A third hypothesis must be taken seriously, namely, deception by god, not out of malice, but for some good purpose we do not understand.[3]

My reply is that I assume the motive for a divine act is the attraction of what is good, including what is beautiful. Hence, the divine goals will be achieved in beautiful ways. Now some acts that break the ethical rules may well have aesthetic value, exhibiting nobility, glory or chutzpah. But, contrary to Plato, lies are never noble. They are an ugly way of achieving some goal. A god, therefore, might well permit false revelation by others but would not deceive. Hence the dichotomy between genuine revelation and a naturalistic explanation is not undermined.

Perhaps readers will propose the Satanic Rejoinder, namely, that some evil being with god-like powers is the author of false revelation, and that god, for some good reason, permits this. Presumably, though, we can tell from the content which scriptures are plausibly Satanic, and that does not include the revelation of divine love.

Individual religious experience

Religious experience would pose a problem for worship if there is an experience contrary to the worship-worthy character of the object of experience. Religious experience varies greatly, however, from the conversion experiences, described along with other kinds by William James (1902), to visions, often of angels, through to the 'ineffable' experiences we call 'mystical'. Not only do the experiences vary, but their interpretation seems to be theory-laden; that is, it reflects the antecedent beliefs of the one having the experiences.

Thus, Christian mystics speak of *union* with God, but Hindu ones often speak of *identity* with God, and those of Buddhists and Jains are non-theistic. What, if any, lesson should we draw from religious experience, then? First, to someone who already believes in God the experience, even though theory-laden, might provide some further confirmation (cf. Alston 1991). Second, the lack of consensus about the experiences exacerbates the Problem of Divine Hiddenness: it seems God is really not that concerned about one to one relations with individual mystics, whose asceticism is therefore wasted. Third, there is the disturbing 'beyond good and evil' experience that R.C. Zaehner links with Charles Manson murders (Zaehner 1974: 306). If god could indeed be veridically experienced as beyond good and evil then that would be proof that god is no God. Given the differences between kinds of religious experience we should not take any of them as establishing anything, either conclusively or probably.

For what it is worth, I think that the common feature of all mystical experiences is the loss of the *sense* of the self/other distinction. This naturally but erroneously gets interpreted as a sense of loss of self and hence union with all else.[4] Ethics is based upon the value of distinct individuals, so the experience of union seems to make ethics irrelevant. Hence the illusion of a god beyond good and evil.

Incommensurable values theodicy

The circumstances of commitment are those in which there is a case 'for' and a case 'against', each persuasive in the absence of the other. The difficulty of the commitment varies with just how persuasive are the respective cases. A good enough theodicy undermines much of the case against worship and so makes the commitment easier. This provides a rationale for the project of speculative theodicy, consisting of hypothetical solutions to the Problem of Evil (and that of Divine Hiddenness). Now, a theodicy is intended not just to argue the consistency of evils with a worship-worthy God but also to explain the origin of the evils around us. The details of theodicy are speculative because we do not have a way of testing the different theodicies to see which of any is true. In this section, I do not go into these details, which are provided in the section Responding to Rejoinders in response to objections. I acknowledge, however, that the Problem of Evil retains considerable intuitive force providing one half of an intellectual dilemma.

An overview

The case for a god is, I say, that it is part of the best ultimate explanation or way of understanding. This case is based on the prior commitment to ordinary human ways of reasoning. Because we rely on these ways of reasoning, and not just strict deductive reasoning from agreed premises, the case for god, and especially for holding god to be God is vulnerable to probabilistic versions of the Argument from Evil and the somewhat similar Argument from Divine Hiddenness (Schellenberg 1993, 2005). Mere logical consistency between God and evil would suffice only for a sceptic not committed to reason and hence lacking any case for there being a god in the first place.

Both the Argument from Evil and the Argument from Divine Hiddenness have immense intuitive force. What reason could god have to allow the emotional horrors that many humans undergo and the immense pain that humans and other animals suffer? And why are good and evil so inequitably distributed? And even if god is worthy of worship, the widespread doubt about the love or even the existence of god suggest that the divine plan is for us to love our neighbours but not concern ourselves with the divine. It is by no means obvious that god would want to be worshipped or that Heaven would consist of anything more than a natural human fulfilment, both individual and collective.

The explication and assessment of the intuitive force of these arguments is extensively debated (see, for instance, Langtry 2008, Tooley 2015). My approach differs in that I have abandoned the omni-God hypothesis, and that I have already provided some grounds for assuming that many values are incommensurable, which will be used to provide a theodicy.

The Problem of Evil is often felt in the context of divine non-intervention ('Did heaven look on / And would not take their part?' *Macbeth* Act 4, Scene 3). My reply is based on god's response to the dilemma of just which individuals there should come to be, namely, to ordain the right sort of laws, providentially ensure a good enough outcome for every individual and then only intervene in ways compatible with those laws.[5] Hence the act of creation is to set up a natural order that not even God can subsequently violate. The constraints on this order are the laws of nature, and they leave room for agents, divine or otherwise, freely to make a difference, but not to perform miracles in the strict sense of law-violations. Often, we do not know if God can intervene, but where it seems things would have been better if God had, then we should infer God could not.

Clearly this reply reinforces the Argument from Evil when applied to the initial divine act: Why set up the Universe with its laws this way? My answer relies on the principle that explanations, even when they are not ultimate, should not be unnecessarily complicated. Hence, god is not posited to start with a moral character. Instead god acts well because agents will choose what seems good unless something interferes. And what seems good to god is good, because god is not subject to illusions. Taking that for granted, I provide a theodicy of incommensurable values based on the many cases of two values that are apparently in tension in the sense that they are neither commensurate nor capable of joint maximization.[6] Consequently, the initial divine decision as to how to create need not be as if god loves us like good parents love their children. For the creator might respond to the tensions differently from human beings. Here I am making an inference from the nature of creation to the character that the creator has acquired. Although much of my work is speculative, I claim that this inference to the divine character is more than speculation, it is a probable inference.

There seem to be four respects in which the initial divine act is markedly unlike the behaviour of a loving parent: the emphasis on the beauty of creation, the ordaining of laws of nature that cannot be broken, the toleration of much suffering at one time provided it is required for some great good later on and a willingness to delay human-divine relations. As the history of the Universe unfolds there come to be individual kinds of organism and individual members of some of these kinds. Only then, I submit, god, either by a radically free choice or merely as a consequence of coming to know these kinds and individuals, seeks a relationship of mutual love with suitable creatures and behaves in a loving way towards them, using preternatural but not supernatural powers. In this way, god became God (see Forrest 2007a).

Would god create all good types of universe?

I used to think that, given incommensurable values, there would be a profusion of creations corresponding to different ways of ranking the incommensurable values (cf. Ahern 1963). In that case not all good types of universe could have instances, because one of the values is that it is good to have individual agents clearly distinguished from other agents. Hence there would not be a continuum of all good types of universes in which each differs negligibly from its neighbours but rather a discrete spectrum of distinct types (see Forrest 1996: Ch. 8).[7] Because this spectrum is not continuous, this would destroy the unity of the divine mind, with its awareness of the various parts of creation. Assuming that it is an overriding good for god to retain existence as the same god, such radical fission is excluded. It follows that my supposition of a profusion of types of universe is incorrect, and god has chosen just one type of universe. More concretely, it is likely that there is the one spatio-temporally connected Hyperverse governed by one set of fundamental laws that holds in all the. A more moderate fission would result in a Trinity of divine persons, but that is not my present topic and may be ignored.[8] The conclusion I draw is that there has to be some divine choice out of an initially infinite array of possible types of universe. This is compatible with the many universes speculation provided these are all parts of the one, connected Hyperverse, with perhaps infinitely many spatial dimensions.

How should god respond to incommensurable values?

The primordial god is, then, faced with a dilemma: different subjective ways of ranking objectively incommensurable values imply different acts of creation. Relying on this dilemma, the theodicy of incommensurable values proposes the following:

1. Where possible god will try to avoid the dilemma of ranking one value higher than another.
2. Hence, god creates a universe allowing a profusion of good ways that agents individually and collectively can complete the divine work.
3. Sometimes, however, god has to rank some values as higher than others. So, a free divine choice has to be made by god with an associated subjective ranking of one value over another.
4. We should conform our ranking to god's if we are to worship god as God.

The Problem of Evil divides, then, into a part where there is a proper human anger at 'God's ways' that need to be 'justified', and the part where we humans are tempted to assert our own subjective comparisons against the divine judgement of values. I now provide some more detail by noting the various tensions between incommensurable values. These enable us to understand the evils we suffer from.

The tension between the collective and the individual

Human beings are valuable as individuals with their histories, but humanity is also valuable with its history. Moreover, our sense of who we are is in part derived from being part of the collective, whether humanity, a nation or some smaller unit. Political ideology has tended to extremes, either of valuing the collective over the individual or vice versa. The former tends to be demonic as in International Socialism or the even more evil National Socialism; the latter promotes a culture of selfishness as in ideological capitalism. (For pragmatic reasons, rather than ideological ones, we might nonetheless have socialist or capitalist leanings.) If god favoured the collective entirely, then our humanist commitment to the worth of individuals would be a mistake. If only individuals with their histories were part of god's plan, then angelic beings, maybe with bodies of light, would make up a superior creation. We may reasonably assume, therefore that god's plan for this planet combines the value both of individuals and of a larger collective, humanity. Most of the evils that beset us would be avoided if we were purely individuals or purely members of a community or society.

It is the tension between the community and the individual that is characteristic of the human condition. One ideal, and the one god seems to have, is that of individuals freely relinquishing autonomy for the sale of a community from which all individuals derive their well-being. This is like the ideal of romantic love but more extensive.

The most surprising divine decision was to set up a community that includes us, other creatures presumably, and God. Someone who had no familiarity with any religion might find preposterous the idea that god would want to have anything to do with us. To set this up, god, I speculate, ordained ethical rules that bind all, not just creatures. Although I say this is surprising, on reflection the history of religions shows that humans have tended to assume a divine-human community long before they had a clear idea of a God. But you might still ask whether the idea that god would want anything to do with us isn't just pride gone mad. I say it is not. Rather it is the humanists' proper pride in the status of human beings. That we differ infinitely from divine persons in power and knowledge in no way detracts from equality of status, not even, I say, our manifest unholiness. I noted in Chapter 6 the corollary of humanism that, in one way, we are god's equals. That is, joy or sorrow for a divine person is no more significant than the same joy or sorrow for a human one. If some Christian readers find this offensive, then I would suggest to them that this humanist thesis is implicit in the doctrine of the Incarnation. Unless we are, in this precise sense, equal to divine persons the Incarnation is as absurd as a man being reborn as a sea-horse in punishment for not taking fatherhood seriously.

This ambitious plan of divine-human community risks the divine suffering likely to result from this involvement with creation and the suffering of individual humans. There is, however, value in there being individuals that are separate from God and yet come both to worship and to love God. This separation from God seems to admit of degree: merely behaving in ways that for one reason or another are not caused by God separates us from God to some slight degree. Radical freedom, the freedom to choose in the context of a dilemma result in even greater separation. The risk with radical freedom is that the creatures will either never or only after much delay come to love and worship God. The extreme case might be Satan or Lucifer if there is such a god-like creature that refused to worship God.

The minimum standard associated with these two incommensurable values is that the overall outcome is one of flourishing at both individual and community level. On my favoured speculation god would, I assume, terminate all universes that fail to meet the minimum standard. This does not exclude either individual or collective choice of a good less than that which god had hoped we would choose, provided this lesser good meets the minimum standard.

A corollary of this minimum standard is that there are no horrendous evils in the sense of evils that make some lives not worth living – with the possible exception, once again, of any who choose damnation. Now, as Marilyn McCord Adams notes (1999), mere compensation cannot confer meaning on a life that is otherwise not worth having. For instance, a brief life of great pain cannot be said to be worth living all things considered if the great joy of an afterlife requires amnesia about that brief life. Compensation requires, in addition, that retrospectively the life, however brief and painful, is *accepted*. And that can only be the case if there is a glorious collective human history, including all the willing, as the individual persons they have become.

The requirement for the minimal standard to be met is, then, that the blessed in Heaven (1) include all who have not freely chosen a different sort of afterlife and (2) will prefer remembering to forgetting the details of their earthly lives. This condition is satisfied provided Heaven is an ideal loving community in which the differences between individuals are cherished. For in that case, the individuals will, in retrospect, be reconciled to the contingent features of their histories that distinguish them. We who are deformed in body and mind should not, for instance, envy those who died in infancy, assuming they are present in Heaven as perfect unblemished adults. For in one sense we could not have been them. That is, although we could have been the same organisms but with greatly different histories, our sense of personhood is made up of the details of our history, especially our acts, something which those who died in infancy lack. This retrospective acceptance of our histories should extend even to free choices that we regret. This is analogous to the thought that had our lives been significantly better in youth, then our children and grandchildren would not have existed.

The tension between the aesthetic and the moral

The omni-God who is the target of the Logical Problem of Evil is said to be perfectly good in a moral way and would not therefore sacrifice moral to aesthetic considerations. But this is far from obvious if we think of a god who does what is good because the good naturally attracts, and acts in a beautiful way to achieve beautiful ends because that too is attractive. If we ascribe no moral character to god, there is no reason to favour moral over aesthetic excellence if they clash. One way in which they clash is that the elegant exceptionless laws that god has ordained greatly reduce god's power subsequently to intervene. Therefore, the details of history are not as god would have wanted even though there is enough providential control to ensure a very good outcome. For instance, the grossly inequitable distribution of suffering should not be thought of as part of the divine plan.

The tension between benevolent and unitive love

The tension between love in the sense of unitive love and love in the sense of benevolence exerts a subtle influence on the Argument from Evil, because it is widely assumed that God would be benevolent. Generically, love is the tendency to derive joy from the object of love. Benevolence is a species of love in that generic sense, for the benevolent person derives joy from the well-being of others. The term 'love' is also used more specifically for the tendency to derive joy from mutual love or, where more than two are involved, a loving community. I call this *unitive love*. (It is similar to the Greek ideal of philia.) Unitive love derives joy from helping others in a community.

To avoid confusion, I should say how unitive love is related to *agape*, for the command to love God and your neighbour as yourself is an injunction to agape, by which I understand the deliberate and active seeking of mutual love even when not yet reciprocated, and so not joyful. This should be compared but not overly contrasted with *eros*, which I take to be a disposition: a desire or yearning for the same sort of mutual love. The reasons for denying that god has (initially) a moral character are also reasons for denying that god has desires that either add or subtract from the motivation provided by the awareness of what is good. We may, however, think of this divine awareness of the good as itself a desire provided that is not contrasted with what is reasonable. Hence, the agape/eros distinction is more important when considering human motives than divine ones.

Both the benevolent and the agapeic person respect others, but in different ways. The benevolent readily acknowledges that often the best way to help others is to help them help themselves, respecting their autonomy. The agapeic might tend to be interfering, offering fellowship where none is wanted. On the other hand, the benevolent might well deceive and manipulate for the sake of the greater good, while the agapeic avoids such impediments towards reciprocity.

The idea that a virtuous superior is benevolent to inferiors is naturally applied to how we might expect God to behave towards us, and that makes the Problem of Evil seem harder than it need be, for a purely benevolent god would not permit present suffering out of a grand plan that leads eventually to loving union between God and humanity, which would be characteristic of unitive love. The initially astounding idea of God who wants unitive love with humanity was shown above to have intellectual and emotional appeal, *given a humanist commitment.*

Even prior to commitment to god being God, we should judge that divine-human unitive love is of surpassing value and well worth whatever suffering required for its achievement. This is an example of the consilience of faith and reason with an astounding proclamation that on reflection is not so improbable. The divine love is seldom taken seriously without prior faith but having been taken seriously it should appeal to us as reasonable. Nonetheless there remains a tension between wanting to help others and the realization that, very often, they should help themselves. In the case of God's love for humanity this tension is, Christianity teaches, resolved by the Incarnation: God incarnate can help us without being an interfering or condescending outsider.

Whether the tension is resolved in the way Christianity teaches or in some other way, it undermines the presumption that God would intervene in ways that undermine the importance of human effort. That in turn helps us understand why the trust that the human story will eventually end well has to be combined with the acceptance that this is a laborious process. The 'end of the world is' not, I say, 'nigh'.

The tension between mercy and justice

The tension between divine mercy and retributive justice is obscured by the contemporary judgement that retributive justice is barbaric and not something an enlightened human being would want, let alone a god. I submit that the contemporary judgement holds for the purely benevolent, and that the tension only arises within the context of unitive love. If we strive for a loving community, how should we deal with free-riders and foul-dealers, who seek to benefit from the community, but either contribute nothing or do harm to others? The ultimate sanction is expulsion from the community, as in the idea of *anathema*. But the value of mutual love implies that we seek to reincorporate those who err. This is the virtue of mercy. To avoid the shame of having been a foul-dealer, a shame that prevents full membership of any community that includes human beings, those who err should have the opportunity to make restoration, tidying up, as it were, the mess they have made. And that, I say, is what justice amounts to: a penalty to be paid in order to be readmitted into full fellowship with the loving community. The alternatives are expulsion or shame.

The need for justice and the resolution of the justice/mercy tension is, then, provided by the mercy involved in restitution. Because we form a collective, namely, humanity, the minimal standard requires collective and individual restitution. Hence, we should expect human history to continue as long as this work remains to be done. I say again that the 'end of the world' is not 'nigh'. As a corollary, whatever divine help is required to achieve the collective goal of achieving a demi-paradise, God's merciful justice requires the maximum human effort as well. Hence, other-worldly 'pie in the sky' religion does not resolve the justice and/or mercy tension, and so should be repudiated.

The tension between joy and suffering

This instance of incommensurability is one that I see no resolution to, and no minimal standard. How much suffering is worth the joy of sharing in the divine life? How long is it worth waiting for? It seems god is forced to exercise radical freedom in these cases. If god has judged that joy is worth much suffering and worth waiting for, then god's worshippers should concur.

Theodicy and the act of creation

The theodicy of incommensurate values provides a hypothesis concerning the act of creation. At the risk of repetition, I shall state this hypothesis to display its coherence with our experience. First, god decides on the physics including any initial conditions for the universe and decides not to create universe-types that are more complicated than is required for aesthetic reasons or other goods that a universe might exhibit. These goods include those that require radical freedom and a heavenly afterlife. That implies setting up a natural order that not even the creator can subsequently break, for breakable laws are less elegant, having a 'nihil obstat' clause built into them. The creator is subsequently constrained to intervene only preternaturally, that is, in ways that do not break the laws, just as we creatures only exert out radical freedom within those same constraints.

I have suggested that to avoid divine fission, there is only the one universe-type created but that it has many domains and so includes great variety. My reflection on the world around us supports the thesis that creation is governed by certain values being promoted over some others. Among the promoted values are the following:

1. The value of free individual persons coming to give up their freedom out of love to form free individual communities that likewise persist and give up their freedom out of love.
2. The aesthetic value of mathematically elegant laws admitting no exceptions.
3. Great joy even if it has to be waited for a long time.

Among the demoted values are the following:

1. Absence of suffering.
2. Equity, in the sense of the good and bad things being equally distributed.
3. Having a good life here and now.

My speculation, then, is that god creates by terminating all universes that do not conform to the beautiful and wisely chosen laws of nature and by terminating all universes that do not meet the minimum standards. Once individual creatures and communities of creatures arise, god seeks to be incorporated with them into a loving community, and so god becomes God.

The tension between the aesthetic and the moral has been resolved because the natural order was chosen aesthetically before there were any individual creatures for whom moral considerations are salient. The primordial god does not know how things will turn out but, at least in our part of the Universe, things seem to have turned out very well aesthetically but too often individuals fail to flourish. Subsequently, God intervenes with preternatural power to help these individuals, including human beings. In addition to the large scale providential intervention in history, we may well suppose there are on a day to day basis many small providential acts, permitted by the natural order. Unfortunately, these are hard to assess unless we make the unwarranted assumption that they only benefit believers. As it is we may hope and pray for such interventions never knowing how frequent or how rare they are.

The divine character

Initially, the speculation goes, god was all-powerful, all-knowing and good in a utilitarian sort of way, knowing what was good and therefore having reason to promote the good. The primordial divine acts not merely limited god's power but established a divine character. To commit reasonably to the worship of god as God we must suppose this character is compatible with god's choosing to ordain ethical rules that are self-binding as well as binding for creatures and, preferably, coming to love both individual humans and humanity as a whole. It would not suffice, for instance, if our misfortunes were *uncompensated* collateral damage in some war between god and Satan. The ethical rules should also prevent god from gross deception for the sake of a good end. Otherwise, we should not trust god enough to worship. The divine character would seem to result in some values being demoted as less important to god than we might have thought, and others promoted. To repeat, among the promoted values are the following:

1. The value of free individual persons coming to give up their freedom out of love to form free individual communities that likewise persist and give up their freedom out of love.
2. The aesthetic value of mathematically elegant laws admitting no exceptions.
3. Great joy even if it has to be waited for a long time.

Among the demoted values are the following:

4. Absence of suffering.
5. Equity, in the sense of the good and bad things being equally distributed.
6. Having a good life here and now.

To worship God requires adopting the divine values. Hence a prior commitment to the superiority of the demoted values is an obstacle to worship. It should be noted, however, that the demotion is only relative: there is no reason to think that the demoted values are of no importance. Nonetheless the divine character is such that although God is not a 'surly tapster' nor is God 'a good fellow'

(Fitzgerald 1995: LXIV). To worship this God and become holy is to adopt the divine character, which is contrary to secular values. It is a genuine cost.

Responding to rejoinders

The Argument from Evil is an objection to the existence of God, that is, a god worthy of worship. The Argument from Divine Hiddenness is an objection to worshipping even a worthy God. My speculative theodicy was a reply based on three premises:

1. There are incommensurable values and the act of creation was motivated in part aesthetically.
2. There are laws that not even God can subsequently break.
3. Radical freedom is of value both because it is required for the good of us not being manipulated into loving god and because it provides a high degree of initial separation from God, increasing the value of a harmonious community.

I anticipate several rejoinders, to which I need to respond.

God is morally perfect, if there is a God

It is characteristic of utilitarianism that the ends justify the means. But most of us judge that sometimes the means are so bad that they should not be employed no matter how good the ends. Thus, in the story 'The Ones who walk away from Omelas', Ursula Le Guin (1975), inspired by Fyodor Dostoevsky and William James, describes a society that would be a utopia except its continued existence requires the misery of a single child. She develops this idea by noting those who 'walk away', going they know not where rather than be complicit in the child's misery.

Even if we distinguish between bringing evils about and merely tolerating them, the creator would seem complicit in the evils of this world and in that respect morally inferior to the 'ones who walk away', who would have refrained from creating at all rather than allow so much evil. I have suggested that the creator lacked any kind of moral character at all and is, for that reason, attracted to the good and repelled by the bad, acting like a good utilitarian. This is central to my theodicy, because the sort of moral perfection of 'those who walk away' is not compatible with the evils we find around us. Hence, the suggestion that God would have to be perfect is a serious objection to that theodicy.

There is a widespread intuition either that there is a perfect being or that a god would be perfect if there is one. Moreover, I hypothesize that god's existence is explained by its being valuable, which, together with Inference to the Best Explanation, would have the corollary that god is something than which there could be no better. In this case, though, I consider that the axiarchist explication replaces the intuition about a perfect being. In addition, the reasons for believing that the creator was perfect do not, however, imply moral perfection, for we should disambiguate the idea of a perfect being, as either one with all perfections or one than which no better is possible. The two differ if, as here envisaged, there are good things that no morally perfect being would bring about, because to do so would result in a moral taint ('dirty hands'). Therefore, moral perfection is incompatible with being a perfect utilitarian, and the axiarchist understanding of god's existence as good cannot decide between moral perfection and being a perfect utilitarian. That supports the initial existence of the character-less all-powerful all-knowing creator that I envisage. Character is acquired by god as a result of the divine choices.

Having given the axiarchist explication of our intuition, I deny that the primordial god was perfect in anything other than the sense of there being no better. The argument from evaluative understanding requires a being with all perfections only if we adopt the strong version of the Principle of Sufficient Reason, which I have rejected. Provided there is nothing better than god, then we have understood as well as required by the weak version.

I anticipate the rejoinder that God must be morally perfect, even if a god need not be. This reminds me of Ivan Karamazov; 'It's not God that I don't accept, Alyosha, only I most respectfully return Him the ticket.' The idea is that even Heaven or God's Kingdom on Earth would be like Le Guin's Omelas and to worship this god as God is to be complicit in the suffering of the innocent. Those, who are tempted to 'return the ticket' should, I say, grant that God is now morally perfect, and forgive God for an earlier utilitarian phase, or, following Ivan more closely, you might refuse Heaven until all those who have been wronged have either forgiven or exercised their right to punish.[9] Fair enough! But to worship is not the same as being part of a heavenly community, and the only forgiveness required for worship is of those who have wronged the worshipper and, if this be appropriate, forgiveness of God.

Divine hiddenness

Good, wise people often fail to find God. This cannot be understood if the primordial god was concerned with individual rather than collective worship. And I have not insisted that God be loving as well as morally righteous. But suppose perhaps as a result of revelation, we now believe there is a loving God. Then it may be objected that the preternatural divine powers should suffice to ensure that human beings know that there is a god and that god is God, a being worthy of worship. Surely, a loving God would reveal this central fact about the meaning of their lives (cf. Schellenberg 1993).

One response is that God has and does, wherever that is possible. A human brain is, however, nearly deterministic and, I conjecture, only open to inspiration in circumstances of deliberation, in which the outcome could go either way. These circumstances do not arise just because the thinker is eager to know the truth. I also note that the struggle with faith is not purely intellectual, as if judging that there is a being worthy of worship is one thing and worshipping that being another. Moreover, not all obstacles to worship are culpable, and many are subconscious. Hence, the scandals of organized religion, especially the Roman Catholic Church, can result in an 'invincible ignorance' that not even God can overcome immediately.

My other response to divine hiddenness is that it refutes the thesis that the primary goal of creation is to establish a series of one to one relationships with individuals. I maintain, therefore, that the divine purpose was to set up of a single community including God, all human beings, and probably other creatures. One concrete expression of this is that love between members of this community should give joy to all who are aware of it, including God. Another is that prayer and other acts of adoration should be of a community not individuals. Hence the knowledge of God by individuals, although a great good, is not our telos, not our *summum bonum*.

The humanist objection

The case for theism presupposes humanism's strong positive assessment of human individuals capable of, albeit limited, self-determination. Yet, my theodicy rests on the importance of the collective. I anticipate the charge of inconsistency. My reply is to repeat what I have already said when considering the tension between the collective and the individual. There is, I say, great value in individual humans, great value in a good society that they form, when they do, and especially great value in individuals freely giving up freedom for the good of some society, and not doing so as a result of coercion. Collective and individual flourishing are in general incommensurable, but the human case is one in which each kind of flourishing requires the other. That god chose to create such beings might show that god did not create like a humanist would have, but the fact that individual humans flourish only in communities shows that subsequently there is no tension and so God now endorses humanist values.

Non-human animals

Non-human animals suffer a great deal of hunger, thirst and pain. My response is that if they are not individuals then there is suffering but no animal suffers. I have previously speculated that their pain is God's pain. Some non-human animals are, however, either individuals or potentially so, and I see no reason to assign them a fate different from human foetuses, the still-born and those who die in infancy. We may speculate either that they reincarnate or, as Dougherty argues (2014), that their potential is developed in Heaven so they can join the community comprising God and creatures. Am I channelling David Lewis or Bruce, his cat? To be sure these animals have the opportunity neither for the glory nor for the shame that responsible adults have, but I do not see that as conflicting with their individuality. One way or another they become persons.

Hume's Dialogues

Michael Bradley (2007) laments our neglect of Philo's argument to be found in Chapters X to XII of Hume's *Dialogues*. This argument is based on Cleanthes's rule that like effects have like causes. Using this rule, we can ask what sort of being would bring about the sort of mixture of good and bad that we find around us. Our assessments might differ somewhat but no one who relied on Cleanthes's rule would infer that the creator was morally good, let alone morally perfect. We need to take Philo seriously even if, like me, we reject Cleanthes's rule in favour of Inference to the Best Explanation. For once we hypothesize an agent as the first cause, using, say, Inference to the Best Explanation, then we should rely on analogy to discern this agent's character.

My rejoinder is that the conclusion of the inference by analogy should be that the creator was either totally lacking in character or was a generous aesthete, like someone who gives away their works of art. This coheres with my speculation that in the beginning there was a god who was no God. Philo might agree.

God the chancer?

The theodicy that I have developed is one in which god takes risks and, as human history shows, things go badly wrong. I have to take seriously, therefore, an objection based on Thomas Flint's accusation that William Hasker's open theist God is 'the bookie than which none greater can be conceived' (Flint 1990: 114). Whether or not this is an objection to Hasker, it seems to hit home at my proposal in which god has abdicated much power by setting up the natural order, for God's character of a chancer is an obstacle to the trust required for worship.

A preliminary response is that the primordial god in setting up the natural order can retain as much providential control as is necessary finally to bring about the divine purpose. If god chooses to allow some creatures to choose a lesser good in place of the good of union with God, then that too is providential. Nonetheless even if god has predestined that all creatures eventually belong to a harmonious community that includes the God who is worshipped, the risk is taken of a deal of suffering meanwhile.

Simplifying matters by ignoring the incommensurability of values, god-the-chancer would act by maximizing expected utility, but therein lies the objection. Suppose your only child needs $500,000 to buy a home, but cannot get a mortgage, and you have only $50,000 savings. You think it unlikely that you will ever save up enough to buy your child a home, but a friend, who is in the know, tells you that a horse actually has 50 per cent chance of winning even though the betting odds are 10 to 1. So, you put all your savings on the horse. Is that rational? Maybe, but if you think so, just modify the example by small degrees until you get to the situation of only $10,000 savings that you 'throw away' on a horse for which the betting odds are 50 to 1, but your friend informs that you have a 10 per cent chance of winning. It does not seem prudent to bet. A standard response to such examples is to appeal to the decreasing marginal utility of money – $1,000 to a billionaire is worth less than $10 to the destitute. But that response does not apply to the home purchase example, for it is many times more important for your child to have the home than you to have some small savings. The irrationality of the bet is due to the thought that very probably you will find yourself with the grief of having wasted your savings.

My response to the god-the-chancer objection is that god took, and God still takes risks, but the risks are not like putting all your savings on a horse. It was a risk taken out of respect for humanity's autonomy. We had a choice between paths, all with good outcomes, with some tougher than others. Considering just two, for simplicity, we may call them the Path of Innocence and the Path of Repentance. The latter comprises (1) *sinning*, that is, disobeying God, which leads to vice, namely, a tendency to further wrongdoing, but (2) *repenting* and after much struggle restoring a virtuous state and friendship with God. This sin-and-repentance outcome is either better than, or more plausibly, incommensurable with, an unfallen innocent state, without the wrongdoing. The Path of Repentance is symbolized by the choice of the fruit of the tree of 'knowledge of good and evil' (knowledge by acquaintance). To have been predestined to follow that path would be both cruel and pointless, but there is a value somewhere between aesthetics and morality in freely repenting and replacing enmity by amity, for love is more valuable if those who love are distinct in various ways, and happy innocently virtuous people are too close to being divine (avatars maybe) to realize the maximum value of a loving union with God. The same applies to the loving union of humanity collectively with God. Because the most valuable kind of loving union requires freedom, god sets up a choice: the good and beautiful innocent life in which no wrong is done versus the glory of repentant sinners.

Having set up this choice there is a risk of iteration, even if that was not god's initial plan, for failure to take the opportunities to repent constitutes a further, deeper fall into sin, repenting from which results in greater glory. I speculate that god had a series of plans: Plan 1, Plan 2 and so on. Each member of the series has a chance of a success, that is, an outcome good enough not to proceed with the next. If there is a last member then its chance of success is 100 per cent. Otherwise there is a chance that the outcome of Plan N is poor enough that proceeding with Plan N + 1 is a good divine act in the circumstances. Moreover, I suggest, the success of Plan N is in the circumstances no worse than the success of any of plans 1 to N − 1. That is, the combined result of Plan 1 failing the way it did with the success of Plan 2 will be no worse than some result considered a success for Plan 1 and so on. It might not be better because I am assuming a variety of goods that are not always commensurable.

Whenever a divine plan for humanity fails because human beings choose poorly there is a 'fall'. By the 'Fall' we mean the first such failure. Now if God loved us just as individuals then the failure of these divine plans and the consequent situation we find ourselves in (with horrible evils and for many the divine silence) would be inexplicable. Here is an analogy. Suppose there is a planet far away with extraterrestrials living good and beautiful lives in accordance with God's initial plan. If we humans make contact and tried out of envy to corrupt them, that would be very wicked, and God should have ensured that they had the resources to rebuff us. It would be most unloving of God if they turned out to be too weak to resist, for they and us are (in this epoch) different communities. Likewise, if we are loved by God only as individuals, then God would not allow each generation to be corrupted by the society they grow up in, for there would be no relevant community. Hence, there could be no falls. Maybe God would start again with a new kind of free creatures each time the plan failed.

An Adam-Eve speculation

Falls only makes sense, if it is as if humanity collectively is itself a free agent. Maybe the best way of explaining this 'as if' is by asserting there really is a collective entity humanity-as-a-person. Call it Adam-Eve. Bearing in mind that this is just speculation, here are some details. God loves us, and we are loveable, but we are not the only creatures that God desires friendship with. There are others. One of these is Adam-Eve who is embodied in humanity going back a million years or so, to whom the divine plan is revealed, namely, that Adam-Eve undergoes a kenosis about 70,000 years ago, a lessening of power giving rise to a multiplicity of human individuals who become the dominant force on Earth. The command is in effect a command to abdicate, to give up some power, just as God gave up power to Adam-Eve long ago. This is intended as part of a process of individuals in turn giving up themselves for each other and so freely forming again the collective being, Adam-Eve. The extent of the revelation of divine love for Adam-Eve is sufficient to enable the right, kenotic, choice to be made but not sufficient to prevent the lesser good of trying to retain power. It is an opportunity for unforced friendship with God, and one that is rejected. Adam-Eve clings to power over individual human beings and as a consequence the balance between the collective and the individual is disturbed.

God's next plan is for both Adam-Eve and us as individuals to make good the mistake, seeing the consequences of the violation of the initial plan and making reparation by serving God by love of neighbour. But this plan fails too. After that, the plan is to choose the people of Israel as servants of the Law. There is yet another fall. It seems that only God can do what we humans must do, repair the damage we have collectively done, or maybe without divine aid it would be possible but so much more difficult. Hence, the master plan, the Incarnation. Jesus can repair the damage, by being divine and by being human ensures we have repaired the damage. I speculate that this is the saving of Adam-Eve along with us individual human beings. But the consequences have to be worked out by us as individuals. Maybe this plan involved the rapid establishment of the Kingdom of God, without the Crucifixion, but this too has failed. Perhaps the next plan involved only a few hundred years more of history. It too failed. We are now involved in a plan in which we become 'as gods' because of our technical prowess, and so are forced to face the fact that in the Leonard Cohen's words, 'Love is the only engine of salvation.'

On this speculation, God's character of valuing the collective coheres with the claim that God subsequently has a loving character, meaning loving individuals, for the love of the collective is the love of a person, Adam-Eve, who pre-existed us as individuals and so was loved before us.

A speculation about Satan

The idea of humanity as itself the body of a creature Adam-Eve might seem too far-fetched; so let me tell a somewhat more conventional story, involving Lucifer.[10] Lucifer is an angelic being whose job is to guide evolution on Earth as painlessly as possible to reach the stage at which, some ten million years after a near collision with an asteroid, intelligent dinosaurs are capable of freely choosing to worship God and capable of developing a technology that ensures that they, not Lucifer, guided the planet. Lucifer is then potentially part of a community with these dinosaurs. God knows that Lucifer will be jealous but hopes for obedience. Lucifer rebels and preternaturally adjusts the path of the asteroid so that it collides with Earth, destroying the dinosaurs. God's plan B is then to save Satan and his cohort by letting them see the consequences of their rebellion. They are forced to guide the evolution of more familiar creatures including us, who unlike the dinosaurs, lead lives in which suffering is not kept to the minimum.[11] Maybe some of them repent at seeing the harm they have done, but Satan, as we now call 'Lucifer', out of further jealousy corrupts the humans who have evolved so that we commit a series of heinous crimes, killing other hominids in Africa when the Mt Toba explosion causes scarcity, and later on committing genocide against Neanderthals, Denisovans and other innocents. Plan B has failed. Plan C is to inspire human beings to progress morally to the point where they shame Satan into repentance, and themselves come to be worthy of sharing in the divine life with all the angels including repentant Satan. Plan C fails; so God redeems by the Incarnation, revealing the divine love and daring Satan to attempt to kill a divine being, in the hope that Satan will repent. This plan, D, fails and human beings at Satan's instigation, crucify Jesus. Plan E is for Jesus to rise, for Christianity to spread quickly in spite of persecution bringing us to a collective acceptance of God's love, all within one generation. It fails. We are now in Plan F, the long haul, in which with increasing power and knowledge we humans come to have to sort of power enjoyed by the angels. We will reach the point of either destroying or restoring our planet, but God's plan is that the events set in motion by God incarnate result in the correct choice. What happens if this too should fail? This is a speculation within a speculation, but there might come a point when the number of those individuals who have gloriously exercised their radical freedom to promote God's kingdom is so great that it is good to bring an end to the era of radical freedom even though the goal of collective salvation has never been achieved.

At each stage success involves not only a total of more misery than the previous stage but also the possibility of greater glory. Gloriously to overcome evil is not better than not experiencing it, but it is not worse either. It is better in one way but worse in another. Our suffering is then a product of God's dealings with Satan. Because God loves Satan, this is compatible with God having a loving disposition towards individuals as well as towards communities.

To sum up, that god was a chancer shows something about the character of God, as being prepared to take risks provided the overall outcome is more suffering in this world but greater glory in the next.

The objection that god overvalues the aesthetic

The world as created by god is astoundingly beautiful in many ways, something that we can appreciate much more than earlier generations: ugliness is almost entirely a human product.[12] Moreover, the human condition, though often miserable, seems intended to provide opportunity for moral heroism, the overcoming of evil, the repenting of wrong doing, the rising above difficult circumstances. As in my rejoinder to Philo, I concede the unprejudiced assessment that the act of creation was by a god who valued the aesthetic: that of the austere mathematical physics, that of life in its variety, that of sensuous beauty and that of the drama of creatures with radical freedom. The same unprejudiced assessment would express surprise at just how much evil in the form of suffering and malice this god allows for these great aesthetic values. This is brought out most acutely by the rather limited ways in which god intervenes. Stories of law-breaking miracles capture our imagination, but I think we should be sceptical. As above, I rely here on reports of miraculous cures at Lourdes, because these reports are assessed rather scrupulously to see if they have a medical explanation or not. Given the sober reporting we should take note of the fact that although many lack medical explanation, and so may properly be taken by the faithful as due to preternatural divine intervention, they do not contravene what we know of physiology. There are no well-documented reports of anyone ever growing a new finger, nor are there such reports in the miracles worked by Jesus. Of these the most striking perhaps are the raising of various people from the dead, but we now know of many cases of those who to all appearances have died but can be revived. Only the resurrection of Jesus himself stands out as a genuine coming back from the dead. That is a special case that might, in accordance with Oddie's Principle, have caused the other divine persons suffering. A sober assessment of reports of the miraculous is that they are evidence for the power of minds over the physiology, even perhaps of paranormal powers, but that god-ordained laws that cannot be broken, so there are no supernatural miracles. This might seem yet another overemphasis on the aesthetic: Why not spoil the beauty of things just a little by ordaining laws that permit exceptions?

If this is taken as an objection to there being a god, my reply is implicit in the minimal standard generated by the tension between the aesthetic and the moral, namely, adequate compensation. It is a more serious objection to worship, to which my reply was that unbreakable laws were ordained, and it so happens that in our part of the Universe they lead to much suffering, which God seeks to alleviate by preternatural intervention. I anticipate the rejoinder that a god who balances the aesthetic and the moral like this is good in a sense but has nonetheless acquired a character incompatible with being worshipped.

As I have said, God intends us to share in the divine life, that is, to be part of a harmonious loving community of which God is a member. That is the beatific vision, the great joy of the blessed in Heaven. But what, I ask, is it like? God must share our joys, and we must share God's. Therefore, there must be divine joy for us to share. Much of this is joy at the beauty of creation and at the glory of the human participation in the war of good against evil. The objector has in effect made the puritanical suggestion that God should not be deriving aesthetic joy from creation but instead do more good. But that would lessen the divine joy that the blessed will share. In short, my reply is that the 'over-valuing' of the aesthetic is for our eventual good not just God's.

The objection that this is not loving

God loves us, so we are told. But this admits of two readings, the distributive and the collective. The first is that God loves each individual, the second that God loves humanity as a whole or creation as a whole. Plan 2, Plan 3 and so on and Plan B, Plan C and so on are good plans only if it is morally acceptable that some suffer, *without their consent,* for the sake of the overall good. Therefore, God, in resorting to these plans exhibits a love for humanity collectively that is opposed to the love for humanity distributively. To be sure there is glory in having suffered for the good of others, but if this is the result of love for individuals then we would require distributive justice, whereby the burden undertaken for the sake of a collective benefit would be equally shared. I draw the conclusion that Plan 2, Plan 3 and so on are motivated by consideration of a collective story of humanity rather than love of individual human beings, nor is this altered by the immense love shown in the Incarnation for that too seems to be part of a divine plan that exhibits the love for humanity collectively.

That the divine love to some extent sacrifices the individual to the collective raises one minor and two major problems. The minor one is that we may well judge that love for other individuals should outweigh the collective good: it would be horrible to save two strangers rather than one person you love. Stated this way the situation with God is rather different: there are no strangers. A closer human analogy is the demonic fascist ideal of individuals serving the state. But this is not what God exhibits, which is love for both the collective and individual. Moreover, God intends a free and loving service of others by humans, not one coerced by the state.

The first major problem is that, it will be objected, we should either not give the collective any value at all or, if we do, it is always outweighed by the value of individuals. Now an intellectually satisfactory account of divine acts will not posit divine mistakes about value. Hence, to accept that Plan 2, Plan 3 and so on are good is to insist that the individual does not always outweigh the collective and so there is a trade-off with some good acts being more for the collective good, others perhaps more for the individual good. That God-worshippers must, I think, make this sort of evaluation might well be taken as a reason for not worshipping. But the attribution of absolute value to the collective and the individual is not so abhorrent for this to be a conclusive reason. Rather it makes theism a genuine commitment for those of individualist leanings.

The other major objection is that, although the idea of divine acts some of which give value to the collective is not absurd, it undermines the propriety of worshipping God. How can you trust a being who might sacrifice your interests for the common good? The answer is that it depends on the nature of the sacrifice. To accept that yours is neither an especially glorious life nor one of great joy but in purely this worldly terms a miserable one can be an entirely consistent with total submission of your will to God's. The proviso is that you trust that God does love us both individually and collectively and draw the conclusion that although others may have a better life in this world and even in the next, yours will still be exceeding good.

Commitment to the worship of God

Ignoring the history of religion and purported revelation, but assuming the commitments to reason and humanism, the case for the existence of god is fairly strong although not conclusive, and for a god who is God somewhat less strong but by no means negligible. Informed by that, an unbiased examination of the history of religion confirms the thesis that there is a God who wants to be worshipped so as to be part of a human-divine community. Against this there are intellectual and emotional considerations that provide a case against worship. The most obvious of these are the residual intuitive power of the Arguments from Evil and Divine Hiddenness. Could not God intervene more to prevent dysfunctional suffering, and why does God hide from wise, good, non-theists? In addition, there is an emotional-cum-intellectual obstacle to loving, or even to obeying, a being so unlike us, especially since that should result in the acquisition of a character like God's. This is shown by an examination of the character-traits that have to be ascribed to God even partially to understand the evils around us. If we ignore divine incarnation, it is clear that God is hard to love. This sets up a dilemma, both intellectual as to the existence of God, and practical as to the decision to at least try to worship.

The Absolute Superiority Condition is satisfied if the worship of God is combined with the expectation of a divine-human community, which far excels the prospect of even a perfect human community in an afterlife. And the history of religions shows, I judge, that this is what God has in mind. The

Pragmatic Condition is harder to assess. History shows that worshipping God can be a disaster. But the various religious wars and persecutions, as well as kill-joy attitudes to art, science and especially the ordinary human pleasures, are the results of religion without constraints. The case for the pragmatic value of religion within the bounds of both reason and humanism depends on just how pessimistic you are for a this worldly good life, for yourself, those you love, humanity and the whole of nature on this planet. Can we make genuine progress without worship? To do so, we must individually and collectively travel along the Razor Edge Path, neither despairing nor overconfident, neither arrogant nor diffident, neither ascetic without reason nor the slave of passion, rejoicing in vindication without being vindictive, and – especially hard – having precisely the right sort of pride in virtue. History shows that progress, though possible, is thwarted by deviation from the path. Now the requirements of the Razor Edge Path could be considered an Aristotelean means between extremes, and Aristotle (*Nicomachean Ethics, X*) rightly sees the need to train children to be virtuous. But that is inevitably of limited success because it is easier to condition the extremes than the mean. I pose the following questions: Are you strong enough to live a genuinely good and beautiful life without worship? Are we collectively strong enough to make progress and to solve the many pressing problems without worship?

One way in which worship can guide those of us who are weak, and know it, is the decision to see our lives as under divine scrutiny (cf. Audi 2011: 239). The strong who do not need God to love their neighbour should, along with the weak, acknowledge that because the weak are many, and because we are collectively weak, the Pragmatic Condition is satisfied, and so it is reasonable to commit to worship. Another help provided by worship is getting the right balance between this life and the next. This life is the only one in which we can help the collective task. But it is not the only one, which gives hope in times of trial.

I reach the conclusion, then, that even by quite rigorous standards, it is reasonable to commit to reason, to humanism within the bounds of reason and to worship within the bounds of both reason and humanism.

9

Corollaries

My proposed criteria permit commitments to reason, to humanism and to God's existence. It remains to note some corollaries of the previous chapters.

Optimism and pessimism

Half-full or half-empty?

The Absolute Superiority Condition reflects a cosmic optimism, differing from axiarchism only in that the latter is a general principle stating that things are as they are because it is good, while the Absolute Superiority Condition applies only in situations of an intellectual dilemma. On the other hand, commitment to God's existence satisfies the Pragmatic Condition only if we are pessimistic about our unaided progress, both individual and collective. Without this combination of optimism and pessimism my case for reasonable commitment to God's existence fails. A corollary of the Pragmatic Condition is, however, that the pessimism does not lead to inaction. Only if we suppose that worshipping God helps us make the desired progress, is the condition satisfied. To those who ask whether the glass is half-full or half-empty, I say it is a quarter-full.

Conservatives and Progressives

It is crass to think you live in a great society or even one in which hardship is the fault of those who suffer it. It is even more crass to think that the global situation is acceptable. Reflective conservatives must therefore be so pessimistic as to think that attempts to improve things just make them worse – David Stove was one such. Equally crass are those progressives for whom politics is a matter of fashion. Reflective progressives must therefore be so optimistic as to think that there is a trajectory of progress on which society is either moving, going forward or, occasionally, going backward. They see their task as pushing society along this trajectory.

There is no clear evidence to support either the conservative or progressivist ideologies, or rather in both cases history is read selectively to support the ideology. A corollary of the combination of cosmic optimism and local pessimism that warrants worship is that worshippers should neither be conservatives nor progressives: God helps us but nonetheless history is full of failure, as often as not due to the hubris that progressives exemplify.

Political non-commitment

Political philosophy is beyond the scope of this work, but my assessment is that the arguments provided are as inconclusive as those of metaphysics. Is it reasonable to commit, then? Perhaps to Marxism, Feminism, Environmentalism or some other political movement? If you hold the ideology then it is unreasonable not to commit to action. But I reject the commitment to a political ideology. History shows that the politically committed tend to take the ends to justify the means. Therefore, political commitment fails the Pragmatic Condition.

A final political corollary. The evils that afflict us would have been easier for god to prevent if either the value of humanity as a whole or of the individual human beings were less. The combination of individual and collective goods is required for any satisfactory theodicy. Worshippers should adopt the divine values. Therefore, their politics should seek the flourishing of individuals in a flourishing community.

Worship, trust and praise; faith, hope and love

It would be most peculiar to commit to there being a God but not worship God, trust God and praise God.

Worship and trust

I define worship as submitting your will to God's, either out of love, fear or some other motive. To do so is reasonable only if you trust God that good will come of this submission, for you and those you love, in this life or an afterlife. And the Abrahamic tradition is that this good either is or requires our loving God individually and collectively. All this presupposes that there is a God. For those who have lost epistemic innocence concerning religion this assent to the existence of God is an act of commitment, as are acts of faith, hope and love.

Clearly, it is foolish to worship a god you do not trust. For instance, suppose god, for utilitarian reasons, deceived humanity with false promises of an afterlife and has no intention of helping us in this life. Then those of us in the know should not worship, although we might decide to further the divine purpose. I have speculated that god ordained universal ethical rules by terminating all the universes in which the breaking the rules has a better outcome than keeping them. Although our grasp of these rules is fallible, this suffices to show that there is no intellectual obstacle to the thesis that god chose to become trustworthy and hence God.

Praise and glory

In addition to doing God's will in so far as we know it and trusting God, worship typically involves praising God. This praise is partly the recognition of what a splendid thing God is, something that the speculation of the Universe as the divine body supports. Worship goes further, though, and it typically requires that God's *glory* be praised. As I understand it, glory is the aesthetic-cum-moral excellence of achieving a good outcome in spite of opposition. Paradigmatically, glory is achieved by defeating a powerful opponent. Therein lies the problem with glorifying God. Who or what could possibly oppose God in such a way as to make the divine victory glorious? The Israelites might have been impressed with their deliverance from Egypt, but what glory is there in God defeating Pharaoh and his army, or, for that matter, Satan and a multitude of fallen angels? It is like a chess grand master playing a beginner, nor is creaturely freedom a sufficient condition for divine glory. By itself it merely provides opportunity for creaturely glory, in overcoming temptation. Nor even is divine kenosis sufficient, for to handicap oneself and then win gloriously only makes sense if you are playing a game. And to think of God as playing a game with humanity is contrary to the humanist commitment to our value and dignity. The problem of how God could be glorious is related to the problem of how creatures can love God, for love of persons, as we usually understand it, is more than the aesthetic enjoyment of the person loved. The one who loves seeks the good of the one who is loved and seeks this good joyfully. And what good can we do God, who it might be thought, can achieve whatever is willed without our help?

Both problems have Fall and Redemption solutions, and I know of no other way of solving them. God both offers creatures a good and beautiful life and commands acceptance. This requires that the divine power be restricted, so that creatures have a choice that will bind. Obedience results in a child-like innocence. Disobedience results in separation from God, which grieves God and leads to creaturely suffering. Disobedience also provides, however, the opportunity for greater joy in the end, as these disobedient creatures freely repent the harm they have done God and each other. In this way they can love God, whereas the child-like unfallen innocents can only enjoy the beauty of God without the love that requires giving. God has to struggle to win back the fallen creatures, and, I assume, success is not inevitable. But if and when the creatures come to love God then that is glorious both for them and for God.

Respect for human dignity and the gravity of human decisions suggests that neither the initial fall nor the subsequent redemption is inevitable. Hence, the praise of God has to be tentative. Worshippers should hold that God has won a glorious battle, but the war is not yet over.

Acts of faith, hope and love

Let me repeat what I have said about commitment in the previous chapters. It should not be controversial that we can choose to say something either publicly or in thought. So, provided the conditions of sincerity and non-pragmatism are satisfied we can commit. Such commitment is required unless the assertion expresses a pre-existing inner state of belief, which state might well be characterized as precisely the disposition to assert. And repeated commitment results in a habit, which is one kind of disposition. Hence commitment is an important exception to the generalization that sincere assertion expresses a prior belief.

The other two defects are insincerity and pragmatism. An assertion of some proposition is insincere if there is a conflicting attitude. The obvious conflicting attitude is disbelief (see Schellenberg 2005: Ch. 8), but it is also insincere to assert if you hold beliefs that you know are incompatible with the assertion. A pragmatic assertion is one primarily for the sake of some real or imagined good external to the context. For example, Henry IVs conversion to Roman Catholicism from being a Huguenot was pragmatic, if it was for the sake of becoming King of

France. ('Paris is worth a mass'.) Likewise, to recite the Creed as a result of being convinced by Pascal's Wager of the need to believe is pragmatic.

But there is more to hope and love, even to faith, than this bare intellectual commitment. Hence, we may ask whether we have the capacity to make an act of faith, of hope or of love. In the Catholic tradition, there are prayers whose assertion is said to constitute such acts, but there is more to faith than asserting that you believe and trust. As with commitment, I distinguish the acts of faith, hope and love from the dispositions to act, which are also called faith, hope and love. And, as with commitment, I take it that although these acts often manifest a prior disposition, they may instead be acts performed deliberately, which, if repeated, result in a habit, which is then one kind of disposition.

By an act of faith, I mean an assertion motivated by an act of trust, which is rather close to an act of hope. As with commitments I say these are genuine *acts* of trust, hope and love provided they are not defective. Therefore, the chief, perhaps only, defects are pragmatism and insincerity. These acts of trust, hope and love are themselves commitments – although not purely intellectual ones – if performed in the face of dilemmas. The reasons for and against trusting god are, trivially, the reasons for and against believing that there is a trustworthy god, God. That is why faith can easily be confused with intellectual commitment. The reasons for and against hope are similar. The difference seems to be that it is a stronger assertion to say god is trustworthy than that god is an object of hope.[1] For it is conceivable that god is, as Whitehead and other process philosophers have described, a god who will not deceive and will help you as much as possible without the power to guarantee what is good for you and those you love. This god would not be powerful enough to trust but could be an object of hope.

Loving God clearly goes beyond worship and requires desiring what God wills, rather than merely submitting to God's will, which suffices for worship. The reason for loving God is that God wills something supremely good for all creatures including us and those we love. The reason for not loving God is the good of autonomy, itself amounting to the preservation of the person characterized by a history of acts, for the saints, that is the habitual lovers of God, lose any will separate from God's. When it is said in *Deuteronomy* 6, 'And you shall love the Lord your God with all your heart, and with all your soul, and with all your might!' this is no less than a command to lose self in God.[2] In a manner of speaking, to love God is to die, as in Jesus's parable of the grain of wheat (Jn 12.24-26). The way that acts of faith, hope and trust are often made in the face of a dilemma should dispel the idea that these acts are performed merely by saying certain prayers. In the circumstance of lost innocence, they take mental effort.

We may illustrate possible defects, note the effort when faced by a dilemma, as well as support the thesis that trust hope and love are acts, by analogies. My first analogy is the act of apologizing. That does not, I say, have to manifest a prior inner repentance, although it is easier to apologize sincerely if it does. To say you are sorry is to apologize provided the act of apology is non-defective. One defect might be insincerity, apologizing when you are convinced you were in the right, or don't care about who was in the right. The other might be saying sorry primarily for pragmatic reasons, to restore good relations. Furthermore, a non-defective apology that does not manifest some inner feeling will take some effort, because there is a dilemma. The reason for apologizing is the belief that you have wronged the other person, but the reason against is the vulnerability of the one who apologizes, namely, that maybe you will not be forgiven. (We ought to forgive those who apologize even if they stumble over the words, but there is a horrible delight in spurning the apology, which hurts the one apologizing.)

Another analogy is the avowal of love in a romantic context. To say 'I love you' will, if you are in love, be effortless and an expression of how you feel. But the beginning of wisdom in human relationships is to extend love beyond the phase of being in love. In that case to say 'I love you' is deliberate, and it is an act of love that does not require some inner feeling that gets expressed. To be non-defective it must not be insincere, that is, there must not be some conflicting state such as hatred. And it is also defective if it is primarily pragmatic, say, a means to sexual gratification. The dilemma is not unlike that of the apology, an attraction to the beloved combined with a sense of vulnerability to rejection.[3]

When it comes to love in a religious context we often get confused. Suppose an evangelical asks, 'Do you love Jesus?' Apart from 'Mind your own business!' the reply might be 'Yes I do'. That would be an act of love, even when an equally correct reply might be 'I am sorry to say I do not' reporting on the lack of the habit or disposition. This confusion between act and disposition also reinforces the widespread but mistaken view that you cannot just decide to have faith, hope or love. I grant that you cannot decide to have faith, hope or love, or to worship, if these acts would be defective. For a defective act of worship, say, is just a pretence at worship. Less obvious but still plausible is the inability to do what is plainly unreasonable. But, provided the acts meet the non-defectivity conditions and are reasonable, then they can be performed freely. An example is the love of step-children or the love of your in-laws. We cannot choose to love them if we find ourselves repelled or have grounds for active hatred. Insincere pretence is the best we can do in such circumstances. But from a neutral start we can love in-laws and step-children for our spouses' sakes and then acquire the disposition to love them. Having acquired the disposition we might then say that we now love them for their own sakes.

A somewhat different analogy is the expression of cosmic optimism, an ur-hope, implicit in an intellectual commitment that satisfies the Absolute Superiority Condition. This ur-hope exhibits the way an intellectual commitment has an emotional component that would be lacking if the same conclusion was reached purely on the balance of probabilities.

In defence of religion

It is fashionable to despise religion but admire spirituality. Much of this is a reaction to the loss of authority of religious organization such as the Roman Catholic hierarchy. Because that authority was based on their supposed holiness, interpreted as a sign of divine approval, their manifest unholiness makes it unreasonable to continue granting this authority.[4] Nonetheless, I claim that a generic, roughly speaking Nicene, Catholicism is the true religion and that all who have made the commitments to reason, to humanism and to God should belong. That is a big claim and not the topic of this work. I shall, however, now defend the human need for religion, with collective worship and a tradition spanning the generations.

Contrasting religion with spirituality

Religions are characterized by some fairly definite public practices (orthopraxy) and assertions (orthodoxy). They involve public religious activity, paradigmatically that of collective worship and praise. And they perform a role that is intended for the general good in this worldly and other-worldly ways, such as giving a sense of belonging. In many cases one of these roles is to be critical of society and government, condemning what is contrary to the divine standards. Spirituality restricts worship, praise and other religious attitudes to that which is not essentially public. So, a non-religious spiritual person might well prefer to express themselves with others of like mind, but that is only because most activities are more enjoyable if done in the company of the like-minded.

The need for religion

Organized religion is open to corruption, and harsh measures will be required in the future to prevent this. Nonetheless there is an important role for a powerful institution based on collective worship that states clearly which beliefs are conducive to our individual and collective salvation. My case for this is based on three reasons for asking what God wants of us collectively. The first is that, as already mentioned, the Argument from Evil is far more serious if we ignore the collective character of humanity, treating us as merely as individuals. Therefore, there is a plan for humanity, or else several plans between which we can choose. The second reason is that the doctrine of *Nulla Salus* is only tenable in an attenuated form, and the self-obsessed piety that strives to avoid final damnation is a waste of a life. Hence, we must ask what the point is of religious practice. The third is that worship involves doing God's will, which presupposes there is something God wills. What is it? One answer is that it is intrinsically good to glorify God, and each other as appropriate. But I have already posed the dilemma. Either what we praise God for is too easy to be glorious, or a task whose success cannot be guaranteed. It follows I think that, while the role of worship in a heavenly state might well be giving glory to God, here and now there is work to be done establishing a loving and wise society. The pessimist in me would despair except that we can rely on God's preternatural help. But given the nature of the task and a pessimistic assessment of achieving it by purely secular means, it follows that there should be organized religion. The urgency of the task is shown by the apocalyptic nature of the threats to society. Only a holy Church suffices.

Conclusion

I conclude that the intellectual commitment to the existence of God is part of a characteristically religious response involving collective worship and acts of faith, hope and love. The commitments to trust in human reasoning, to humanism and to the existence of a worship-worthy God combine to form the theocentric world view, one that may be defended by, but does not imply, metaphysical speculations such as the Multiverse and theological theses such as the Incarnation that are treated as speculations in this work.

To call theocentrism a world view is to say that it provides a way of understanding the universe and our place in it, with at least a sketch of the 'meaning of life', that is a grasp of our individual and collective tele (ends) as loving each other and God. This understanding is partial in that we humans do not in general understand things by seeing that they are good. That we should understand in this way remains a speculation, supported by the special case of understanding by seeing the beauty in things. Hence, agency and radical freedom remain mysteries.

In addition to the sequence of commitments that have been made, we can commit to the world view as a whole, aware that there are considerations for and against. Such an integrated commitment would be undermined if one of the parts did not meet the conditions for a commitment. Therefore, it is not a rival to a sequential commitment, although it might better reflect the practice of many.

Notes

Chapter 2

1 Cartesian dualism is the thesis that mind and body are distinct *substances*, so I think of it as an explication of radical dualism.

2 Zombies are also discussed by Keith Campbell (1970), who calls them imitation men.

3 I am ignoring the case from qualia as expressed in Frank Jackson's famous papers (1982, 1986) because the sort of physicalism that they refute is stronger than the supervenience thesis, which is in turn stronger than the rejection of Radical Dualism, for the supervenience of the mental on the physical would hold even given Cartesian dualism – provided the laws of nature, including the psycho-physical interaction laws, were taken to be metaphysically necessary.

4 I have defended theism without radical dualism in earlier work (Forrest 1996, 2007a).

5 In that case the physical Universe would be a necessary being. Many philosophers (e.g. Audi 2011: 243 n.7) assert that physical things must be contingent. Now, the ordinary physical things, such as rocks, are, I assume, contingent, but I do not think we can extrapolate to the whole Universe. To be sure, if both the laws and initial conditions were necessary and the laws deterministic, then all details of the physical, including the existence of the rocks around us would likewise be necessary. This is not, however, a reductio ad absurdum of the thesis of a necessary Universe but rather of deterministic laws. For intuitively the laws and the initial conditions would be symmetric and so, given deterministic laws, the whole Universe would be symmetric, contrary to observation.

6 Note, though, that the universes are concrete four-dimensional things not abstract ones such as sets of propositions. Calling them stories is a tad misleading.

7 I call it *Delayed* Collapse because the termination occurs after the passage through the slits. Hence, we retain the Many Worlds explanation of quantum probabilities.

8 The difference between worlds and universes seems so be that a possible world could be the sum of disjoint universes. I shall stick with possible universes.

9 John Leslie (1979) treats theism of the sort I am propounding in Chapter 6 as *moderate* axiarchism, on the grounds that theistic explanations rely both on god's existence and the values god is aware of. That is not what I mean by axiarchism.

10 John Bishop and Ken Persyck (2017) propose *eutelelogy* as an alternative to personal theism. This is the position that the Universe's history is influenced by its telos, which is to evolve towards a splendid final state. Although not the same as Leslie's extreme axiarchism, it is open to the objection I raise in Chapter 6, where I explain the advantage of theism over axiarchism.

11 The naturalness of manifolds was something I failed to grasp in Forrest 2012. Mea Culpa!

12 Draper (p. 56) suggests that coherence supports the requirement of naturalness. Maybe, but it does not enable us to discover what classification is natural unless we already have a modicum of a priori insight into naturalness.

13 Following Kant, I distinguish the judgement that something is agreeable from the judgement that is beautiful. The latter includes a claim to objectivity. I also note that much of aesthetic interest is beautiful by *pros hen* analogy: it expresses or causes something beautiful.

14 I argue for them not being equal using a method I owe to Keith Lehrer. If we add just a little to one of the two values then it is still intuitive to deny that one outweighs the other. Suppose the artist is not merely poverty-stricken but the use of turpentine has resulted in a permanent running nose. Is that the last straw? No, I say there is still no objective preference for the wealthy twin's life.

15 I have provided a more detailed defence of the method of speculation in Forrest 2007a Introduction. A good example of the method of speculation is provided by Peter van Inwagen (1991: 41–2):

> Suppose that Jane wishes to defend the character of Richard III, and that she must contend with evidence that has convinced many people that Richard murdered the two princes in the Tower. Suppose that she proceeds by telling a story, which she does not claim to be true, or even more probable than not, that accounts for the evidence that has come down to us, a story according to which Richard did not murder the princes. If my reaction to her story is, 'For all I know, that's true. I shouldn't be at all surprised if that's how things happened', I shall be less willing to accept a negative evaluation of Richard's character than I might otherwise have been.

His critique of the Argument from Evil (2008) is based on a series of speculative 'just so' stories, not unlike those I have presented (Forrest 2007a) and will be presenting in this work.

16 If there are a large number of explanations none better than any other then the criterion is too lax because each of them is highly improbable.

17 A similar problem holds if we qualify theories by saying they are close to the truth.

18 Descartes may be interpreted as claiming that even the acceptance of core epistemology requires trust in providence, but it is less controversial to consider the use of reason more generally as presupposing trust in providence.

19 Imre Lakatos (1970) answers a slightly different question: When should we continue with a research program in the face of anomalies? His answer that we should do so only unless the program is degenerating is sensible enough but not applicable to the question of believing the theory to be true.

Chapter 3

1 For the sake of a clear example, I consider the position of someone not persuaded by *Dialethism*, the position that there are true contradictions. As presented by Graham Priest (2006) Dialethism provides the required synthesis, or so I say, for it turns out that the law of non-contradiction and its negation are both true. While I have a firm intuition that the law of non-contradiction is true, it's mind-boggling negation is up for negotiation.

2 Clearly, prior to belief in God any prayer must be conditional: God, if there is a God, help me decide.

3 If we consider inferences to have logical probabilities, then we might follow Henry Kyburg (1974) and represent the probabilities as intervals. Then for two completely incommensurable inferences the combined probability is represented by the smallest interval containing the intervals for the two inferences. For commensurate inferences the combination has a smaller interval. In the case of an intellectual dilemma the epistemic probability is judged to be somewhere in the range represented by the logical probability.

4 An exception is the unfortunate person worried that Solipsism might be correct. Commitment against Solipsism requires no dismissal of others.

5 Suppose there are abundant and striking religious experiences agreed upon by all inhabitants of the island, and that in this context everyone reasonably holds there are gods and demons. Each nation argues from experience that the other's gods are their demons.

6 Pathological cases such as the Liar Paradox are not the stuff of commitment.

7 Traditionally that claim has been made by Catholics. I think it should be rejected, not on general grounds, but because of a more specific incompleteness: reincarnation is as plausible a speculation as Limbo.

Chapter 4

1 Audi (2011: 56) in his subtle typology of faith notes, 'Attitudinal faith is not just a position of the mind, but partly *a state of will.*'

2 It may well be that no one admits to being a Wittgensteinian fideist in this sense (see Amesbury 2017: §2.2.4).

3 In the next chapter I make a similar criticism of Stephen Jay Gould's NOMA (Non-overlapping Magisteria) thesis (1999).

4 The complexity of faith is illustrated by Robert Audi's careful elaboration (2011).

5 Given transubstantiation we would have to say, 'just so long as their accidents survive'.

6 *Ultimism* (Schellenberg 2005) is the thesis that there is some ultimate source of good. It is agnostic over whether this something is a god.

7 As Nils Franzén (2018) points out, if this was a straightforward case of Gricean implicature it would not be peculiar to say, 'The Mona Lisa is somewhat over-rated. Anyway, the crowds have prevented me seeing it whenever I have been to the Louvre'. On the other hand, I note that there is nothing peculiar about saying, 'Almost certainly the Mona Lisa is somewhat over-rated, like the vast majority of famous art works'.

Chapter 5

1 See Stove (1986) for a defence of Donald Williams's (1947) justification of extrapolation as sampling. Now I take it that probable inferences from a sample to the population are justified using core epistemology, but there is a problem, however, with using this to justify an inductive extrapolation, namely, excluding novelty.

2 The metaphysically possible universes, which I am positing, should not be confused with possible worlds, which may well be fictions. A possible world would, for instance, contain a sequence of sums of universes, corresponding to changes in time.

3 The idea of ontological dependence has been extensively debated in recent years (see Tahko and Lowe 2016).

Chapter 6

1 Maybe it's a reaction to teaching about 'original sin', or maybe it's just whistling in the spiritual dark.

2 See Joyce (2015) for the point that relativism does not entail subjectivism.

3 I owe this principle to Tony Lynch.

4 If a cause could be later than its effect, then foreknowledge would be compatible with moral responsibility but such foreknowledge could not, on pain of circularity, be used to affect the choice.

5 See Zagzebsky (2017: §2.5) for the link between Frankfurt examples and divine foreknowledge.

6 To be sure, the advice to toss a coin can be used to focus the ditherer on one outcome, to decide if there is an all-things-considered reason for acting one way or another. But if this advice helps, then there is no dilemma.

7 Alexander Pruss defends the Principle of Sufficient Reason against Peter van Inwagen's claim that it leads to the thesis that there are no contingent truths. His defence (Pruss 2006: 192) takes the proposition that god 'appreciated the reasons for actualising BCCF and chose accordingly' as a sufficient explanation for BCCF (Big Conjunctive Contingent Fact). If god was in a dilemma then appreciating the reasons coheres with the Weak not the Strong Version.

8 Oppy (2008) complains that I *dismiss* atheism in my (2007). Mea culpa!

9 With the standard stipulation that X_{T^*}'s being part of X_T includes the case of $X_{T^*} = X_T$.

10 An example of the tenseless use of the grammatical present is provided by mathematics. If a teacher mentions that π is irrational, a student might ask, 'What has π gone and done – invested in bit-coins?' A more philosophical wag might ask, 'When did that happen and why wasn't I told?' Another example of the tenseless is when we ask whether there are non-simultaneous events x and y such that neither is earlier than the other. As the second example shows, this usage is not the same as the ómni-temporal, defined as past, present or future.

11 By Desmond Fearnley-Sander in conversation.

12 We require a suitable group of symmetries on the sum of all nomically possible universes. In that case we can substitute the Haar measure for frequencies.

13 I favour the identification of the mental states with the brain processes, treating the elusive *qualia* as the way the brain processes appear. But a mere correlation would suffice.

14 I have previously (Forrest 1996) referred to this as the Principle of Harmony, but I have renamed it because Oddie's principle is also one of Harmony.

15 Following Donald Davidson (1980) we might say the mental state *rationalizes* the behaviour as action. I, however, take the word 'rationalize' always to be pejorative.

16 To reply to the swap objection, we would have to posit 'indelible marks on the soul', properties that it is possible to acquire but impossible to lose. While coherent this would be an unwarranted metaphysical posit.

17 In this work, by Utilitarianism I mean Act Utilitarianism understood as starting that we ought not to perform an act if there is some other act we could perform and that has better consequences.

Chapter 7

1 Our body awareness depends on various interconnected neural maps in the brain. Our sense of having a body supervenes on the activity in these maps. Analogously, I am supposing that activity in the whole Universe manifests as the divine body image.

2 See Jantzen (1998) for an extended treatment of the thesis that the universe is the divine body. Audi (2011: 258–60) has recently expressed some sympathy with the idea.

3 It does not come with a distinguished set of coordinate axes, but it might help to think of it as having an infinite sequence of coordinates $t = x_0$ and $x_1, x_2, \ldots$. The metric assigns either a positive (space-like), zero or a negative (time-like) measure of separation between two points. If the two points have coordinates $t, x_1, x_2, \ldots$, and $t', x_1', x_2', \ldots$, respectively, then the measure of separation is: $-(t-t')^2 + \sum_n (x_n - x_n')^2$.

4 The things that belong to a given kind share a common nature, which is essential to each of them. For example, portions of water form a kind, and to a first approximation we may say the essential property is being largely made up of H_2O molecules. (A puzzle case is provided by gels made of mostly H_2O.)

5 Even a rather extreme version of Social Trinitarianism is acceptable. This is that there are three gods but they are only one God, meaning one focus of worship, because appropriate worship of any of them is also worship of the others.

6 So initially David Lewis's Modal Realism holds. As a realist about the past, I take it that Modal Realism is still correct because terminated universes exist in the past.

7 Rowe argues that a god who created a given universe would be less good than a god who created a better one. If we think of moral perfection as a propensity to act, a better god might create less well, but Rowe's conclusion still follows. Suppose there were possible acts of creation labelled by the integers in order of increasing goodness. Then god, we all agree, prefers an act corresponding to a positive integer to the zero-goodness act or to a negative goodness act. If god had a disposition to choose better rather than less good then there would, it seems, be a probability p less than 100 per cent of god deciding to create a universe better than a given one. If p was as low as 50 per cent there would be a rather disappointing result, namely 50 per cent chance of the least good act, that is number 1, a 25 per cent chance of the next one up and so on. If, however, p was 99 per cent then there would only be a 1 per cent chance of act one, slightly less than 1 per cent of act 2 and so on. The more virtuous god is, the higher p is. No value less than 100 per cent will represent moral perfection but 100 per cent implies repeated deferral and hence no act at all.

8 Choosing at random from an infinite array requires suitable mathematical structure. If for instance the array has a structure of a compact Hausdorff group then it has an invariant probability measure so it makes sense to choose at random, although that does not explain how god would do it.

9 A tribe does not usually hunt its own totem, so the function is that of preserving the species that a group of tribes hunt, by giving protection to each species in a certain region. We may speculate that in the Australian case this arose because of an awareness of the many splendid species that were going extinct.

10 This bears on Christianity in two ways. The doctrine of the Trinity shows that concern for other divine persons' suffering will motivate each not to jointly perform

highly improbable miracles. The second is that the Resurrection of Jesus might be an exception, in which case the second person suffers on the cross but the other two suffer, not merely by knowing what the second person is going through, but also in raising Jesus from the dead.

11 A recent critique of the specious present (Arstila 2018) undermines the thesis of a short specious present (of the order of magnitude a second or less) but leaves intact the case for the long specious present (of the order of magnitude a minute).

12 I take the calculus of probabilities to be an idealization of the thought of reasonable human beings, providing qualitatively correct results. Suppose, then, the probability of evil given theism is less than 1 per cent of the probability of evil given atheism, and that the probability of theism bracketing off evil is no more than 90 per cent. Then the probability of theism given evil is less than 9 per cent.

13 An interesting alternative to the thesis that god chooses not to be able to intervene is the thesis that god chooses ignorance of various details, knowledge of which would occasion intervention (see Audi 2011: 242–3).

14 I failed to acknowledge the work of various theologians who have described creation as kenosis (see Polkinghorne 2001). Mea culpa! I was especially remiss not to mention Jürgen Moltmann, the leading exponent of kenotic theology (e.g. Moltmann 2001). Mea maxima culpa!

Chapter 8

1 Here I ignore the possibility of delayed divine kenosis, not because it is silly, but because there is no need to multiply speculations. Delayed kenosis would occur if god did not love all of humanity but only the people of Israel, until the Incarnation.

2 I here assume that Abraham was not an innocent worshipper but one who *committed* to worship.

3 Hud Hudson (2014) argues that 'skeptical theists' are in no position to reject the idea of a deceiving god.

4 David Armstrong calls this 'the Headless Woman illusion': not observing what you expect to observe can lead to the illusion that you have observed its absence.

5 As always, there might be an exception for any who damn themselves – not that I have any candidates.

6 Alexander Pruss relies on this lack of commensurability to argue for divine freedom (Pruss 2016).

7 There I assumed that the value of distinctness *was* commensurable to other values and pointed out that we humans were unable to work out how they would be jointly maximized.

8 My current proposal is that the values of moral perfection and perfect love are in enough tension to cause fission into two persons but not so much as to destroy the unity of god, and that this then requires a further value of harmony between the persons, which is again in enough tension to result in a third person. This goes beyond (Forrest 2009b).

9 The right to exert retribution rather than to forgive has been developed by Thurow (2017) into a case for Purgatory.

10 For some recent Satan theodicy, see Boyd (2001). Satan theodicy is also considered by van Inwagen (2008).

11 Earlier in this work, I judged implausible the attribution of suffering to the supernatural intervention of Satan. Let me now clarify this. What is implausible is the attribution of *supernatural* powers to Satan that are misused directly to cause us suffering. Instead I am proposing that God had a plan that avoided excessive suffering, but Satan meddled with it *preternaturally* so the natural order now produces this suffering.

12 If we think the Blob Fish is ugly that is because a human being who looked like one would be ugly. Ugliness in the natural world is always due to a defect, like a five-legged frog.

Chapter 9

1 Robert Audi (2011: Ch. 3) exhibits hope on a spectrum that includes trust and propositional faith.

2 Maybe this makes the command too much to bear. If so I note that the Christian doctrine of the Trinity exhibits a middle path between full autonomy and absorption by God. The blessed are the persons incorporated along with the divine persons into a community that is God.

3 Famously Ovid said 'Odi et amor', 'I hate and I love'. This might reflect that dilemma. Alternatively, it might be said by someone in love who despises the beloved.

4 The Catholic Church itself teaches that the marks of the true church are being one, holy, universal and apostolic.

References

Ahern, M. B., 1963, 'An Approach to the Problem of Evil', *Sophia*, 2: 18–26.

Alston, William, 1985, 'Functionalism and Theological Language', *American Philosophical Quarterly*, 22: 221–30.

Alston, William, 1991, *Perceiving God: The Epistemology of Religious Experience*, Ithaca, NY: Cornell University Press.

Amesbury, Richard, 2017, 'Fideism', in Edward N. Zalta (ed.), *The Stanford Encyclopedia of Philosophy*, Fall 2017 edn, https://plato.stanford.edu/archives/fall2017/entries/fideism/.

Anderson, Robert, 2014, 'Is the Molinist Account of God Manipulative?' *Conference paper*, Religious Studies @ 50, University of Leeds, 25–27 June 2014.

Arstila, Valtteri, 2018, 'Temporal Experiences without the Specious Present', *Australasian Journal of Philosophy*, 96: 287–302.

Audi, Robert, 2011, *Rationality and Religious Commitment*, Oxford: Oxford University Press.

Barrett, Justin, 2004, *Why Would Anyone Believe in God?* Walnut Creek, CA: AltaMira Press.

Baum, Lauris and Frampton, Paul, 2007, 'Turnaround in Cyclic Cosmology', *Physical Review Letters*, 98 (7): doi:10.1103/PhysRevLett.98.071301.

Bishop, John, 2002, 'Faith as Doxastic Venture', *Religious Studies*, 38: 471–87.

Bishop, John, 2007, *Believing by Faith*, New York: Oxford University Press.

Bishop, John and Persyck, Ken, 2017, 'The Divine Attributes and Non-personal Conceptions of God', *Topoi*, 36: 609–21.

Blackburn, Simon, 1993, *Essays in Quasi-Realism*, New York: Oxford University Press.

Boyd, Gregory, 2001, *Satan and the Problem of Evil: Constructing a Trinitarian Warfare Theodicy*, Downers Grove, IL: InterVarsity Press.

Bradley, Michael C. 2007, 'Hume's Chief Objection to Natural Theology', *Religious Studies*, 43: 249–70.

Briggs, Rachel and Forbes, Graeme, 2012, 'The Real Truth About the Unreal Future', *Oxford Studies in Metaphysics*, 7: 257–302.

Brown, Harold A., 1993, 'Theory-Laden Observation Can Test the Theory', *The British Journal for the Philosophy of Science*, 44: 555–9.

Buchak, Lara, 2014, 'Rational Faith and Justified Belief', in Laura Frances Callahan and Timothy O'Connor (eds), *Religious Faith and Intellectual Virtue*, Oxford: Oxford University Press: Ch. 2.

Campbell, Keith, 1970, *Body and Mind*, London: Macmillan.

Carnap, Rudolf, 1950, *Logical Foundations of Probability*, Chicago: University of Chicago Press.

Chakravartty, Anjan, 2017, 'Scientific Realism', in Edward N. Zalta (ed.), *The Stanford Encyclopedia of Philosophy*, https://plato.stanford.edu/archives/sum2017/entries/scientific-realism/.

Chalmers, David J., 1996, *The Conscious Mind: In Search of a Fundamental Theory*, New York: Oxford University Press.

Chalmers, David J. and Jackson, Frank, 2001, 'Conceptual Analysis and Reductive Explanation', *The Philosophical Review*, 110: 315–60; reprinted in, T. Gendler and J. Hawthorne (eds), 2002, *Conceivability and Possibility*, Oxford: Oxford University Press: 145–200.

Chisholm, Roderick, 1976, *Person and Object: A Metaphysical Study*, LaSalle, IL: Open Court.

Chisholm, Roderick, 1991, 'On the Simplicity of the Soul', *Philosophical Perspectives*, 5: 157–81.

Clifford, William K., 1887, 'The Ethics of Belief', *Contemporary Review*, 29: 289–309.

Coady, C. A. J., 1992. *Testimony: A Philosophical Study*, Oxford: Clarendon Press.

Daniels, Norman, 2013, 'Reflective Equilibrium', in Edward N. Zalta (ed.), The *Stanford Encyclopedia of Philosophy*, http://plato.stanford.edu/archives/win2013/entries/reflective-equilibrum/.

Davidson, Donald, 1980, 'Mental Events', in *Essays on Actions and Events*, Oxford: Clarendon Press: 207–24.

Dawkins, Richard, 2006, *The God Delusion*, London: Bantam Books.

Dennett, Daniel 1991, *Consciousness Explained*, Boston, MA: Little, Brown and Company.

Deutsch, David, 1998, *The Fabric of Reality: The Science of Parallel Universes and Its Implications*, London: Penguin Books.

De Witt, Bryce Seligman, 1970, 'Quantum Mechanics and Reality: Could the Solution to the Dilemma of Indeterminism be a Universe in which all Possible Outcomes of an Experiment Actually Occur?' *Physics Today*, 23: 30–40.

Dougherty, Trent, 2014, T*he Problem of Animal Pain: A Theodicy for All Creatures Great and Small*, Basingstoke: Palgrave Macmillan.

Draper, Paul, 2016, 'Simplicity and Natural Theology', in Michael Bergmann and Jeffry E. Brower (eds), *Reason and Faith: Themes from Richard Swinburne*, Oxford: Oxford University Press: Ch. 3, 48–63.

Durkheim, Émile, 1995, *The Elementary Forms of the Religious Life*, trans. Karen Fields, New York: Free Press.

Elga, Adam, 2010, 'How to Disagree about How to Disagree', in Richard Feldman and Ted A. Warfield (eds), *Disagreement*, Oxford: Oxford University Press: 175–81.

Evans, C. Stephen 1998, *Faith Beyond Reason: A Kierkegaardian Account*, Grand Rapids, MI: Eerdmans.

Everett, Hugh, 1957, 'Relative State Formulation of Quantum Mechanics', *Review of Modern Physics*, 29: 454–62.

Fales, Evan, 1990, *Causation and Universals*, London: Routledge.

Feldman, Richard and Warfield, Ted A. (eds), 2010, *Disagreement*, Oxford: Oxford University Press.

Feyerabend, Paul, 2010, *Against Method*, 4th edn, London: Verso Books.

Fitzgerald, Edward, 1995, *The Rubaiyat of Omar Khayyam*, Project Gutenberg.

Flint, Thomas, 1990, 'Hasker's God, Time, and Knowledge', *Philosophical Studies*, 60: 103–15.

Flint, Thomas, 1998, *Divine Providence: The Molinist Account*, Ithaca: Cornell University Press.

Fogelin, Robert J., 2009, *Hume's Sceptical Crisis: A Textual Study*, New York: Oxford University Press.

Forrest, Peter, 1991, 'Aesthetic Understanding', *Philosophy and Phenomenological Research*, 51: 525–40.

Forrest, Peter, 1996, *God without the Supernatural: A Defence of Scientific Theism*, Ithaca: Cornell University Press.

Forrest, Peter, 2006, 'Epistemic Bootstrapping', in Stephen Hetherington (ed.), *Aspects of Knowing: Epistemological Essays*, Amsterdam: Elsevier: 53–66.

Forrest, Peter, 2007a, *Developmental Theism: From Pure Will to Unbounded Love*, Oxford: Oxford University Press.

Forrest, Peter, 2007b, 'The Tree of Life: Agency and Immortality in a Metaphysics Inspired by Quantum Theory', in Peter van Inwagen and Dean Zimmerman (eds), *Persons: Human and Divine*, Oxford: Oxford University Press: 301–18.

Forrest, Peter, 2008, 'Relativity, the Passage of Time and the Cosmic Clock', in Dennis Dieks (ed.), *The Ontology of Spacetime II*, Amsterdam: Elsevier: 245–53.

Forrest, Peter, 2009a, 'Razor Arguments', in Robin Le Poidevin, Peter Simons and Ross P. Cameron (eds), *The Routledge Companion to Metaphysics*, London: Routledge: Ch. 25.

Forrest, Peter, 2009b, 'Divine Fission: A New Way of Moderating Social Trinitarianism', in Michael C. Rea (ed.), *Oxford Readings in Philosophical Theology, v. 1: Trinity, Incarnation, and Atonement*, Oxford: Oxford University Press: 44–46.

Forrest, Peter, 2012, *The Necessary Structure of the All-pervading Aether: Discrete or Continuous? Simple or Symmetric?* Frankfurt: Ontos.

Forrest, Peter, 2016, 'The Personal Pantheist Conception of God', in Andrei Buckareff and Yujin Nagasawa (eds), *Alternative Concepts of God: Essays on the Metaphysics of the Divine*, New York: Oxford University Press: 21–40.

Frankfurt, Harry, 1969, 'Alternate Possibilities and Moral Responsibility', *Journal of Philosophy*, 66: 829–39.

Franzén, Nils, 2018, 'Aesthetic Evaluation and First-Hand Experience', *Australasian Journal of Philosophy*, 96: 669–82.

Freud, Sigmund, 1959, *Totem and Taboo: Some Points of Agreement between the Mental Lives of Savages and Neurotics*, trans. James Strachey, Abingdon: Routledge & Kegan Paul.

Gaita, Raymond, 2000, *A Common Humanity: Thinking about Love and Truth and Justice*, 2nd edn, London: Routledge.

Gaita, Raymond, 2004, *Good and Evil: An Absolute Conception*, Revised edn, London: Routledge.

Ginsborg, Hannah, 2014, 'Kant's Aesthetics and Teleology', in Edward N. Zalta (ed.), *The Stanford Encyclopedia of Philosophy*, https://plato.stanford.edu/archives/fall2014/entries/kant-aesthetics/.

Gosse, Philip, 1857, *Omphalos: An Attempt to Untie the Geological Knot*, London: John Van Voorst.

Gould, Stephen Jay, 1999, *Rocks of Ages*, New York: Random House.

Hare, Richard Mervyn, 1952, *The Language of Morals*, Oxford: Oxford University Press.

Harman, Gilbert, 1986. *Change in View, Principles of Reasoning*, Cambridge, MA: MIT Press.

Harper, Leland Royce, 2016, *Multiverse Deism*. PhD thesis, University of Birmingham.

Hasker, William, 1998, *God, Time and Knowledge*, Ithaca: Cornell University Press.

Hasker, William, 2004, *Providence, Evil and the Openness of God*, London: New York: Routledge.

Herbermann, Charles (ed.), 1913, 'Faith', *Catholic Encyclopedia*, New York: Robert Appleton Company.

Hudson, Hud, 2014, 'The Father of Lies?' in Jonathan Kvanvig (ed.), *Oxford Studies in Philosophy of Religion*, Oxford: Oxford University Press: 147–66.

Hume, David, 1975, *A Treatise of Human Nature*, ed. L. A. Selby-Bigge, rev. P. H. Nidditch, Oxford: Clarendon Press.

Hume, David, 1998, *Dialogues Concerning Natural Religion*, ed. Henry Aiken, New York: Hafner Pub. Co.

IHEU 2002, *Amsterdam Declaration*, IHEU Congress.

Jackson, Frank, 1982, 'Epiphenomenal Qualia', *The Philosophical Quarterly*, 32: 127–36.

Jackson, Frank, 1986, 'What Mary Didn't Know', *The Journal of Philosophy*, 83: 291–5.

James, William, 1896, 'The Will to Believe', *The New World*, 5: 327–47.

James, William, 1902, *The Varieties of Religious Experience: A Study in Human Nature*, London: Longmans Green & Co.

Jantzen, Grace, 1998, *Becoming Divine: Towards a Feminist Philosophy of Religion*, Manchester: Manchester University Press.

Jaynes, Edwin T., 1982, 'On the Rationale of Maximum-Entropy Methods', *Proceedings of the* IEEE, 70: 939–52.

Jaynes, Julian, 1976. *The Origin of Consciousness in the Breakdown of the Bicameral Mind*, Boston, MA: Houghton Mifflin.

Johnston, Mark, 1989, 'Relativism and the Self', in Michael Krausz (ed.), *Relativism: Interpretation and Confrontation*, South Bend, IN: University of Notre Dame Press: 441–72.

Joyce, Richard, 2015, 'Moral Anti-Realism', in Edward N. Zalta (ed.), *The Stanford Encyclopedia of Philosophy*, http://plato.stanford.edu/archives/fall2015/entries/moral-anti-realism/.

Kane, Robert, 1985, *Free Will and Values*, Albany, NY: SUNY Press.

Kerade, Baba Ifa,1994, *Handbook of Yoruba Religious Concepts*, Red Wheel.

Kraay, Klaas J. (ed.) 2015, *God and the Multiverse: Scientific, Philosophical and Theological Perspectives*, London: Routledge.

Kuhn, Thomas, 1962, *The Structure of Scientific Revolutions*, Chicago: University of Chicago Press.

Kyburg, Henry E. Jr, 1974, *The Logical Foundations of Statistical Inference*, Dordrecht: Reidel.

Lakatos, Imre, 1970, 'Falsification and the Methodology of Scientific Research Programs', in Imre Lakatos and Alan Musgrave (eds), *Criticism and the Growth of*

Knowledge: Volume 4: Proceedings of the International Colloquium in the Philosophy of Science, London, 1965, Cambridge: Cambridge University Press.

Langtry, Bruce, 2008, *God, The Best, and Evil*, Oxford: Oxford University Press.

Le Guin, Ursula, 1975, 'The Ones Who Walk Away from Omelas', in *The Wind's Twelve Quarters*, New York: Harper Perennial: 275–84.

Leslie, John, 1979, *Value and Existence*, Oxford: Blackwell.

Leslie John, 2002, *Infinite Minds: A Philosophical Cosmology*, Oxford: Clarendon Press.

Lewis, C. S., 1947, *Miracles: A Preliminary Study*, London: Collins.

Lewis, David, 1986, *On the Plurality of Worlds*, Oxford: Blackwell.

Lipner, J. J., 1984, 'The World as God's "Body": In Pursuit of Dialogue with Rāmānuja', *Religious Studies*, 20: 145–61.

Lipton Peter, 2004, *Inference to the Best Explanation*, 2nd edn, London: Routledge.

López-Sandoval, Eduardo, 2008, 'Static Universe: Infinite, Eternal and Self-Sustainable', arxiv.org/pdf/0807.1064.

Lovejoy, Arthur, 1936, *The Great Chain of Being*, Cambridge, MA: Harvard University Press.

Lycan, W. 1987, *Consciousness*, Cambridge, MA: MIT Press.

Mackie, John, 1977, *Ethics: Inventing Right and Wrong*, Harmondsworth: Penguin Books.

MacMurray, John, 1957, *The Self as Agent*, London: Faber & Faber.

Marquis, Don, 1950, *The Lives and Times of Archy and Mehitabel by Don Marquis*, illustrations by George Herriman, introduction by E. B. White, Garden City, NY: Doubleday & Company.

McCall, Storrs, 1994, *A Model of the Universe: Space-time, Probability, and Decision*, Oxford: Clarendon Press.

McCord Adams, Marilyn, 1999, *Horrendous Evils and the Goodness of God*, Ithaca: Cornell University Press.

Mellor, D. Hugh, 1971, *The Matter of Chance*, Cambridge: Cambridge University Press.

Moltmann, Jürgen, 2001, 'God's kenosis in the Creation and Consummation of the World', in John Polkinghorne (ed.), *The Work of Love: Creation as Kenosis*, Grand Rapids, MI: Eerdmans: 137–51.

Mulgan, Tim, 2015, *Purpose in the Universe*, Oxford: Oxford University Press.

Newton-Smith, William H., 1981, *The Rationality of Science*, London: Routledge & Kegan Paul.

Oppy, Graham, 2008, 'Review of *Developmental Theism: From Pure Will to Unbounded Love*' *Dialectica*, 62: 549–3.

Pearson, Oley, 2018 *Rationality, Time, and Self*, Basingstoke: Palgrave Macmillan.

Peirce, Charles S., 1908, 'A Neglected Argument for the Reality of God', *Hibbert Journal*, 7: 90–112.

Perry, John, 1979, 'The Problem of the Essential Indexical', *Noûs*, 13: 3–21.

Pinnock, Clark H., 2001, *Most Moved Mover: A Theology of God's Openness*, Grand Rapids, MI: Baker Books.

Plantinga, Alvin, 1965, 'Free Will Defence', in Max Black (ed.), *Philosophy in America*, Ithaca: Cornell University Press.

Plantinga, Alvin, 1974. *God, Freedom, and Evil*, New York: Harper and Row.

Plantinga, Alvin, 1983, 'Reason and Belief in God,' in Alvin Plantinga and Nicholas Wolterstorff (eds), *Faith and Rationality*, South Bend, IN: University of Notre Dame Press.

Plantinga, Alvin, 1993, *Warrant and Proper Function*, New York: Oxford University Press.

Polkinghorne, John (ed.), 2001, *The Work of Love: Creation as Kenosis*, Grand Rapids, MI: Eerdmans.

Pollock, John, 1986, *Contemporary Theories of Knowledge*, Lanham, MD: Rowman and Littlefield.

Priest, Graham, 2006, *In Contradiction*, Oxford: Oxford University Press.

Pruss, Alexander, 2006, *The Principle of Sufficient Reason: A Reassessment*, Cambridge: Cambridge University Press.

Pruss, Alexander, 2016, 'Divine Creative Freedom', in Jonathan Kvanvig (ed.), *Oxford Studies in Philosophy of Religion*, vol. 7, Oxford: Oxford University Press: 213–38.

Pullman, Philip, 2008, *His Dark Materials, Gift Edition including all Three Novels: Northern Light, The Subtle Knife and The Amber Spyglass*, London: Everyman.

Quine, Willard V. O., 1969, 'Epistemology Naturalized', in *Ontological Relativity and Other Essays*, New York: Columbia University Press: 69–90.

Rawls, John, 1971, *A Theory of Justice*, Cambridge, MA: Harvard University Press.

Rowe, William L., 1979. 'The Problem of Evil and Some Varieties of Atheism,' *American Philosophical Quarterly*, 16: 335–41.

Rowe, William L., 1986. 'The Empirical Argument from Evil,' in R. Audi and W. Wainwright (eds), *Rationality, Religious Belief, and Moral Commitment*, Ithaca: Cornell University Press: 227–47.

Rowe, William L. 1996, 'The Evidential Argument from Evil: A Second Look,' in Daniel Howard-Snyder (ed.), *The Evidential Argument from Evil*, Bloomington: Indiana University Press: 262–85.

Rowe, William, 2004, *Can God Be Free?* Oxford: Oxford University Press.

Ryrie, Charles C., 1999, *Basic Theology: A Popular Systematic Guide to Understanding Biblical Truth*, Chicago: Moody.

Sartre, Jean Paul, 1973, *Existentialism and Humanism*, trans. Philip Mairet, London: Eyre Methuen.

Schellenberg, John L., 1993, *Divine Hiddenness and Human Reason*, Ithaca: Cornell University Press.

Schellenberg, John L., 2005, *Prolegomena to a Philosophy of Religion*, Ithaca: Cornell University Press.

Schucman, Helen, 2007, *Course in Miracles*, 3rd edn, Mill Valley, CA: Foundation for Inner Peace.

Shallis, Michael, 1986, 'Time and Cosmology,' in Raymond Flood and Michael Lockwood (eds), *The Nature of Time*, Oxford: Basil Blackwell: 63–79

Shoemaker, Sydney, 1998, 'Causal and Metaphysical Necessity,' *Pacific Philosophical Quarterly*, 79: 59–77.

Smart, J. J. C. and Williams, Bernard, 1973, *Utilitarianism: For and Against*, Cambridge: Cambridge University Press.

Spelke, Elizabeth S. and Kinzler, Katherine D., 2007, 'Core Knowledge', *Developmental Science*, 10: 89–96.

Steinhardt, Paul and Turok, Neil, 2004 'The Cyclic Model Simplified', *New Astronomy Reviews*, 49: 43–57.

Steinhardt, Paul and Turok, Neil, 2007, *The Endless Universe: Beyond the Big Bang*, New York: Doubleday.

Stove, David, 1985, 'Why Have Philosophers?' review of S. A. Grave, *A History of Philosophy in Australia*, *Quadrant*, 29 (7): 82–3.

Stove, David, 1986 *The Rationality of Induction*, Oxford: Oxford University Press.

Swinburne, Richard, 1984, 'Personal Identity: The Dualist Theory', in Sydney Shoemaker and Richard Swinburne (eds), *Personal Identity*, Oxford: Blackwell: 1–66.

Swinburne, Richard, 2005, *Faith and Reason*, 2nd edn, Oxford: Clarendon Press.

Swoyer, Chris, 1982, 'The Nature of Natural Laws', *Australasian Journal of Philosophy*, 60: 203–23.

Tahko, Tuomas E. and Lowe, E. Jonathan, (2016) 'Ontological Dependence', in Edward N. Zalta (ed.), *The Stanford Encyclopedia of Philosophy*, https://plato.stanford.edu/arc hives/win2016/entries/ dependence-ontological/.

Thurow, Joshua, 2017, 'Atoning in Purgatory', *Religious Studies*, 53: 217–37.

Tooley, Michael, 2015, 'The Problem of Evil', in Edward N. Zalta (ed.), *The Stanford Encyclopedia of Philosophy*, http://plato.stanford.edu/archives/fall2015/entries/evil/.

Tryon, Edward P., 1973, 'Is the Universe a Vacuum Fluctuation?' *Nature*, 24: 396–7.

Vaihinger, Hans, 1924, *The Philosophy of 'As if': A System of the Theoretical, Practical and Religious Fictions of Mankind*, trans. C. K. Ogden, New York: Barnes and Noble, 1968.

van Fraassen, Bas C. 1980, *The Scientific Image*, Oxford: Oxford University Press.

van Inwagen, Peter, 1991, 'The Problem of Evil, The Problem of Air, and the Problem of Silence', *Philosophical Perspectives*, 5, Philosophy of Religion: 135–65.

van Inwagen, Peter, 1975, 'The Incompatibility of Free Will and Determinism', *Philosophical Studies*, 27: 185–99.

van Inwagen, Peter, 2008, *The Problem of Evil*, Oxford: Oxford University Press.

van Til, Cornelius, 1967, *The Defense of the Faith*, Phillipsburg, NJ: Presbyterian & Reformed Publishing Company.

Walls, Jerry and Dougherty, Trent (eds), 2018, *Two Dozen (or so) Arguments for God: The Plantinga Project*, New York: Oxford University Press.

White, Stephen, 1989, 'Metapsychological Relativism and the Self', *Journal of Philosophy*, 86: 298–323.

Williams, Donald, 1947, *The Ground of Induction*, Cambridge, MA: Harvard University Press.

Wolf, Susan, 1990, *Freedom within Reason*, New York: Oxford University Press.

Wolterstorff, Nicholas, 1976, *Reason within the Bounds of Religion*, Eerdmans.

Zaehner, R. C., 1974, *Our Savage God: The Perverse Use of Eastern Thought*, London: Collins.

Zagzebski, Linda, 2017, 'Foreknowledge and Free Will', in Edward N. Zalta (ed.), *The Stanford Encyclopedia of Philosophy*, https://plato.stanford.edu/archives/sum2017/e ntries/free-will-foreknowledge/.

Index